Dr. Tevfik Dalgic, BA, MBA
Editor

Handbook of Niche Marketing
Principles and Practice

Pre-publication
REVIEWS,
COMMENTARIES,
EVALUATIONS . . .

Best Business Books®
The Haworth Reference Press™
Imprints of The Haworth Press, Inc.
New York • London • Oxford

Handbook of Niche Marketing
Principles and Practice

THE HAWORTH PRESS

Haworth Series in Segmented, Targeted, and Customized Marketing: Conceptual and Empirical Development

Art Weinstein

Editor

Handbook of Market Segmentation: Strategic Targeting for Business and Technology Firms, Third Edition by Art Weinstein

Handbook of Niche Marketing: Principles and Practice edited by Tevfik Dalgic

Lifestyle Market Segmentation by Dennis J. Cahill

Segmentation Strategies for Hospitality Managers: Target Marketing for Competitive Advantage by Ron Morritt

Handbook of Niche Marketing
Principles and Practice

Dr. Tevfik Dalgic, BA, MBA
Editor

Best Business Books®
The Haworth Reference Press™
Imprints of The Haworth Press, Inc.
New York • London • Oxford

For more information on this book or to order, visit
http://www.haworthpress.com/store/product.asp?sku=5475

or call 1-800-HAWORTH (800-429-6784) in the United States and Canada
or (607) 722-5857 outside the United States and Canada

or contact orders@HaworthPress.com

Published by

Best Business Books ® and The Haworth Reference Press™, imprints of The Haworth Press, Inc.,
10 Alice Street, Binghamton, NY 13904-1580.

Cover design by Lora Wiggins.

Library of Congress Cataloging-in-Publication Data

Handbook of niche marketing : principles and practice / Tevfik Dalgic, editor.
    p. cm.
    Includes bibliographical references and index.
    ISBN-13: 978-0-7890-2329-2 (hc. : alk. paper)
    ISBN-10: 0-7890-2329-6 (hc. : alk. paper)
    ISBN-13: 978-0-7890-2330-8 (pbk. : alk. paper)
    ISBN-10: 0-7890-2330-X (pbk. : alk. paper)
    1. Market segmentation—Case studies. I. Dalgic, Tevfik.

HF5415.127.H36 2005
658.4'02—dc22

2005006261

CONTENTS

PART I: BACKGROUND CONCEPTS
AND APPLICATIONS

**Chapter 1. Niche Marketing Revisited: Concept,
Applications, and Some European Cases**   **3**
    Tevfik Dalgic
    Maarten Leeuw

PART II: EMPIRICAL RESEARCH IN NICHE MARKETING

Chapter 5. A Visual Approach for Identifying Consumer Satisfaction Niches   105

Hooman Estelami
Peter De Maeyer

Chapter 6. High Tech, High Performance: The Synergy of Niche Strategy and Planning Focus in Technological Entrepreneurial Firms   129

Karen Bantel

PART III: NICHE MARKETING CASES

ABOUT THE EDITOR

Tevfik Dalgic, PhD, is currently a professor with the Department of Organization, Strategy, and International Management at the University of Texas at Dallas Management School. He teaches global economy, marketing, international marketing, and international strategic management subjects for graduate classes. Dr. Dalgic has worked as a consultant for the WTO of the United Nations for several countries in the field of international trade and has also been a consultant for the Dutch government on international projects in the field of international marketing and training. He is the Founder and Editor of two academic, refereed business journals: *Advances in Business Studies— An Irish Review* and *Utrecht Business Review.* He has published works in several journals, including *Columbia Journal of World Business, Journal of International Marketing, International Marketing Review, Management International Review, European Journal of Marketing, Advances in International Marketing,* and *Journal of Market Segmentation.* His research papers have been presented at the Academy of Marketing Science, American Marketing Association, European Marketing Academy, and the Consortium of International Marketing and Research. Dr. Dalgic also has a consultancy practice, International Management Training Organization (IMTO). His current research includes ethnicity in international business, international software marketing, and chaos theory and international business.

CONTRIBUTORS

Karen Bantel serves as the president of CyberMichigan. Previously she was executive director of the Michigan Entrepreneurship Education Network (MEEN), a program funded by the State of Michigan's MEDC (Michigan Economic Development Corporation), and sponsored by the University of Michigan Business School's Samuel Zell & Robert H. Lurie Institute for Entrepreneurial Studies. In her teaching role, she taught several courses in entrepreneurship and strategic management, including business planning, acquisitions, and high growth strategies. Dr. Bantel holds a PhD and MBA from the University of Michigan Business School.

Michael Beverland is a senior lecturer in marketing with the Department of Management at the University of Melbourne. He earned his PhD from the University of South Australia. His articles have been published in *Business Horizons, European Journal of Marketing, Industrial Marketing Management, Journal of Management Studies, Journal of Personal Selling and Sales Management,* and the *Journal of Product Innovation Management.* Dr. Beverland's research interests include customer-desired value change, consumer values, niche marketing, luxury branding, and brand evolution.

Blaine J. Branchik, an assistant professor of marketing at Quinnipiac University School of Business, is an expert on buyer decision making, market segments, business marketing, and marketing history. He has taught undergraduate and graduate courses on marketing strategy, Internet marketing, business-to-business marketing, and principles of marketing. Prior to pursuing his doctoral studies, he spent over fifteen years in various technology marketing management positions for companies including IBM, Siemens, and Oracle.

Peter De Maeyer received his PhD in marketing at Columbia Business School. His areas of interest are services marketing and advertising, and his research has been published in the *Journal of Service Research, Journal of Consumer Satisfaction and Dissatisfaction,* and the *Journal of Retailing.* He is currently an assistant professor of marketing at Singapore Management University. Previously, he held positions as an assistant professor of marketing at Georgetown University, and as a management consultant with the Monitor Group. His consulting experience includes assisting organizations such as Coca-Cola, Heineken, Safeway, Office Depot, and France Telecom.

Hooman Estelami is an associate professor of marketing and the codirector of the Pricing Center at Fordham University in New York. He received his PhD in marketing from Columbia University. His research has been published in the *Journal of Retailing, Journal of the Academy of Marketing Science, International Journal of Research in Marketing, Journal of Business Research, Journal of Service Research, Journal of Financial Services Marketing, Journal of Services Marketing,* and elsewhere. He also serves as an associate editor of the *Journal of Product and Brand Management.*

Isil Hezar is a graduate of business administration from the School of Management at the University of Texas at Dallas. She has a BSc from Bogazici University, Istanbul, and an MBA from Marmara University, Istanbul.

Gary Knight is an associate professor of international marketing and works at Florida State University, College of Business, Tallahassee. His area of interest covers international marketing strategy; exporting and foreign market entry strategies; international strategy of the "born global" firm, and international entrepreneurship and international services marketing. He completed various export and international business-related seminars through the U.S. Department of Commerce, International Trade Administration.

Maarten Leeuw currently serves as the interim manager at Nuon Business, the largest energy company in the Netherlands. He is owner and managing director of his own company, Partners in Sourcing, which focuses on executive search, interim management, contracting, and coaching. Over the past two decades, he has been active mainly in the IT industry and has held several national and international senior management positions in areas such as marketing, sales and delivery, and people and resource management. He has been published in several international journals in the fields of marketing, quality, and strategy. He is frequently invited as a guest lecturer for several MBA courses. He received a PhD from Henley Management (UK) and Brunei University.

Lawrence S. Lockshin is a professor of wine marketing at the University of South Australia, and he is also the director of the Wine Marketing Group. He received his masters in viticulture from Cornell University and his PhD in marketing from The Ohio State University. His research interests are consumer choice behavior for wine and wine industry strategy. He is currently studying market-based assets in the wine industry, brand and regional cues in consumer wine choice, wine/alcohol awareness of health and societal control as it relates to wine purchase behavior, success factors for small and medium-sized wineries, and modeling of consumer choice based on large panel data sets.

Charlotte H. Mason, marketing professor, focuses her research on the development and testing of marketing models and applications of multivariate statistics to marketing problems. She is currently investigating issues relating to the analysis and use of large customer databases. She and marketing colleague William Perreault are the authors of *The Marketing Game!,* a strategic marketing simulation. Dr. Mason is chair of the MBA concentration in customer and product management and an award-winning teacher. She offers courses in data, tools, and decisions; research analysis for marketing; and customer relationship management. Prior to her academic career, Dr. Mason was a management scientist for Proctor & Gamble, where her projects included simulating the production facilities of a pulp and paper plant prior to start-up, developing production planning models, and assessing the sales force's productivity. She also worked as a consultant for Booz, Allen, and Hamilton, focusing on operations management problems. Dr. Mason continues to consult for a variety of businesses, including GlaxoSmithKline, American Express, and the American Bankers Association. She received her PhD in business, her MS and BS in industrial engineering and engineering management, and an MS in statistics from Stanford University.

George R. Milne is an associate professor of marketing at the Isenberg School of Management at the University of Massachusetts,

Amherst. He received his PhD from the University of North Carolina, Chapel Hill. His articles have been published in the *Journal of Marketing, Journal of Public Policy and Marketing, Journal of Academy of Marketing Science, Marketing Letters, Journal of Interactive Marketing, Journal of Consumer Affairs, Journal of Business Research, Journal of Managerial Studies,* and others. George's research interests include privacy, database marketing, niche marketing, and consumption experiences.

Ron Morritt is currently a marketing consultant for Global Marketing Solutions of Fort Lauderdale, Florida. He teaches marketing, strategy, and international marketing at the University of Phoenix, Florida International University, and Nova Southeastern University. He has also served as a reviewer for the *Journal of Segmentation in Marketing.* Previously he was CEO of a New York real estate development firm and has also served as CFO and chairman of the board for a resort condominium hotel in Montego Bay, Jamaica. Dr. Morritt's academic credentials include several publications and presentations in the area of hotel marketing strategy. His interests in marketing include customer value, customer retention, strategic partnerships, segmentation, and marketing strategy.

Steven Phelan joined the faculty of the University of Nevada, Las Vegas, in July 2003 as an assistant professor of strategic management. Previously he held tenure-track appointments at the University of Texas at Dallas and La Trobe University in Melbourne. He has been a visiting professor at Bocconi University in Milan, Italy, and Queensland University of Technology in Brisbane, Australia. Prior to joining academia, he worked in the telecommunications and airline industries and was a principal partner in Bridges Management Group, a consultancy specializing in strategic investment decisions.

Foreword

It would not be an exaggeration to say that the topic of niche marketing itself has been somewhat of a niche market. Indeed, its importance far exceeds the attention it has received in academic journals, curricula, and textbooks. The business press, on the other hand, has been more receptive to the concept but has made it into something of a buzzword. It is therefore a credit to Dr. Tevfik Dalgic that he has taken the initiative of editing this handbook to hopefully induce niche marketing to take its proper place in the mainstream of marketing consciousness.

The handbook collects previously dispersed references in the literature and some new material into a single convenient repository that will immeasurably aid current niche practitioners as well as managers who have been waiting to adopt the methods of niche marketing. Few people are better qualified to lead us to a finer and deeper understanding of niche marketing than Professor Dalgic. Two of his co-authored papers, including the famous "Niche Marketing Revisited" article, are in the collection. Also included are carefully selected published seminal articles written by well-known marketing experts, as well as some unpublished forward-looking articles written specially for the handbook.

The two review chapters co-authored by Dalgic emphasize up front the differences between segments and niches, as these differences are not properly appreciated by many. An important inclusion is the use of quantitative methods to define niches. The two suggested approaches are based on evolutionary principles by Milne and Mason and kernel methods by Estelami and De Maeyer. The handbook is made more useful for managers and students by the inclusion of a large number of examples, cases, and several detailed studies of niche marketing implementation for the wine industry by Beverland and Lockshin, the hotel industry by Morritt, and the gay consumer market by Branchik.

This handbook combines theoretical and pragmatic issues in niche marketing and includes both conceptual and empirical articles and practical cases of successful niche marketing applications. It provides guidelines for niche marketing strategies to assist marketers to be successful in today's turbulent and highly competitive environments. This handbook will likely inspire marketing scholars to conduct research in the area of niche marketing.

Suresh Sethi
Ashbel Smith Professor and Director
Center for Intelligent Supply Networks (C4ISN)
School of Management
The University of Texas at Dallas

Introduction

ABOUT THE PROJECT: THE NEED FOR A BOOK ON NICHE MARKETING

My personal interest in niche marketing has a history of about 20 years. During my earlier studies, I came across the concept and its practices; after 1992, I focused entirely on the issue and tried to read every conceptual and empirical paper published in academic journals, which are very few. Later, I concentrated on the practical applications of niche marketing and found several important examples, many of which were included in my previous writings. On the practical side, the concept of niche marketing has gained widespread acceptance in business. Due to increasing competitive pressures, many company leaders have tried to apply this approach with mixed results.

The Internet has brought a new dimension to the issue. It has empowered e-marketers with new marketing tools that help them target very narrow, well-defined niches. A simple Internet search of the term "niche" via the Google search engine provided about 1,740,000 results (September 21, 2003)—almost all of these were about businesses and practical issues or promotional materials of companies all over the world marketing niche-related products, services, or training. A week later this number skyrocketed to 2,480,000 hits (September 28, 2003). As of May 20, 2005, this figure was 4,320,000 hits. The Web sites were mostly companies claiming to be niche marketers, software vendors selling Web-based niche-finding programs, and the like. To find items of substance was virtually impossible.

Then it hit me. How is it that the number of practitioners and niche marketers is so large and fast growing, but no single comprehensive book covers this important subject? This edited book aims to provide an answer to this need. In order to find high quality, unpublished works, I placed a "call for papers" on the electronic marketing list (ELMAR e-mail list of American Marketing Association) and received several papers from respected marketing professors. The best ones are included in the book.

With ever-changing customer needs and hypercompetition, company leaders need to find new ways to attract, satisfy, and retain customers. Most companies, whether big or small, local or foreign, some gradually and some at an increasing speed, direct their marketing efforts to select niche customers. Even the largest manufacturers target carefully selected market niches to maximize the effectiveness of their programs and often aim at creating different niches for each product group. For example, Hewlett-Packard Company markets all-in-one machines that print, fax, photocopy, and scan to segments of the home office market, while targeting larger offices for higher-priced, single-function units, such as laser printers, fax machines, and scanners. Niche marketing is being accepted as one step closer to the concept of "one-to-one" or "tailor-made" marketing, which is hailed as the marketing approach for the twenty-first century.

Niche marketing is no longer confined within national market boundaries; new emerging firms or even existing firms are finding new niches that go beyond national boundaries, thus creating international or "global nichers." A unique product for a group of unique customers is the essential element of niche marketing. Research shows that niche marketing firms are also market-oriented ones (Leeuw, 1997).

Although the majority of the chapters presented in this book are "classics" and were published in the 1990s, by no means have they lost their importance. Limited new insights have been made over the past five years on niche marketing. Hence, I have selected the most important essays both from theoretical and practical perspectives to provide readers with a comprehensive collection of work on niche marketing. The *Handbook of Niche Marketing* will be a valuable resource to both practitioners who want to learn how to do a better job of niche marketing and scholars who do academic research in this field.

ABOUT THE READINGS

The book consists of three parts: Part I, *Background Concepts and Applications,* includes an overview of what niche marketing is, issues, current research, and global niche marketing applications and examples. Part II, *Empirical Research in Niche Marketing,* includes academic studies covering several applications of the niche marketing concept and relevant research methodologies. Part III, *Niche Marketing Cases,* discusses applications of niche marketing for specific market sectors/conditions.

The following is a brief explanation for the relevance of the nine chapters selected.

Chapter 1: This very comprehensive conceptual work combines the foundations and essential issues of niche marketing with practical examples, methodology of application, and updated literature for the day. Many researchers and practitioners have used this article since its publication. I co-authored this chapter with my PhD student Dr. Maarten Leeuw, who studied specifically niche marketing subjects in his PhD thesis at the Henley Management College of the United Kingdom.

Chapter 2: In this study we take the concept of niche marketing to international markets, trying to find principles and practices of becoming international niche marketers. Several case stories explain why and how they have become international niche marketers. Some conclusions were drawn from the cases as well as from well-documented empirical works.

Chapter 3: As a recent development, manufacturers, retailers, and consumers are increasingly concerned about product proliferation and parity products. Constraints on retail shelf space and manufacturing considerations are examples of pressures leading firms to prune items from their product lines. When reviewing strategy and performance, a critical issue is cannibalization, or the extent to which one product's customers are gained at the expense of other products offered by the same firm. With the exception of new product models, little research could be found on cannibalization. In this chapter, authors propose an approach for identifying cannibalization in mature markets by using an ecological niche approach. They empirically illustrate an approach for the cigarette market with 188 brands and brand variants.

Chapter 4: Authors Milne and Mason continue the extended use of ecological theory to study markets in their second empirical chapter. They apply ecological theory to product markets by quantifying concepts such as niches, niche breadth, and niche overlap and propose a new approach for measuring competitive intensity and identifying competitive submarkets. The authors define competition among brands as the extent to which brands compete for the same customers. Their approach is suitable for both durable and nondurable goods, as well as for markets with many brands, and it can be used to assess competition between existing and hypothetical brands. They illustrate this approach using data on the magazine market and offer suggestions for future research.

Chapter 5: Authors Estelami and De Maeyer in this chapter prove that using the existing approaches for obtaining the shape of the distribution of consumer satisfaction ratings often results in ambiguous and unreliable interpretations of the data. They propose a new approach for estimating the shape of the distribution of consumer satisfaction ratings. The proposed approach, based on an established nonparametric method in econometrics, is shown to have superior properties to existing approaches used for graphing consumer satisfaction response distributions. Benefits of the proposed approach are demonstrated and replicated in this study in two different consumer satisfaction settings. The application of the method on consumer satisfaction data in two separate scenarios helped to identify underlying consumer segments. These segments were further differentiated based on the dynamics by which satisfaction is derived. As a result, the proposed method facilitates the study of heterogeneity in consumer satisfaction data, an issue of equal concern to academics and practitioners. Moreover, it facilitates the development of segment-based and focused quality improvement programs in consumer services.

Chapter 6: This chapter explores the influence on a technological entrepreneurial firm's performance of a specific product/market strategy, the quality/service niche, and one aspect of strategic implementation capabilities: breadth or focus in strategic-planning processes. Further, reflecting the resource-based view of firms (i.e., that synergies exist between strategy and implementation characteristics), the effect of the interaction of these variables is examined. Because the strategic benefit of implementation skills can be understood only in reference to the firm's competitive context, the contextual influences of the environment (instability and munificence) and the product stage of development are also examined, as the organizational context of age and size.

Technological entrepreneurial firms are the subjects of this study because they are an increasingly important segment of international economies (although little is known about them) and achieving strategic success is particularly challenging for them. Technology-based industries, with their rapidly changing environment, require that firms make highly flexible and rapid strategic moves, which can be difficult for young firms with few surplus resources. Entrepreneurial firms also have the difficulty of the "liability of adolescence" in which failure is high during the firm's early years. Insight into strategic success for such firms has potential business and public-policy value.

Chapter 7: This chapter reports on the case of Palliser Estate Wines of Martinborough, an established niche producer and exporter of ultrapremium wines. The case study is appropriate for several reasons. First, the world wine market is undergoing substantial change, with an increasingly clear partition emerging between large and niche players. Second, research suggests that wineries of all sizes will need to increase their market orientation, and focus simultaneously on building market awareness and relationships necessitating an increased strategic focus. Third, this case has been developed longitudinally and as such provides one of the few longitudinal examples of strategic emergence and evolution in a field dominated by cross-sectional research. Longitudinal studies are important, as competitive advantage is built over time and is often an emergent process. Finally, this case is a successful niche marketer and, as such, offers insights into how such firms craft strategy in an increasingly competitive market.

Chapter 8: This chapter is another practical example that examines the strategy of niche marketing for competitive advantage in the consolidation phase of the 1990s hotel market. It tracks the evolution of segmentation strategy in the U.S. hotel market from price segmentation to integrated niche marketing. Different types of segmentation used in both the U.S. and Caribbean hotel markets are cited as examples of successful segmentation and niche marketing in the hotel industry. Benefits and liabilities associated with niche marketing are summarized. The need for empirical support for the selection of a target niche is emphasized using different types of market research. The chapter concludes with a review of four niche selection methods for hotel managers and owners. These methods include (1) adapt and modify a successful segmentation formula; (2) use your hotel guest history/database to profile your best customers; (3) identify segmentation gaps in your local market; and (4) contract with a reputable consulting firm to do a segmentation study. The use of at least two of these methods is recommended.

Chapter 9: This chapter deals with a specific niche market: gays in the United States. The gay market has been recognized in publications and businesses as large and lucrative. The widespread corporate interest and associated targeting activities are less than thirty years old; however, U.S. businesses have been marketing to gay consumers for well over 100 years. This market segment has developed as a result of a series of historical and societal events, paralleling the development of the gay community, and involving activities on the part of both buyers and sellers. This chapter traces the evolution of the gay market segment from the late nineteenth century to the beginning of the twenty-first century through three historical phases: (1) the Underground Phase, pre-1941; (2) the Community-Building Phase, 1941-1970; and (3) the Mainstream Phase, 1970-2000. A conceptual framework linking buyer and seller activities to historic events in these three phases is presented along with examples of products and services marketed to gay Americans within each phase.

REFERENCE

Leeuw, M. (1997). Unpublished doctoral dissertation. Henley Management College, United Kingdom.

PART I:
BACKGROUND CONCEPTS
AND APPLICATIONS

Chapter 1

Niche Marketing Revisited: Concept, Applications, and Some European Cases

Tevfik Dalgic
Maarten Leeuw

INTRODUCTION

Niche marketing is an approach which has been applied success-fully by several companies around the world. Despite its growing in-terest and increasing popularity there seems to be limited research on this subject. Although several papers have been published in this area, they are predominantly from a practitioner's point of view. From an academic perspective research publications seem to be lim-ited to some general definitions and brief explanations, under the general heading of "segmentation" or "positioning," in some market-ing textbooks. This chapter will attempt to bring together both the practical and conceptual aspects of niche marketing, leading to a set of guidelines which may be used as a deliberate marketing strategy. Niche marketing has been with us for some time. What is new, how-ever, is the increased diversity of markets, advanced technologies en-abling new marketing approaches, and the deterioration of large com-panies and their traditional marketing approaches. Niche marketing seems an appropriate method to be employed in this changing envi-ronment. It also seems appropriate with the unification of the present markets of the European Union and future enlargement toward the

This chapter was originally published in *European Journal of Marketing* (1994), Vol. 28, No. 4, pp. 39-55. Reprinted with permission.

creation of Euromarketing,[1] as well as further globalization of other markets and an increase in competition among companies active in these markets.

Due to this intensification of competition a shakeout may take place in these markets, leaving only the strongest. Niche marketing may help companies to remain among the healthy survivors. Companies which want to survive, grow, and be profitable may be forced to find markets which have

- sufficient size to be potentially profitable;
- no real competitors, or markets which have been ignored by other companies;
- growth potential;
- sufficient purchasing ability;
- a need for special treatment;
- customer goodwill; and
- opportunities for an entrance company to exercise its superior competence.[2,3]

These characteristics may be termed niche characteristics. They could, however, just as well apply to a market segment. A further analysis of the differences between a segment and a niche, in the section titled Niche Marketing versus Segmentation, will clarify this issue. Another characteristic, according to Kotler,[3] is that niches are relatively small. Although niches might be comparatively small initially, they might grow to become large markets. According to McKenna,[4] "most large markets evolve from niche markets."

What Is Niche Marketing?

Target marketing, focused marketing, concentrated marketing, and micromarketing are all used as synonyms for niche marketing. Although they exhibit substantial similarities, they differ to some extent. In this section we will not attempt to explain these differences. We will however attempt to define niche marketing. In order to do so, we have to establish the meaning of the word *niche*.

What Is a Niche?

Webster's dictionary[5] describes a niche as "a recessed space or hollow, specifically a recess in a wall for a statue or the like; any position specifically adapted to its occupant." According to the *Penguin Dictionary of Biology,*[6] an ecological niche has the following meanings: a particular role or set of relationships of organisms in an ecosystem which may be filled by different species in different geographical areas. Some marketers have long advocated the use of ecology or biological theory in marketing in order to study markets. A relationship may be drawn between the ecological niche and the market niche.[7] This refers to ecological niche and market niche similarities. In both cases, organisms and organizations live in their immediate physical environment and are able to continue their life forms in a changing environment. An ecosystem in biology may serve as an analogy for the macroenvironment of an organization which continues its life without being threatened by the environmental forces. Another definition is given by Keegan et al.[8] They define a niche as "a small market that is not served by competing products." Hooley and Saunders[9] use the word "pocket" to define a niche.

We consider a niche to be a small market consisting of an individual customer or a small group of customers with similar characteristics or needs. In niche marketing a company focuses on a market niche exhibiting the aforementioned characteristics. In such marketing we can make a distinction between two approaches:

1. To see niche marketing as a creative process, as Chalasani and Shani[10] termed nichemanship, which is "a process of carving out a small part of the market whose needs are not fulfilled. By specialization along market, customer, product or marketing mix lines, a company can match the unique needs."
2. To see niche marketing as the last stage of segmentation, taking place in the following sequential stages: segmentation, targeting, positioning, and niching.[8]

A more general definition of niche marketing is provided by Stanton et al.[11] as a method to meet customer needs through tailoring goods and services for small markets. Figure 1.1 depicts the development of a niche marketing strategy in support of the first approach.

NICHE MARKETING VERSUS SEGMENTATION

It is often assumed that segmentation is a starting point in niche marketing. Chalasani and Shani,[10] however, hold a different view. According to them, "segmentation is the process of breaking a large market into smaller pieces. It is a top-down approach." They further state that "niche marketing is a bottom-up approach where the marketer starts from the needs of a few customers and gradually builds up a larger customer base"; this is in contrast to breaking up a market into smaller markets. In this respect niche marketing may be termed as inverted or reversed segmentation. This view opposes the concept which perceives niche marketing as the last or final stage of segmentation.

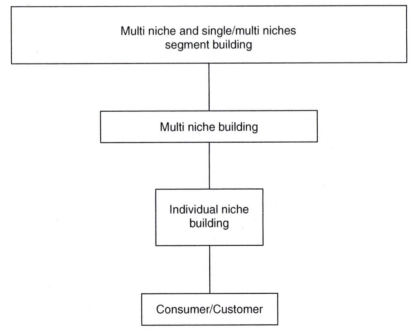

FIGURE 1.1. Niche Building Strategy—Bottom-Up Approach

Other observed differences are that

- a niche is usually smaller in size compared with the size of a segment;
- a niche focuses on individuals—in a segment we focus on a so-called homogeneous group; and
- a niche fulfills a specific need in contrast to a segment where the emphasis is on being a manageable part of the market.

Kotler[3] suggests that the key idea in niche marketing is specialization and he provides the following ways in which to specialize:

- end-user specialization;
- vertical-level specialization;
- customer-size specialization;
- geographic specialization;
- product or product-line specialization;
- product-feature specialization;
- job-shop specialization;
- quality/price specialization;
- service specialization; and
- channel specialization.

Kotler's[3] idea of specialization leads us to the distinctive competencies a firm needs to possess to pursue niche markets. According to Pavitt,[12] innovating small firms are typically specialized in their technological strategies, concentrating on product innovation in specific produced goods such as machine tools, scientific instruments, specialized chemicals, and software. Their key strengths are in their ability to match technology with specific customer requirements. We may conclude that niche marketing could be defined as positioning into small, profitable homogeneous market segments which have been ignored or neglected by others. This positioning is based on the integrated marketing concept and the distinctive competencies the company possesses. The previous definition addresses five essential elements of niche marketing:

1. positioning;
2. profitability;

3. distinctive competencies;
4. small market segments; and
5. adherence to the marketing concept.

These ideas have been incorporated within the guidelines we developed for practical application. (See Practical Guidelines, Step 1.) Other essential elements not mentioned explicitly in this definition, although included, are long-term relationships and company reputation. This brings us to the concept of relationship marketing which can be defined as "a marketing strategy that seeks to establish an ongoing business relationship with customers whereby the product becomes the total relationship."[8] In niche marketing, long-term, strong relationships are key. In order to develop them, we have to practice relationship marketing. In this approach we try to build a relationship for the mutual benefit of both parties. Through this win-win situation the niche marketer can build a barrier to deter potential competitors and sustain long-term profitability as well as customer retention and supplier relationships.[13] According to Copulsky and Wolf[14] the relationship marketing process incorporates three key elements:

1. identifying and building a database of current and potential customers,
2. delivering differentiated messages to these people, and
3. tracking each relationship to monitor the cost of acquiring the consumer and the lifetime value of his purchases.

In relation to the first element, Blattberg and Deighton[15] stressed the need for a customer database in order to keep track of customer preferences and increase marketing effectiveness. They claim that "niches too small to be served profitably today will become viable as marketing efficiency improves." Without further embarking on this process it must be clear that the central theme in relationship marketing is that those companies which can relate to and satisfy the customer in the most comprehensive way over a period of time will survive and thrive competitively. (See Practical Guidelines, Steps 2, 4, and 7.) The other concept of major importance to niche marketers is reputation. In niche marketing you do not only market your product, you also market your business; reputation is key. According to

McKenna,[4] "niche marketing depends on word-of-mouth references and infrastructure development, a broadening of people in related industries whose opinions are crucial to the product's success." We may conclude that a solid reputation in the minds of the customers is essential to be successful as a niche marketer.

EVOLUTION OF NICHE MARKETING

General Observations

Since the 1980s mass-marketing companies have been under enormous pressure from niche marketers, who are nibbling away at the major markets of these mass-marketing companies. These niche marketers are steadily eating up parts of formerly traditional mass markets. New demands, changing customer motivations, and further individualization (both business-to-business as well as business-to-consumer marketing) have created a multitude of diverse and fractured markets in contrast to what once was a simple mass market. This fragmented market, also termed "multiple option society" by Naisbitt in his book *Megatrends,*[16] is mainly technology driven. These new markets need a new nontraditional approach of marketing from these larger companies in order to keep and expand their currently held markets. According to Sheth,[17] changing macroeconomic forces are reshaping marketing strategies. Consequently, doing faster and better may not be sufficient and, instead, businesses will be required to develop new marketing concepts and practices.[18] American and European mass markets have been broken down into fragmented markets due to several causes since the Second World War; these causes, as identified by Linneman and Stanton,[19] McKenna,[4] and Rapp and Collins[20] which have led to this profusion of smaller markets, are

- single-parent households, families with double income and no children, yuppies;
- working women, overweight people, tall people;
- increasing minority markets;
- technological advances;
- the evolution of consumer countervailing power;

- changing demographics and lifestyles;
- the demands on personal time;
- overcrowding by too many products, services, and stores;
- the weakening of the magic in network television advertising;
- the decline in brand loyalty;
- advertising clutter, overkill, and waste; and
- feeding the discount promotion monster.

To fulfill the demands of these newly emerging markets requires, among other things, flexibility and differentiation. In today's fragmented market we have to tailor our products and marketing mix to suit the different tastes of the customers. In niche marketing the focus is on the customer and on profit; niche marketers specialize in serving marketing niches. Instead of pursuing the whole market (mass marketing), or large segments of the market, these firms target segments within segments or, for the sake of simplicity, niches. This is true for small firms in particular due to their often limited resources, but it also applies to business units within large firms.

Underlying Trends

Smaller companies do not have a monopoly on niches but they may be better focused and equipped to serve these specific markets, in contrast to their big brothers. There are smaller, nimbler companies, termed the "Third Force" by Ferguson and Morris,[21] which have gained ground from the bigger U.S. and Japanese computer giants, for example. Dalgic[22] likens this competition with niche marketers to guerilla warfare and labels it as "guerrillas against gorillas," gorillas being the giants. Larger companies such as IBM and Philips may also make use of niches but they, like most large companies, will have to change their ways of doing business and adapt their organizations to enable them to take hold of niches as a part of repositioning. IBM, in its quest for profit and IT leadership, has announced further decentralization and the formation of strategic business units to enable them to carry out this process. The former chief executive officer (CEO) of IBM, Aaker,[23] said: "We expect that more independent businesses will make better investment decisions because they are more agile, faster and closer to the markets they choose to serve."

Whether the proposed actions of CEO Aaker will prove successful remains to be seen. However, we may conclude that large mass-marketing firms will need to adapt to this change from uniform markets to individualized/fractured markets. Niche marketing for larger firms, among others, could mean

- new opportunities for healthy profits in smaller markets;
- a new approach to the market from uniform to fractured;
- smaller profits per market, but more markets;
- an easier defense against potential competitors, by creating safe havens; and
- structural internal organizational adaptation which, due to inherent cultural changes, could be a lengthy process.[4,8,11]

An example of a large company pursuing and organized for a niche strategy is Johnson & Johnson, the health care company. It consists of 170 affiliates (business units), most of which pursue niche markets. In a 75 percent response survey conducted by Linneman and Stanton[19] among all Fortune 1,000 firms, the results showed that almost all these firms have, in some way, started to serve smaller segments. This indicates that most of these companies are abandoning traditional mass-marketing techniques and are steadily switching over toward niche marketing. Niche marketing, from the viewpoint of larger firms, may be seen as selling big by selling small, meaning selling to as many niches as possible, where each niche is a small market aggregating into a large one.

As Kotler[24] observed, companies usually have niche markets at the initial stages of their product life cycles as in the case of The Body Shop. This company has leapt from being a local niche marketer to an international niche player. It has found a niche market in cosmetics. As reported by Dibb and Simkin,[25] "based on a clear understanding of certain customers' needs and a very distinctive positioning strategy, The Body Shop is one of the world's fastest growing and most successful niche retailers." Customer focus helps companies to respond faster to the dynamic changes in customer demand, but it takes more than customer focus to become a successful niche marketer as McKenna[4] points out: "An essential requirement for approaching markets however is for the company to focus on the fragmented, ever

evolving customer base as if it were part of the own organization."
According to Piercy:[26]

> being market-led is simply about putting the customer at the top
> of the management agenda and list of priorities. It is about focus
> on the customer, specializing on the customers' unique needs,
> finding better ways of doing what the customer values, educat-
> ing and informing the customer, commitment and care. This is
> the only thing we have that genuinely makes sense of our busi-
> ness operations.

(See Practical Guidelines, Step 2). In order to create a better positioning for your product in the marketplace you have to differentiate your
product from your competitors'. Your product should not be just a
"thing" but should include added values such as service, good customer perception, quality, word-of-mouth references, company image, etc. In niche marketing you market not only your product; you
also market your business. In niche marketing you focus on the customers and you provide the customers with the products they need,
now and in the future. If you can involve your customer in the design
of your product you are halfway there. Some IT companies such as
Apple have done this. They worked with the customer to create new
applications and as a result found new niche markets, such as desktop
publishing. (See Practical Guidelines, Step 5.)

NICHE MARKETING AND MASS MARKETING: A COMPARISON

In marketing management we have moved through several stages:
from the production concept to the selling concept, and from the selling concept to the marketing concept. The marketing concept holds
"that the key to achieving organizational goals consists in determining the needs and wants of target markets and delivering the desired
satisfaction more effectively and efficiently than your competitors."[3]
It may be argued that this concept is better suited to niche marketing
than mass marketing, as an approach to present-day fragmented markets, because niche marketing functions closer to the customer. Niche
marketing has recently become a trend as a result of severe competi-

tion in mature markets. Standardized mass production and trying to sell the same product to masses of consumers seems to become less profitable in these mature markets.

Most managers were taught that mass production and mass marketing were the most advanced and efficient methods to produce and market products. In today's competitive world there still is a strategic debate about the desirability of mass marketing, focusing on standardization, or niche marketing, focusing on customization or tailored products for niche markets. Although there can be benefits to mass marketing it may be argued that niche marketing is more equipped to deal with the existing and rapid changing minimarkets. As stated by Kotler,[24] mass-marketers "engage in the mass production, mass distribution and mass promotion of one product for all buyers." Verhage et al.[27] state three arguments in favor of the mass-marketing strategy:

1. Economic advantages can be gained through economies of scale and experience curve effects.
2. Strategic price mechanism.
3. Competitive—if the economic and strategic argument has been achieved, the company can be competitive, through offering the "best" product at the "best" possible price.

In mass marketing—undifferentiated marketing—a company attempts to reach buyers with one product with one marketing mix. In the product-oriented era of marketing the so-called mass marketing strategy was pursued by many companies. Coca-Cola, for example, was available in only one flavor and in one type of bottle. In this era, entrepreneurs perceived the market as one aggregated market, predominantly focusing on the common needs of customers instead of focusing on differences. Mass marketing does still take place, especially with "undifferentiated" products such as sugar, salt, and milk. But even these are becoming more and more differentiated. According to Porter,[28] by making units of a fairly standardized product and underpricing everybody else, you can attain overall cost leadership; this is one of the most important arguments in favour of undifferentiated marketing.

The difference between mass marketing and niche marketing can be characterized by differences in organizations. A mass-marketing company can be characterized as being centrally led and bureaucratic, which may lead to inflexibility. Niche marketing organizations can be characterized as being decentralized, with several strategic business units if the company is large. If the company is small it can be characterized as being concentrated on one part of the market. This entails anticipative decision making which constitutes responsiveness and flexibility. In *The Third Wave* Tofler[29] talks about the de-massified society as a part of the corporate identity crisis. He states that "the mass society, for which the corporation was designed, is beginning to de-massify. Not merely information, production and family life, but also the market place and the labour market as well are beginning to break into smaller, more varied pieces." The beginning of de-massification has created a plethora of smaller markets which demand continuous change and customization.

An economic argument in favour of niche marketing, in contrast to mass marketing, is "greater profits." As Kotler[3] suggests: Why is niching profitable? The main reason is that the market nicher ends up knowing the target customer so well that he meets their needs better than other firms that are casually selling to this niche. As a result, the nicher can charge a substantial markup over costs because of the added value. The nicher achieves high margin, whereas the mass marketer achieves high volume. Many companies (Campbell, Coca-Cola, IBM, for example) are changing or have adapted from what once was viewed as a single mass market toward a multitude of smaller markets. Some are still focusing on too large segments but this differs depending on whether the product is classified as a commodity or a specialty product. Jain[30] points out that a firm which chooses to serve commodity markets must be the low-cost producer. Specialty manufacturers are less concerned with cost; they must isolate the customer segments they wish to serve and develop a superior product at an appropriate price.

But even when a product can be classified as a commodity a niche-marketing approach can be successful—such as Diet Coke or Nutrasweet. Diet Coke contributes only 4 percent of Coca-Cola's sales volume and might be considered as a narrow segment or niche, but it contributes "more net profit from in-home sales than did the mainstream product, Coke," as reported by Linneman and Stanton.[19] Another group of researchers, Hammermesh et al.,[31] after analyzing successful niche marketers, found the following niching characteristics:

- an ability to segment the market creatively, focusing activities only on areas where a company has particular strengths that are especially valued;
- efficient use of R&D resources, using them where they can be most effective; and
- thinking small: adopting a "small is beautiful approach."

If the marketing concept is adhered to, it is clear that a marketing strategy must be adjusted or tailored to the markets. Recent research results support this view and investigate the constructs and antecedents of market orientation which show us that adherence to the marketing concept, known as market orientation, is a basic requirement for success.[32,33,34] It is often argued that niche marketing is only for small firms. It is interesting to know, however, that most of the successful medium-sized companies today are niche marketers. There are some common factors observed among them. These firms are offering high value; charging a premium price; and creating new experience curves and shaping a strong corporate culture and vision.[35]

According to Tom Peters,[36] the backbone of German economic success is the small and mid-sized companies, almost all of which are niche marketers. Linneman and Stanton[20] also reported a study, carried out by the Strategic Planning Institute, called "Profit Impact of Marketing Strategy" (PIMS), which investigated hundreds of business units from different types of businesses: "It was reported that the return on investment from larger markets averaged 11 percent. By contrast, the return on investment from smaller markets was 27 percent." This supports a niche-marketing approach.

We can draw a parallel between mass marketing and niche marketing in that niche marketers often evolve to mass marketers and mass marketers return to be niche marketers. It seems that most companies start out as niche marketers and evolve into mass marketers as their product life cycles tend to develop into maturity. Once maturity is reached and saturation starts, innovation occurs and former mass markets tend to return to niche markets. A similarity which can be notified between a large niche marketer and a mass marketer is that they both control a large market; the niche marketer however controls aggregated/linked niche markets in contrast to just one large market. (See Practical Guidelines, Step 9, and Figure 1.1.)

A combination mass marketing and niche marketing approach can be found in mass customization. Technological advances such as CAD/CAM have made it possible for marketers to customize their offerings for individual buyers. Some car manufacturers, for example, BMW and GM, offer their customers, within some constraints, the opportunity to custom design their own cars.

CHOOSING A NICHE STRATEGY

When do we choose a niche strategy? According to Leeflang,[2] a niche strategy is selected under the following conditions: (1) if the company concerned has the ability to approach a niche in a specific manner, better and different than others, and (2) if the company is able to create a considerable amount of goodwill in a relatively short period, in order to deter potential competitors.

Jain[30] labeled a niche strategy as a single marketing strategy which can be employed for the following reasons: (1) to avoid competition/confrontation with larger competitors and to devote its energy to serving a unique market; (2) to enhance an opportunity; and (3) survival.

Another reason for choosing a niche strategy, in our opinion, is its use as a competitive strategy. It can be used to penetrate large markets or existing segments, as was done with Oral-B, the children's toothpaste: a weak spot was discovered in the toothpaste market and was subsequently filled by positioning Oral-B as a niche brand. (See Practical Guidelines, Step 3.) Leeflang and Beukenkamp[37] warn against choosing a niche strategy and the inherent danger of hypersegmentation—i.e., selecting niches that are too small. This can, however be countered through contra-segmentation—joining several niches. Leeflang[2] suggests the following points to be taken into account when identifying and selecting a niche strategy:

- realizing sustainable competitive advantages with products in specific markets;
- basing advantages on long-term interests of customers;
- transforming long-term interests into long-lasting relationships with different interest groups; and
- taking initiatives to sustain relationships.

MAKING A NICHE MARKETING STRATEGY WORK

General Examples

The slogan "getting bigger by acting smaller" is one that can literally be applied to niche marketing. Large companies, as well as medium-sized and smaller ones, see the opportunities niche marketing can provide. Consider the following examples:

- American Express introduced several credit cards applicable to as many niches, e.g., the gold card for moderate users, the corporate card for business users, and the platinum card for heavy users. This has been followed by other credit card companies such as Visa and Access. (See Practical Guidelines, Step 11.)
- Niche publishers have arisen, e.g., *Woman's Day, Better Homes and Gardens.* (See Practical Guidelines, Step 8.)
- BMC Software Inc. jumped into a niche which IBM created through producing mainframe software that is not as efficient as it could be. BMC filled that gap with packages that let mainframes run faster, pack more data onto disks, and make databases easier to update. This saves the customer money and helped BMC into a niche of US$90 million. The company's earnings jumped by 50 percent to $1 million in one year. (See Practical Guidelines, Step 3.)

Some European Cases

Due to its fragmented character, old traditions, regional differences, and different nationalities, Europe could be considered a breeding ground for niche marketers. Although used by several marketers, mass marketing as opposed to niche marketing is not really suited to Western Europe. National identity, regional characteristics, and traditional business practices have played, and do play, important roles in the formation of successful Euro-niches. These traditions and fragmented national markets may hinder the application of large-scale mass-marketing techniques in the Euromarket and postpone the realization of expected benefits of Europe-1992 measures. However, Euro-niches may be found across the Euromarket which may give the same economic benefits as mass marketing as well as the benefits of niche marketing. Consider the following examples:

- The Dutch banking organization Direktbank uncovered a niche through focusing on a market other bankers ignored. They concentrated on the growing market for loans to the elderly which seems to be a very profitable market. The same approach could be used in other European countries with a high proportion of elderly citizens. (See Practical Guidelines, Steps 10 and 11.)
- The Dutch supermarket chain Albert Heyn introduced some special programs enabling customers to select their own amounts of products (e.g., vegetables, dog food, sweets). This is profitable for Albert Heyn and also profitable for the customer; it makes the products more accessible to customers, resulting in increased usage and decreased costs for the retailer. The same method has been followed by other European food retailers. (See Practical Guidelines, Step 11.)
- Bavaria, a Dutch beer producer, identified the need for an alcohol-free beer, due to the fact that people want to drink and drive—a key buying motive for purchasing beer without alcohol which proves to be a very successful niche market in the Netherlands. The same method has been applied in other European markets. During the Gulf War, Bavaria also exported a million cans of alcohol-free beer per week to the Gulf for consumption by the Allied Forces. (See Practical Guidelines, Step 11.)
- Pickwick is a Dutch tea brand of Douwe Egberts, a Dutch food producer. The company found a niche market through producing tea with specific tastes such as strawberry, melon, orange, lemon, etc., with which they found new niches. (See Practical Guidelines, Step 11.)

- Linx Printing Technologies is a UK-based company in the industrial inkjet market with an estimated value of $50 million. Industrial inkjet printing is a niche technology which has so far escaped the attention of the big battalions of the electronics industry. (See Practical Guidelines, Step 7.)
- The German firm Scharman, producer of machine tools, found an opportunity by solving an intractable problem for Caterpillar Inc.'s Belgian operations. This job convinced the company to focus on high-quality products that it could sell at a premium. This strategy has been an undeniable success. In 1970 Scharmann sold 150 machine tools for $18 million. In 1987 sales totaled $100 million. (See Practical Guidelines, Step 11.)
- SAP, a German software firm, specializes in writing special software for IBM mainframes and, as a result, uncovered a very profitable niche market. Today SAP is one of the most successful software houses in Europe. (See Practical Guidelines, Step 5.)

PRACTICAL GUIDELINES

Here, we would like to elucidate some practical guidelines for using a niche marketing strategy. There are many pitfalls to niche marketing, and to avoid them, Linneman and Stanton[19] have provided us with some essential guidelines to develop and successfully implement a generic niche marketing strategy. We have used these guidelines and some others, together with the experience of real-life examples, to create a step-by-step approach. They by no means represent the ultimate and only method to make a niche-marketing strategy work. However, they provide a general checklist to prevent potential marketing mistakes.

Step 1: Know Yourself

Know your company's strengths and weaknesses, its uniqueness, competitive advantages, distinctive competencies, regional and traditional characteristics.

Step 2: Know Your Customer

To be able to focus on specific niches or customer groups you need exact information on these customers. Unlike mass-marketing techniques we cannot make assumptions about specific customer groups. You have to know your market and you have to know it better than your competitor. The key to getting to know your customers is through talking and listening to them. This can be the key to success because it will provide the necessary information on which to focus. Proposed actions include the following:

- Gain economies of knowledge in contrast to economies of scale.
- Know your customers and their business; become a specialist in the business of your customers.
- Know your competitor.
- Know your environment.
- Customize your product to suit the customer's business: do not suit it to suit your own business.
- Focus on the customer; be market driven.

Step 3: Know Your Competitors

Find out why customers do not use your products but use competitors' goods and find out how you can persuade them to purchase your products. This might be accomplished through repositioning your offering or through other means.

Step 4: Develop a Continuous Information System

Present-day database techniques can provide us with a comparatively cheap, efficient marketing tool. This database can register prospects and customer traits. The types of data needed, however, are the data needed for decision making. In niche marketing we do not need sales volume but profit figures. This is due to the fact that in niche marketing we make a decision based on profit and not on sales volume, which is of secondary importance. Customer databases need to be linked to other marketing information systems and business intelligence systems in order to be responsive to the marketplace.

Step 5: Apply Differentiation

Be differentiated, not just different; offer significant benefits to your customers. Determine what your customers' real values are and appeal to these values better than anyone else. Position by differentiation and segmentation. Position on your own strengths and the weaknesses of others. Develop a clear product image for each niche. Communicate how your product can fulfill key buying motives.

Step 6: Do Not Compete in the Same Market Segments with Yourself

Avoid competing with your own products in the same market segments. Do not let your "soldiers" fight with each other; be specific in defining your own niches.

Step 7: Create Your Safe Haven

Create high entry barriers through building a close relationship with your customers, patents, copyrights, alliances, and relationship marketing. Cover all the bases to deter potential competitors.

Step 8: Do Not Spread Too Thin

If you have discovered one niche you'll probably end up finding more, but make sure that you do not exceed your limit by expending all your abilities and resources; stay flexible.

Step 9: Develop a Corporate Marketing Strategy

You cannot develop your niche markets as stand-alone markets but you have to link them to gain synergies and create efficiency. For large firms this could entail linking the SBU's niche marketing plans into a corporate plan.

Step 10: Be Alert; Be in Control

It is essential to watch constantly for shifts in the marketplace and to respond to them.

Step 11: Do Not Be Static; Look for New Pastures Continuously

In addition to the methods already mentioned for locating niches, here are some further approaches to locate niche markets. It should be determined why those who use your competitors' products do not use yours and how you can turn them to your products; this might be done through repositioning your marketing offer or through other means. Regarding those who don't use your or your competitors' products— find out why. Consider the possibility that creating new products/services for an old category may mean new solutions to old problems. Consider conglomerate diversification (be careful; watch your resources). Look at emerging markets.

Step 12: Minimize Your Dependence on Any One Customer or Product

Do not put all the eggs in the same basket. Try to increase your alternatives. Create more room to maneuver.

CONCLUSIONS AND RECOMMENDATIONS

Niche marketing could be viewed as the implementation of the marketing concept, in that niche marketing requires a customer/market-oriented organization which is customer focused, competitor oriented, responsive, anticipative, and functions in balance with the market and with internal resources, in pursuit of long-term relationships and sustainable profitability. Niche marketing is a continuous process.

In this chapter, we tried to cover all the important studies to reach a general understanding and develop basic guidelines for the application of niche marketing strategies. This is only a start. Further empirical and theoretical research is needed to determine the success factors of this strategy.

NOTES

1. Dalgic, T. (1992). "Euromarketing: Charting the Map for Globalization," *International Marketing Review,* Vol. 9 No. 5, pp. 31-42.

2. Leeflang, P.S.H. (1990). "Market Segmentation," unpublished European Business Studies Seminar (03-1990).

3. Kotler, P. (1991). "From Mass Marketing to Mass Customization," *Planning Review,* September/October, pp. 11-47.

4. McKenna, R. (1988). "Marketing in an Age of Diversity," *Harvard Business Review,* November-December, pp. 88-95.

5. *Webster's* Dictionary (1992). New York: Pamco Publishing Co.

6. Crambie, M.A., Hickman, C.J., and Johnson, M.L. (1978). *Penguin Dictionary of Biology,* 6th ed., London: Penguin.

7. Lambkin, M. and Day, S. (1989). "Evolutionary Processes in Competitive Markets: Beyond the Product Life Cycle," *Journal of Marketing,* July, pp. 4-20.

8. Keegan, W., Moriarty, S., and Duncan, T. (1992). *Marketing,* Englewood Cliffs, NJ: Prentice Hall.

9. Hooley, J.G. and Saunders, J. (1993). *Competitive Positioning: The Key to Market Success,* London: Prentice Hall.

10. Chalasani, S. and Shani, D. (1992). "Exploiting Niches Using Relationship Marketing," *The Journal of Consumer Marketing,* Vol. 9 No. 3, pp. 33-42.

11. Stanton, W.E.J., Etzel, M.J., and Walker, B.J. (1991). *Fundamentals of Marketing,* New York: McGraw-Hill.

12. Pavitt, K. (1990). "What We Know About the Strategic Management of Technology," *California Management Review,* Vol. 32, pp. 17-26.

13. Davis, S.M. and Davidson, W. (1990). *2020 Vision,* New York: Simon and Schuster.

14. Copulsky, J. and Wolf, J.M. (1990). "Relationship Marketing: Positioning for the Future," *The Journal of Business Strategy,* July/August, pp. 16-20.

15. Blattberg, R.C. and Deighton, J. (1991). "Interactive Marketing: Exploiting the Age of Addressability," *Sloan Management Review,* Vol. 33 No. 1, pp. 5-14.

16. Naisbitt, J. (1982). *Megatrends,* New York: Warner Books.

17. Sheth, N.J. (1992). "Emerging Marketing Strategies in a Changing Macroeconomic Environment: A Commentary," *International Marketing Review,* Vol. 9 No. 1, pp. 57-63.

18. Thurow, L. (Ed.) (1985). *The Management Challenge,* Cambridge, MA: MIT Press.

19. Linneman, R.E. and Stanton, J.L. (1991). *Making Niche Marketing Work,* book and audiotape, New York: McGraw-Hill.

20. Rapp, S. and Collins, T. (1990). *The Great Marketing Turnaround: The Age of the Individual and How to Profit,* Englewood Cliffs, NJ: Prentice Hall.

21. Ferguson, H.C. and Morris, R.C. (1993). *Computer Wars,* New York: Times Books.

22. Dalgic, T. (1993). "European Marketing Strategies: Guerillas Against Gorillas," unpublished lecture notes, Henley Management College—Nederland, Zeist, the Netherlands, and Hoogeschool voor Economie en Management (HEM), Utrecht, the Netherlands.

23. Aaker, A.D. (1984). *Strategic Marketing Management,* New York: John Wiley & Sons.

24. Kotler, P. (1989). *Marketing Management,* 7th ed., New Jersey: Prentice Hall.

25. Dibb, S. and Simkin, L. (1991). "Targets, Segments and Positioning," *International Journal of Retail & Distribution Management,* Vol. 19 No. 3, pp. 5-10.

26. Piercy, N. (1991). *Market-Led Strategic Change: Making Marketing Happen in Your Organization,* London: Thorsons.

27. Verhage, J.B., Dahringer, B.J., and Cundiff, E.W. (1989). "Will a Global Marketing Strategy Work? An Energy Conservation Perspective," *Journal of the Academy of Marketing Science,* Vol. 17 No. 2, pp. 129-136.

28. Porter, M.T. (1980). *Competitive Strategy: Techniques for Analyzing Industries and Competitors,* New York: Free Press.

29. Tofler, A. (1980). *The Third Wave,* New York: Bantam Books.

30. Jain, C.S. (1985). *Marketing Planning and Strategy,* 2nd ed., Cincinnati, OH: South-Western Publishing.

31. Hammermesh, R.G., Anderson, M.J., and Harris, J.E. (1978). "Strategies for Low Market Share Businesses," *Harvard Business Review,* Vol. 50 No. 3, pp. 95-102.

32. Kohli, K.A. and Jaworski, J.B. (1990). "Market Orientation: The Construct, Research Propositions and Managerial Implications," *Journal of Marketing,* Vol. 54, April, pp. 1-18.

33. Narver, C.J. and Slater, F.S. (1990). "The Effect of a Market Orientation on Business Profitability," *Journal of Marketing,* Vol. 54, October, pp. 20-35.

34. Jaworski, J.B. and Kohli, K.A. (1993). "Market Orientation: Antecedents and Consequences," *Journal of Marketing,* Vol. 57, July, pp. 53-70.

35. Clifford, K.D. and Kavanagh, E.R. (1985). *The Winning Performance: How America's Hi-Growth Midsize Companies Succeed,* New York: Bantam Books.

36. Peters, T. (1990). "The German Economic Miracle Nobody Knows," *Across the Board,* April, pp. 16-23.

37. Leeflang, P.S.H. and Beukenkamp, P.A. (1981). *Probleemgebied marketing, een management benadering,* Leiden: Stenfert Kroese.

SUGGESTED FURTHER READING

Porter, M.E. (1980). *Competitive Advantage: Creating and Sustaining Superior Performance,* New York: Free Press.

Chapter 2

Principles of Global
Niche Marketing Strategies:
An Early Conceptual Framework

Isil Hezar
Tevfik Dalgic
Steven Phelan
Gary Knight

INTRODUCTION

The ever-increasing diversity in consumer tastes and habits as well as changing needs of business and organizational markets, coupled with cutthroat competition, structural changes in markets, continuous advancement in information, and production technologies do not only create new marketing approaches and methods but also threaten large companies and question the validity of their traditional marketing methods and practices. Niche marketing is among the most frequently mentioned marketing methods in the business press recently (see *Forbes* issues in 1991-2005, *The Wall Street Journal,* 1996-2005). However, academic journals seem to ignore this popular business choice, and the literature of marketing is lacking in this field (Dalgic, 1998). When it comes to international markets, the need for new marketing approaches and methods becomes more urgent due to the fact that many companies from different countries compete for the same host markets. International marketers need applicable, operationalized methods to be more successful in foreign markets.

Most international management theory focuses on large, established multinational corporations (Oviatt and McDougall, 1994). Existing internationalization theory highlights slow and incremental foreign market commitment because such behavior has been frequently observed and because internationalization seems so risky for small and new ventures (Johanson and Vahlne, 1990).

According to a study by the Organisation for Economic Co-operation and Development (OECD), more than a quarter of the world's small manufacturing firms already derive more than 10 percent of their revenue from foreign sources, and at least one-third of them are predicted to do so by 2005. One to two percent of small manufacturing firms are estimated to be international at inception. Although that percentage may seem small now, it represents at least 30,000 to 40,000 firms worldwide. Niche marketing has been identified in small and medium-sized enterprises' (SME) success strategies by different studies. Several authors identified successful niche strategies at national markets in general terms (Stanton, Etzel, and Walker, 1991; Stanton and Linneman, 1991; Shani and Chalasani, 1992; Dalgic and Leeuw, 1994; Dalgic, 1998). As we stand at the threshold of a new millennium, the number of young firms experiencing rapid internationalization appears to be increasing, yet our understanding of them is rudimentary.

Although niche marketing is applied by several companies around the world, today we do not have any information on how to operationalize it, nor any idea on how to apply in international markets properly. This chapter is an early conceptual assessment of literature in this area trying to develop a framework for evaluation, development, and application of international generic niche marketing strategies. A niche strategy or focus strategy as termed by Porter (1980) concentrates on serving a particular market niche, which can be defined geographically, by type of customer, or by segment of the product line. Biggadike (1977) defined niche as using narrow product lines and narrow market segments. Leduc's (1998) definition of a niche market covers a group of potential customers who share common characteristics making them especially receptive to a product, service, or opportunity. Johnson and Scholes (1993) define niche strategy as an extreme example of focus. Similarly, according to Bantel (1997), complementing a niche strategy is a highly focused strategic planning process in which the narrow scope of the firm is the guiding principle. On the application side, Clifford and Cavanagh (1985) found that mid-sized companies attributed their success directly to the way in which they niched within a market rather than trying to go after the entire market. As Dalgic and Leeuw (1994) concluded, niche marketing strategy also requires establishing long-term, one-to-one relationships with customers where possible, and adopting a customer focus.

Most of us are aware that certain items are consistent sellers. This is one reason why potters make so many coffee mugs, even though supermarket shelves are always well stocked with serviceable industrial products. Many are made, at astronomical rates, on computer-controlled, robot-equipped production lines. Yet the very weight of this mass production opens up markets for goods of high quality, good design, appropriate decoration, and originality. Success comes from an ability to make a rapid response, manufacturing short runs of products that customers need—in other words, exploiting niche marketing (Lewis, 1998).

Niche Marketing in General

An understanding of niche marketing at national-market levels is the first step in the development of an understanding of international niche marketing. Only recently have the large consumer-brand marketers, dissatisfied with the erosion in their brands, begun to speak in terms of niche marketing strategies. There is a proliferation of niche products and services, some successful and some not, as large consumer marketers face the realization that their brands cannot be all things to all people. Tapping particular niches can also help companies stand out from the crowd. "A business must differentiate itself in ways that are important to the customer," concludes Kotler (2003, p. 48). "Concentrate on one or two areas in which you can excel or stand out, such as speed, reliability, service, design, relationships, features, personality, or technology. That is the key to success."

A West Coast company called Natural Nectar with about 50 years of existence situated in City of Industry, California, achieved extraordinary success by focusing on product differentiation and niche positioning. According to Maynard (1993), Natural Nectar's owners wanted to serve niches with special products aimed at satisfying certain customer needs. They developed strategies to provide more fiber products to their targeted niche. Natural Nectar introduced FI-BAR, a low-fat, cholesterol-free, high-fiber granola snack bar. The main reason for the company success was studying the competition and trying to see the unsatisfied, overlooked mini segment in the market. Natural Nectar's management discovered that granola bars aimed at the crowded children's market were dominated by the big food companies. So they decided to go for the less-competitive mini segments, mainly young-adult and senior markets (Maynard, 1993). They made some adjustments to the selected niche needs and adopted a product differentiation strategy for the targeted niches' tastes by developing bars with only almonds. Later on, the company introduced a product containing fruit and nuts (Maynard, 1993). They could not compete head-on with the big companies, so they found a little niche that worked. Instead of creating a "me-too" product they differentiated themselves (Maynard, 1993). Natural Nectar has continued to do extensive marketplace homework and creative marketing, including an emphasis on product samplings designed to counter assumptions that healthful products are not tasty.

Philip Kotler is the only marketing academic who devoted large coverage to niche marketing (2003). As he points out, "whereas segments are fairly large and normally attract several competitors, niches are fairly small and normally attract only one" (2003). His definition of an attractive niche is characterized as, "The customers in the niche have a distinct set of needs; they will pay a premium to the firm that best satisfies their needs; the niche is not likely to attract other competitors; the nicher gains certain economies through specialization; and the niche has size, profit and growth potential" (Kotler 2003, p. 280).

Let us take the example of Chrysler Corporation, which was merged with the German luxury auto maker Mercedes. Chrysler, relying on its ability to mass market millions of cars, produced the Dodge Viper, a niche vehicle that sells in extremely limited quantities to hard-core automotive enthusiasts. Although niche strategy theoretically seems to be a good idea, in practice there are some pitfalls and other specific factors that may play important roles in applying this strategy.

INCREASING SEGMENTATION OF MARKETS

In the new competitive landscape, many firms have become adept at identifying precise differences among customers' needs. Armed with these understandings, companies segment customers into competitively relevant groups—groups of customers with unique needs (Hitt, Ireland, and Hoskisson, 1999). In the United States, estimates are that at least 62 distinct classes of citizens exist, each with its own beliefs, aspirations, tastes, and needs. Some believe that, if anything, the trend toward fragmentation into smaller classes and subgroups is accelerating in the United States and throughout the world's markets (Labich, 1994). As McKenna (1991) pointed out, to focus on the fragmented, over-evolving customer base as if it were part of the organization is an essential requirement for approaching markets. Consider examples from the toothpaste market. The recent proliferation in niche toothpastes include special interests such as tartar control, or people with sensitive teeth, or people who have dentures, or people who smoke or have gum disease.

As markets fragment, profitable positions become available. There is no need to go head-to-head against a strong competitor. Markets constantly evolve, and each new evaluation generates opportunities. The results of a 75 percent response survey conducted by Stanton and Linneman (1991), among all Fortune 500 firms, showed that almost all of these firms have in some way started to serve smaller market segments to be closer to their customers. Today's segmented society has room for many positions, but each position has room for only one occupant. When company leaders know which positions their competitors occupy, they will not waste valuable time and resources trying to fill the same slots. Room exists even in a highly competitive market. One can succeed in a market dominated by large players. Like the 600-pound gorilla that can sleep anywhere he wants, the big companies can successfully occupy a limited amount of space at any one time. The success comes by giving them the position they have picked and looking for a niche too specialized or too small to attract their attention (Reynolds, 1993).

Successful organizations have become so by better meeting the needs of some group or segment. According to Kadens (Glascoff, 2000), one way for a health care organization to become successful is to find a niche that is currently underserved (in terms of number of competitors). To do this, he suggested organizations be assessed on six different dimensions identified as the six Cs of e-health organizations, which seems to be defined as an organization actively involved in some manner in electronic commerce. The six Cs of e-health organizations are connectivity, commerce, community, content, care, and consulting. Organizations can be classified by the extent to which they provide each of them. After examining 39 different organizations on those six items, the author created 16 "clusters" or niches depending on the mix of online services each offered. Two of the clusters had six or more organizations (suggesting customers desiring those sets of services were well served), while eight companies were singular in providing a particular mix of Cs—thus suggesting that opportunities might exist in those eight niches.

The author predicted successful e-health organizations would be those emphasizing business customers, rather than final household consumers, and/or were the result of mergers and acquisitions rather than start-ups. Interestingly, no mention was made of groups of Cs that did not exist as opportunities (i.e., no organization provided all six or even five of the six Cs, and no organization was alone in focusing on only one C in the case of connectivity, community, or consulting). The logic of segmentation and focusing would suggest those "empty" areas might represent niche opportunities to be better served by a single-function provider rather than looking at what competitors are currently doing (Glascoff, 2000).

Maynard (1993) provides another successful niche marketing case, this time from Atlantic Publication Group, Inc. (APG), in Charleston, South Carolina. This company is a good example of how small companies succeed by taking advantage of their flexibility and tailoring their goods and services for market segments. As Maynard (1993) reports, APG spent four years offering broad-based, general-interest magazines on a variety of subjects before Marvin Jenkins, the president of APG, began developing products for particular niches in 1989. In 1993, this small company was producing twenty-eight publications for different organizations. APG grew from four to eleven employees, and revenues tripled. The company first identified prospective readers and tried to determine what they were looking for. APG looked for groups that have a database of readers and needed means to communicate with their readers. Company President Jenkins made arrangements to produce publications over several years for trade associations, economic development entities, municipalities, regulators, architects, and other groups.

NICHE AS SURVIVAL STRATEGY

Weak organizations are unlikely to survive through the product life cycle unless they identify and exploit a market niche and, effectively, become a strong provider within that niche. A declining business could search for some niche in which to survive, as Motorola in Case 1.

Case 1: Motorola has pursued a declining niche strategy in deciding to stick with the basic transistor business. Since integrated circuits and advanced semiconductors have long replaced basic transistors in most electronic applications, many of the original firms producing basic transistors have finally exited. Motorola is now the last niche producer of basic transistors that still have a tiny market—mostly hobbyists—in the United States (Pitts and Lei, 2000).

A small entrepreneurial company can outperform its competitors if employees develop special skills and knowledge to serve a narrow market. Developing an effective niche strategy, including achieving high market share in a targeted segment, can lead to high performance, save time and expense, and reduce management complexity and duplication of effort (Bantel, 1997).

Domino's Pizza is a good example of how to grow in a market with a strong competitor, Pizza Hut, by focusing on home delivery as explained by Case 2.

Case 2: Domino's Pizza began with a pizza parlor in Ypsilanti, Michigan. When owners wanted to grow, they knew that they could not compete head-to-head with Pizza Hut; therefore, they narrowed their focus. They selected a market segment that was not being featured by their competitors, a segment they could dominate with their limited resources. Domino's Pizza chose home delivery. Home delivery was not new; other pizza parlors delivered as well, but no other pizza company focused all their efforts and resources on the home-delivery market. Domino's differed from its competitors who were trying to do it all: in-store pizza, takeout pizza, delivery pizza, and other food choices. Domino's redesigned its operation to accommodate the home-delivery niche (Reynolds, 1993).

More effort focused on narrower choices leads to greater productivity and therefore higher profits. It is that simple, and it is that hard. Many companies start out to focus on a single position but get off the track (Reynolds, 1993). Chrysler need look no further than American Motors, a company it absorbed, to see what can happen when a company insists on competing in a desperate market at the expense of losing its niche position as explained in Case 3.

Case 3: American Motors owned the four-wheel drive vehicle market position with the established Jeep. Instead of focusing on this position and further strengthening it, American Motors threw its Jeep profits into a hopeless passenger car battle against the big three car makers, General Motors, Ford, and Chrysler. American Motors was destroyed and Chrysler absorbed the pieces. Since its rebirth, Chrysler's sales successes have been with unique vehicles such as the Jeep, minivans, and convertibles. Instead of focusing its efforts on expanding these successes, Chrysler continued its fruitless battle against Ford and General Motors and poured money into unsuccessful diversification efforts. While Chrysler was pursuing this strategy, Ford improved the Explorer (Reynolds, 1993).

Great Transaction Costs for Small and Medium-Sized Enterprises

SMEs are confronted by greater transaction costs than larger enterprises not only because they cannot enjoy economies of scale, economies of scope, and economies of experience, but also because they are more sensitive to uncertainty. They are also more vulnerable to opportunism and they raise higher suspicions of opportunism. Small firms therefore cannot target a low-cost strategy in large market commodities, but rather need to focus on product differentiation or a niche strategy. The propensity to be involved with a specialized product requiring specialized assets targeted for a narrow group of consumers tends to increase for smaller firms (Fujita, 1998). Niche retailing also uses a simple rule of business: Stick to those who seek your product and need your service. Franchisees of Aaron Rental Purchase in Atlanta point out that rent-to-purchase furniture and appliance is a niche without a season. Aarons gives its target market, consumers with blemished credit, the opportunity to rent and purchase items. Aarons has carved its niche against its competitors by opening 8,000-square foot stores, compared to the industry standard of 2,000 square feet. The customers can own items within 12 months rather than anywhere from 18 to 24 months (Shubart, 1998).

Another example is a Houston home improvement company, which is a niche retailer by providing four different concepts with four different franchises for four different customer segments (see Case 4).

Case 4: A Houston, Texas, company, Franchise Concepts Inc., developed a new approach to franchising by creating four franchises each appealing to a different customer segment. They are operated in different locations. Franchise Concepts Inc. deals with home-improvement franchises with the following names: Deck the Walls, Great Frame Up, Framing and Arts Centre, and Ashley Avery Collectibles. The management of the company knows about identifying and expanding their target markets. Shubart (1988) reported that custom art framing at Deck the Walls and Ashley Avery were located in shopping malls, self-framing at Great Frame Up, and Framing and Arts Centres were located in strip malls. The company CEO believed in niche marketing and niche retailing. Customization worked especially well with the art concepts because no one wanted the same art as everyone else (Shubart, 1998).

EXPLOITING: CARVING NICHES BY EXISTING COMPANIES

Exploiting a narrow, specialized segment of a broad, diverse market can bring in solid profits. Delaney (1995) provides several examples. One comes from the Plaza Bootery in downtown Larchmont, New York, which had been selling expensive designer handbags off nails on the walls. In addition to its large stock of moderately priced shoes, the management of the company figured out that there was a market for an upscale women's shop. Instead of copying the similar merchandise sellers, they opened an upscale store, Plaza Too, without conducting market research. They sell $12 hosiery, $200 shoes, and $300 handbags in an affluent community within commuting distance of New York City (Delaney, 1995). Their secret for success is targeting the customer who is fashion conscious and has money to spend. Their customers can shop locally instead of having to drive to malls. This is another successful niche marketing experience in the retail merchandise sector by a small firm aimed at exploiting a small segment of a large, diverse market which is generally served by only the biggest companies. By targeting a well-defined niche, the business can then offer specialized goods and services to a specific group of customers. To succeed, however, a niche business must stand out in the crowded retail marketplace (Delaney, 1995).

Niche businesses do not need a good economy to succeed; they can also be successful during economic downturns according to their niche market characteristics. Delaney (1995) provides some examples for those successful niche marketers. For example, gas utility businesses must maintain lines and repair leaks even in a bad economy and even in the worst weather conditions. Their service trucks typically haul air compressors on trailers to operate equipment at work sites. Mr. Patrick Wilkens, an employee in the marketing and sales staff of the utility company Sulair Corporation, which manufactures air compressors in Michigan City, Indiana, designed a way to mount compressors under a truck's hood. Because of an economic recession, utility companies were looking for ways to be more cost-effective. Mounting compressors under the trucks' hoods have made them more efficient and less costly. Mr. Wilkens quit his job and started a new business with his brother, Paul, a certified public accountant. They developed a detailed business plan and a five-year forecast with $75,000 in savings and $500,000 in loans guaranteed by the Small Business Administration (SBA). Their business venture was based on their knowledge of the industry; they easily recognized a niche and took advantage of this underserved market. This new firm aggressively marketed their modified compressors to gas companies, offering a year's free tryout. They knew that once a crew got used to not hauling a compressor, they would want the new product. The new firm set up distributor networks in Canada and the United States and demonstrated their machines at trade shows. Their first year's sales were eighty compressors at $7,500 each. In 1994, combined sales for compressors, parts, and service came to almost $5 million.

Take another example from the pet care business. Veterinary technician Peggy Swain and her business partner Julie Getz started a niche business of a different sort: specialized care service for pets. Their company, Pet Pals Inc., provides lodging, grooming, and home-care visits when owners of pets are away. For $11/hour, they visit a home, feed, walk, and brush the pets, change their litter boxes, water plants, take in the mail, and put out the trash. Their business idea is based on the belief that people look at their pets as their kids and they want them pampered. Their pet hotel offers forty pet rooms for $7 to $11 a night, plus a grooming salon, an exercise area, and twenty-four-hour supervision (Delaney, 1995). Dogs in their pet hotel are walked individually four times a day and they also receive nondairy treats. Peggy Swain and Julie Getz launched their company with $90,000 of their own money plus $135,000 in SBA-guaranteed loans. They advertised in newspapers and with fliers, but mostly word-of-mouth. This has attracted 4,000 clients (Delaney, 1995). Locals were not sure whether they could pull it off in a small community, but they did. In the long run, these entrepreneurs plan to add an emergency clinic for pets, with veterinary care open from dusk to dawn (Delaney, 1995).

Here is another niche marketing success example that started with limited resources and a well-defined target market. In 1989, Andrew and Thomas Parkinson pioneered the online grocery delivery concept, establishing Peapod in Evanston, Illinois. Combining backgrounds in consumer product marketing (Andrew was a brand manager with Procter & Gamble and Kraft) and technology expertise (Thomas was the founder of a software company), the brothers established Peapod as a lifestyle solution for busy families. In 1990 Peapod partnered with Chicago-area Jewel Food Stores to fulfill orders. Peapod began test marketing to about 400 households in Evanston. The company provides software and modems for customers who have to dial in directly to the Peapod shopping system. During the early days, Andrew, Thomas, and their families did the picking and packing—making deliveries with their own cars. In 1991, with the success of the Evanston location, Peapod expanded its service to the surrounding suburbs. Chicago Peapod launched service in San Francisco in collaboration with Safeway in 1993. In 1995 Peapod launched its first advertising campaign; the company gained 4,600 members. The same year Peapod initiated service in Columbus, Ohio, with the Kroger Company. In 1996, Peapod reached a customer base of 43,200, and partnered with Stop & Shop to offer "Peapod by Stop & Shop" in the Boston metro area. Later, Peapod developed its own Web site (www.peapod.com) and *Journal Inc.* named Peapod in the "Inc. 500" list of the fastest-growing U.S. private companies. A year later, Peapod opened the first Stop & Shop wareroom in Watertown, Massachusetts, just outside Boston, and in June, Peapod completed a successful initial public offering by listing its shares on the NASDAQ. After a steady increase in its coverage in 2000, famous Dutch food retailer Royal Ahold took a 51 percent ownership. Peapod is one of the success stories of Web-based niche marketers.

Many entrepreneurs typically fall in love with their products or services, but that doesn't mean the consumers will do the same. Do some homework. Delaney (1995) offers some ways to determine if there is a niche for you: Size up the market. Describe your market in terms of growth, trends, and demographics. Identify your target customers, their per-capita income, age, sex, geographic locations, and attitudes. Supporting data can be obtained from trade associations, trade journals, government statistics, and surveys. Marketing consultants probably can do research faster than you can. Business owners should know the other players, their strategies, strengths, and weaknesses. You won't be able to compete on every front, so try to match your strengths—people, product, and service—against your competitors' weaknesses. Make sure your product or service—your niche— has staying power and won't be overtaken or made obsolete in a world of rapidly changing technology. Try to stay on top of the current market. Make a list of the barriers that could prevent you from reaching your marketing goals. Insufficient capital, lack of management experience, or too much competition can spell failure. Savvy entrepreneurs know their limitations and do their best to overcome them (Delaney, 1995).

An industry's structural attractiveness is determined by five underlying sources of competition (Porter, 1985):

- the intensity of rivalry among existing competitors;
- the barriers to entry for new competitors;
- the threat of substitute products and services;
- the bargaining power of suppliers; and
- the bargaining power of buyers.

An examination of a wide range of industries that are applying niche strategy may reveal some clear views. If we apply Porter's Internet model (Porter, 2001, p. 67), we see that some of the industries could be negative for a nicher if a nicher is out-focused by other nichers. Another risk is shifting the strength to other products. There are two reasons for this: First, the niche is too specific for the customers and the product value is not providing enough attractiveness. Second, the technology and/or trends affect the position of the products dramatically. In addition, if the supplier is also a nicher, the power shifts to the supplier.

However, most of the forces seem to be positive. Niche marketing provides high barriers for entry as long as the niche is well defended. By successful specialization and focus, niche marketing prevents threats of substitute products or services. The competition between the suppliers increases. Nichers can charge premium prices as well as eliminate powerful channels or improve bargaining power over existing channels. The companies using niche strategy defend their own territory, where they may shift to other niches; they become multi-nichers.

Two approaches are used by companies deploying niche strategy: up-down approach and bottom-up approach. The following figures illustrate the flow of this strategy. The up-down approach is deduction, where the companies diversify customer segments. They go from mass markets to niche markets. These companies become big by being big in small markets. The second approach, the bottom-up approach, is induction, where the companies start with the individual customer and build a niche strategy around it. Then they search for similarities among customers to obtain customer clusters, where they go from single niches to multiple niches. These companies become big by being small in small markets. Figure 2.1 illustrates this concept in detail.

NICHE MARKETING STRATEGIES
IN INTERNATIONAL MARKETS

International marketing literature also lacks the studies showing characteristics and operationalization methods of niche strategy. Leontiades (1986) identified four generic international competitive marketing strategies as shown in Figure 2.2. Also, some reported cases and empirical studies provided clues about the characteristics and managerial issues related with niche marketing strategies.

In an empirical study of internationalization of 533 German medium-sized enterprises, the authors illustrated a deficit in the field of strategic planning of internationalization. Although the individual planning activities are attested as being of major importance, deficits in implementation are evident (Behnam and Gilbert, 2000).

Business-level strategies are concerned with a firm's industry position relative to competitors. Companies that have established favorable industry positions are better able to cope with the competition.

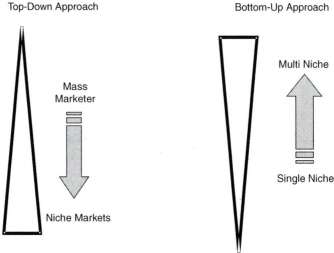

FIGURE 2.1. Top-Down and Bottom-Up Approaches (*Source:* Adapted from Dalgic and Leeuw, 1994, p. 41.)

		High	Low
Scope	Global	Global high share strategy	Global niche strategy
	National	National high share strategy	National niche strategy

Configuration of Activities

FIGURE 2.2. Generic International Competitive Strategies

By using niche marketing strategies, SMEs develop strategic advantages through targeting specific market segments based on

- customer characteristics and unique customer needs,
- specific or differentiated product(s) designed to solve these specific needs,
- geographic locations, sometimes ignored by the large companies,
- lower overhead costs,
- better coordination and communication,
- flexibility and ability to move fast,
- competitive advantage based on skills, expertise, service quality, and customer relations, and
- preventing head-to-head confrontation with the large companies.

This makes niche marketing strategy a customer-focused or customer-oriented strategy at national markets. This conclusion is also found to be correct for international markets (Dalgic, 1998). Some authors have even labeled these companies as "guerillas" fighting a war against the gorillas—the big companies (Dalgic, 1988; Dalgic and Leeuw, 1994; Kotler, 2003). The main issue then becomes how to operationalize niche marketing strategies in international markets.

International niche marketing is concerned with marketing a differentiated product or service overseas using the full range of market entry and marketing mix options available. Exporting is primarily concerned with selling domestically developed and produced goods and services abroad. Domestically delivered or developed niche services can be marketed or delivered internationally to potential visitors.

Direct marketing including electronic commerce allows firms to market products and services globally from a domestic location. Participation in the international supply chain of a multinational enterprise (MNE) can lead to SMEs piggybacking on the MNE's international development. This may involve either domestic production or establishing a facility close to where the MNE's new locations are established in other countries. For international niche marketing to be successful, the product or service must be distinctive, highly differentiated, and recognized by consumers and other participants in the international supply chain, and have clear positioning (Doole and Lowe, 1999).

BMW is one of the most successful vehicle manufacturers in the world, although by no means the largest. BMW protects its niche position by engineering, manufacturing, and developing advertisement campaigns as explained in Case 5.

Case 5: On July 21, 1917, Rapp-Motorenwerke was renamed Bayerische Motoren Werke GmbH. It is the company name for the famous BMW brand cars. Their manufacturing plants were originally located in Germany. Recently they opened new manufacturing plants in South Africa, the United States, and China. Up to 20,000 parts travel the pressings plant and are then painted and assembled to become a perfect whole—a unique BMW. Every vehicle that rolls off the line is tailor-made according to the customer's wishes in terms of model, color, interior furnishing, accessories, and engine type. With this special care, BMW cars over the years have developed a high-speed, sleek-looking, exciting brand image. The cars and the current company success have come from the development of a long-term-oriented niche marketing strategy.

International business is considered inherently risky because it involves potential loss of profits and/or assets as a result of potential changes in political, legal, economic, and social factors in foreign markets where firms compete (Cosset and Roy, 1991; Ghoshal,

1987). However, there is little theory about managing international risk for firms experiencing the accelerated internationalization that has become apparent in recent years. Since the phenomenon will likely be increasingly prevalent in the new millennium (OECD, 1997), theory development and testing would appear to be valuable for both academics and entrepreneurs (Shrader, Oviatt, and Mc-Dougall, 2000).

In a study by Litvak (1992) with 29 small technology-based companies, one of the common corporate strategies among successful survivors was to pursue a global marketing niche strategy. Benefits for new technology firms with a niche planning strategy include a higher number of employees, greater productivity per employee, and higher performance on operational efficiency, sales growth, market development, profitability, and future prospects (Bantel, 1997).

Winterhalter Gastronom, a German dishwasher company, shows how to boost the market position by focusing on a narrow product line in depth (see Case 6).

Case 6: Winterhalter makes dishwashers for commercial use. Many different markets exist for such a product—hospitals, schools, companies, public organizations, hotels, restaurants, military installations, and so on. Therefore, the market potential is large, but the customers' requirements vary from segment to segment. Many different products are available in the market for the various segments. When Winterhalter analyzed the total market for commercial dishwashers, they found that their world market share was about 2 percent. This led them to totally redirect their strategy. They focused solely on hotels and restaurants. They even renamed the company Winterhalter Gastronom. They then defined their business as a supplier of clean glasses and dishes for hotels and restaurants and took full responsibility. They included water-conditioning devices and their own brand of detergent in their product line. They offered excellent service around the clock. Winterhalter Gastronom's world market share in the hotel/restaurant segment rose to 15 to 20 percent and was climbing (Simon, 1996).

Small and medium-sized firms are often better suited for global expansion than huge firms with high overhead, bureaucratic slowness, and inflexibility. Small firms are usually better positioned and able to meet similar niches in other countries than large firms are as well.

The same niche that created high growth in the domestic market can be achieved not once but repeatedly in many other countries if the owners understand the realities of global business expansion (Blackwell and Stephan, 1990).

Two of Porter's (1985) generic strategies, focus and differentiation, are used efficiently by many SMEs in international niche marketing. Cost leadership is a very difficult strategic option to utilize in international markets due to the limited resources of these companies.

The foundation of focus strategies is that a firm can serve a particular segment of an industry more effectively or efficiently than can industry-wide competitors. Success with a focus strategy rests on a firm's ability either to find segments where unique needs are so specialized that broad-based competitors choose not to serve them or to locate a segment being served poorly by the broad-based competitors. The unique attributes and characteristics of a firm's product (other than cost) provide value to customers by differentiation strategy. Because a differentiation product satisfies customers' unique needs, firms implementing the differentiation strategy charge premium prices. The ability to sell its differentiated product at a price that exceeds what was spent to create it allows the firm to outperform its rivals and earn above-average returns (Hitt, Ireland, and Hoskisson, 1999).

An empirical survey covering 242 affiliates owned by 97 SME transnational companies in foreign direct investment areas concluded that cost leadership strategy was not favored by these companies due to limited resources, but differentiation and focus strategies were favorable (Fujita, 1998).

According to Simon (1996), the world's 500 best unknown companies or hidden champions apply Porter's generic narrow scope strategies, which cover both differentiation and focus. Simon (1996) concluded in his empirical study among German SME companies who are active in international marketing that they are successful because they are either "supernichers" or "ultraspecialists." They are market leaders in their narrowly defined markets and their relative market shares are three times bigger than their nearest competitors. As "market owners," they created their own niche markets by highly specialized products, and they have no competitors at all. Some small U.S. companies have become very successful in international markets by customizing products for the specific foreign market, something the larger firms often do not do (see Case 7).

Case 7: Adolph Hertrich, who owns a small lumber mill in Boring, Oregon, switched to metric sizing for his lumber and mastered Japan's complicated grading system. He even stacks his Japan-bound wood to suit the market there with only vertical grain surfaces exposed. He generates 70 percent of his sales in Japan (Blackwell and Stephan, 1990).

In a study by Keogh, Jack, Bower, and Crabtree (1998) involving operators, contractors, and SMEs within the oil and gas industry, the organizations studied claimed their long-term aim was to establish themselves in a global market, while surviving in an increasingly constrained local market. All six companies, which were regarded as being among the most innovative, noted the importance of maintaining their niche position. Due to the global nature of the industry, these leaders appeared to have been aware of international opportunities from their companies' inception and of the importance of their particular differentiated products and services. Thus they were closer to the model of Oviatt and McDougall (1994).

With the globalization of markets, international demand for customized products appears to be growing (Dalgic and Leeuw, 1994; Dunning, 1993; Oviatt and McDougall, 1995). Technology is facilitating greater specialization and the appearance of an increased number of small firms supplying products occupying narrow, cross-national niches (Dunning, 1993; Kotler, 1991). Indeed, with heightened competition in many industries and advances in production technologies, small entrepreneurs are leveraging highly specialized knowledge bases to define and serve market segments small enough to go unnoticed by larger rivals. As McKenna (1991) notes, such knowledge can be applied to generating "niche thinking" in the identification of global niche markets that the small player can own (Knight, 1997).

Thinking globally means having the ability to understand markets beyond one's own country of origin, with respect to sources of demand, sources of supply, and methods of effective management and marketing. Global thinking can enable contemporary organizations to sustain long-term growth and profitability. In today's slower growth markets, firms are looking for new ways to increase their

business. The identification of new markets is an increasingly important way to grow profits (Blackwell and Stephan, 1990). For example,
in the software industry dominated by U.S. companies, European
companies occupy niches rather than challenging the large players as
Case 8 explains.

Case 8: Germany's SAP is the biggest software company in Europe. SAP
makes enterprise resource planning software used by manufacturers to coordinate their processes and customer relationship management software
for marketing departments (Blackwell and Stephan, 1990).

Corporations such as Coca-Cola, IBM, Gillette, Nestlé, Sony,
Phillips, and Unilever could derive over 50 percent of their sales outside their country of domicile. They are not alone. Many small companies with specialized niches that transcend national boundaries do
so also (Blackwell and Stephan, 1990). A wholesale meat distributor
and a dry cleaning company are two of the many examples of companies who gained competitive advantage by going outside their national borders; Case 9 explains how.

Case 9: A small dry cleaning firm discovered that Swiss and German equipment was superior to equipment available in the United States. By taking
the time to understand foreign availabilities and standing ready to adapt
them to the U.S. operating environment, this firm has grown far faster than
most of its competitors. Similarly, a Midwestern distributor of wholesale
meats found that a grinder made in Denmark had many superior characteristics to domestic equipment. This small firm bought the machine at a greatly
reduced price by agreeing to demonstrate it as a sales tool for the manufacturer. This small firm has grown into a medium-sized firm, partly as a result
of its early adoption of a more efficient grinding process for hamburger. Resource capabilities may emphasize labor costs in one country, raw materials
in another, and information technologies in still others (Blackwell and
Stephan, 1990).

Another example comes from the cable industry. Cable industry
executives agree that cable networks need to specialize in a particular

field holding global appeal to cultivate a strong market identity. Executives believe networks need to develop long-term business plans that ensure that their development will not be held captive by limited, demographically specific audiences. Niche marketing is seen as the key to cable network growth. For cable, effective branding means cultivating network identity around a narrowly targeted concept with global appeal, say leading cable network executives. Whether the services offer 24-hour news or nonstop cartoons, the goal is to become recognized as an authority in the field, said Betty Cohen, president of Cartoon Network Worldwide, during a panel session on cable marketing and promotion in Los Angeles (see Case 10).

Case 10: Cartoon Network, which has a presence in Latin America, Europe, and Asia, is branching out into the online world, home video, and other licensing and merchandising. Effective marketing of niche services was the driving force behind cable's growth in the past and likely will pave the way for the dominant players of the future (Littleton, 1996).

Management thinkers concluded long ago that the dominance of today's global giants is rooted in their first-mover status. There are, however, some distinct advantages to turning up late for the global party. Bartlett and Ghoshal (2000) observed that the emerging multinationals typically exploited late-mover advantages in one of two ways. One of these is starting by benchmarking the established global players and then maneuvering around them, often by exploiting niches that the larger companies had overlooked.

Taking on the soap giants is no mean feat, but Benckiser (Amsterdam) is successfully doing just that. Granted, the company is not competing in the branded laundry detergent markets. It has, however, been doing well in attractive niche markets such as automatic dishwashing detergents, where it has built its global market share to 34 percent, well ahead of giants Procter & Gamble (P&G) and Unilever. Benckiser claims an 85 percent share of the water softener market and boasts leading positions in fabric treatments and specialty cleaners, such as lime and rust removers.

Founded by Johann A. Benckiser in 1823 in the Netherlands with limited resources, the company's core business was derived from industrial chemicals. Benckiser diversified into consumer goods and industrial cleaning products. In 1956, Benckiser launched Calgon Water Softener and made a name for itself globally as the Calgon maker.

Ten years later Benckiser developed and launched Calgonit Automatic Dishwashing Detergent and Quanto Fabric Softener. All the time the company did not divert from its focused and well-defined product lines. Benckiser continued its expansion into consumer goods via acquisitions and divestitures and in 1985 acquired St. Marc S.A.France.

As Hunter (1997) reported, the company was looking for growth by enlarging its share of markets, including the U.S. automatic dishwasher detergents segment, and by developing business in new regions. In 1990, Benckiser acquired Beecham Household Products in the United States and Canada. In 1991 Benckiser began its expansion strategy toward Eastern Europe and five years later continued its expansion into the Baltic countries, Belorussia, China, and Israel.

Benckiser's main growth markets are Turkey, Poland, the Czech Republic, and Hungary. The company's strategy for most markets is to enter with its value laundry detergents, line-branded products selling at 15 to 40 percent below the big soapers' top-line brands and when it has a good market share, to add on its premium niche products. More than two-thirds of Benckiser's sales in the United States are made up of dishwashing detergents and specialty cleaners, backed by strong positions in smaller niches. They have seen very good growth in automatic dishwashing detergents, registering 13 percent/year during the past two years. The company increased market share from 15 percent in 1990 to 23 percent in 1996. It is number two in the U.S. market, behind P&G but ahead of Unilever. The company had high hopes for its latest offering, Electrasol, to further boost its sales. Benckiser's Lime-A-Way specialty cleaner is number one in the United States and is expected to still see significant growth opportunities. Hunter (1997) reported that future development in the United States would focus on two categories.

As Hunter (1997) reported, Benckiser has continued to grow in different directions and dimensions. In 1999 Reckitt & Colman plc (UK) and Benckiser N.V (Dutch), after a lengthy negotiation process, decided to merge to create Reckitt Benckiser plc—the number one leader in household cleaning.

In the international arena Cooper Tire & Rubber Company has set a good example of niche marketing success by concentrating on the replacement tire market instead of the original equipment (OE) market segment (see Case 11).

Case 11: John F. Schaefer and Claude E. Hart, brothers-in-law, purchased the M and M Manufacturing Company in Akron, Ohio, producing tire patches, tire cement, and tire repair kits in 1914. A year later Schaefer and Hart acquired The Giant Tire & Rubber Company of Akron, a tire rebuilding business. The firm's name changed to Cooper Tire & Rubber Company in 1946. They specialized in the manufacturing and marketing of rubber products for consumers. Products include automobile, truck, and motorcycle tires, inner tubes, NVH control systems, automotive sealing, and fluid delivery systems. Cooper markets its products nationally and internationally through well-established channels of distribution. Among its customers are automotive manufacturing companies, independent tire dealers and wholesale distributors, and large retail chains. After acquiring a Mexican-based inner tube manufacturer in 1985, it went to Singapore to open a purchasing office for raw materials in 1993 and later expanded its territory by acquiring British-based Avon Tires.

One factor in Cooper's success was confining itself to the replacement tire market. The J.D. Power and Associates 2002 Replacement Tire Customer Satisfaction Study SM ranked Cooper the highest light truck replacement tire in a tie. CooperWorld.Net, a free business-to-business Internet site, was launched in August, 2002, providing dealers with a quick and easy way to order tires, access information, and communicate after hours. This secure site enhances Cooper's top-rated customer service. The company steers clear of the low margin business of making OE tires for new cars. Instead, it concentrates on the replacement tire market, which is about four times larger than the OE market, and growing faster because the owners of today's highly durable cars are keeping them longer (Hill and Jones, 1998).

Klebnikov (1997) presents an interesting case to show how an expensive, high-quality niche marketer is trying to be a full-line car manufacturer—Mercedes-Benz AG Corporation. The A140 model symbolizes the continuing move of Daimler-Benz AG's car operations away from being exclusively a manufacturer of Mercedes-Benz luxury cars to becoming a full-line producer more along the lines of General Motors, Ford, or Toyota. At the same time, Mercedes aimed at a niche market with its A140: Europeans who can afford the highest quality car want a small car for maneuvering around their narrow roads and crowded streets. The A140 is small but quite roomy inside and drives with a real "Mercedes feel." That is the new Mercedes strategy: to produce a full range of cars aimed at a niche within every category—people who will pay a premium for prestige and perceived quality. The company is letting demand outrun supply.

To achieve this tough goal of producing cheaper cars without penalizing profitability, Daimler-Benz is breaking many of the rules of how to succeed in the auto business. According to Klebnikov (1997), an automaker should reduce the number of platforms on which it builds its different chassis as Toyota, Chrysler, and VW have done. However, Mercedes is producing a new platform for each of its new car lines and expects to make money on each at a production level that would spell insolvency for the bigger, full-line manufacturers. Some warn that there are obvious risks. For example, Packard, which hastened its demise by trying to compete in the midprice range, and Cadillac's mistake with Cimarron. In this new strategy, Mercedes-Benz hopes to capitalize on the Mercedes image and at the same time enhance it. Mercedes-Benz management wants to add a little sportiness and youth to its brand by exploiting the consumer franchise and enriching it (Klebnikov, 1997).

Dawar and Frost (1999) reported on Asian Paints, which controls 40 percent of the market for house paints (in its home base, India) despite aggressive moves by major multinationals such as ICI, Kansai Paints, and Sherwin-Williams. After its success exporting to neighbors such as Nepal and Fiji, the company is now pursuing joint ventures abroad. Asian Paints brings substantial advantages to these countries by localizing its overall strategy. Its managers are used to dealing with the kind of marketing environment characteristic of this region—thousands of scattered retailers, poorly educated consumers, and customers who want only small quantities of paint that can then be diluted to save money. However, its multinational competitors, by contrast, have built their operations around the demands of affluent customer segments looking for a large selection of colors and finishes. Multinational expatriate managers are used to air-conditioned offices and bottled water that costs more per liter than most customers are willing to pay for paint. Even after they develop a low-end paint product, the multinationals will still have a long way to go to catch up in some emerging markets as in the case of Nepal and Fiji. Asian Paints knows well how to speak the language of these customers (Dawar and Frost, 1999).

INTERNATIONALIZATION PROCESS IN NICHE MARKETING

International marketing of goods usually starts with indirect exporting and goes through the modes of direct exporting, licensing, joint venture, sales and service subsidiary, assembling, and finally reaches the local production mode in the foreign markets. Ayal and Zif (1979) define "concentration" and "diversification" as alternative options. In concentration, a company starts by selling to a few carefully selected countries, while diversification signifies simultaneous market entry in several countries. Concentration is more time-consuming but less demanding on capital and human resources (Ayal and Zif, 1979). Attiyeh and Wenner (1981) extended the concept to "sequential concentration," in which at any given point resources are focused on one country; once the "critical mass" has been reached there, that is, once the business has become self-sustaining, internationalization proceeds to the next country. The "sequential concentration" also consumes a great deal of time since it ordinarily takes four to six years per country to reach critical mass (Simon, 1992).

Simon found in his study that the globally successful German SMEs rarely follow such ideal patterns. Rather they started to internationalize very early, very rapidly, and often chaotically (Simon, 1996). A recent study of small and medium-sized firms in 26 developed and developing countries makes the case that an era of accelerated firm internationalization is upon us and will make its effects felt even more in the twenty-first century (OECD, 1997).

Some researchers also argue that some firms might skip stages because global niches have become narrower and transportation and communication costs have rapidly decreased (Oviatt and McDougall,

1994). Cavusgil (1993) lists several trends of recent decades that help explain why smaller enterprises can successfully cultivate export markets. First is the development of niche markets. Customers in mature economies are increasingly demanding specialized or customized products. The second trend relates to changes in process technology. Advances in numerical controls, electronic control devices, and similar areas mean that low-scale, batch-type production can be economical. The new machine tools now allow manufacturing of complex, nonstandardized parts fairly easily. Third are advances in communications technology. Gone are the days of large, vertically integrated firms where information flows were expensive and took considerable time to be shared. With the latest telecommunications and computer technology, managers can manage operations across firm boundaries. Information is now readily and more quickly accessible to everyone. Finally, inherent advantages of small enterprises—quicker response time, flexibility, adaptability, etc.—facilitate smaller firms' international ventures (Cavusgil, 1993).

In a study by Karagozoglu and Lindell (1998), a majority of the small and medium-sized technology-based companies did not view "threats from multinational firms on the domestic market" and "the rapidity of technological developments" as significant pressures to internationalize since these firms tend to carve out well-defined niche markets (Baird, Lyles, and Orris, 1994).

The rise of small and medium-sized enterprises that achieve considerable success in export markets is exciting. The experience suggests that, in spite of small size and inexperience in international transactions, high value-added manufacturing firms can outperform their larger, more resourceful counterparts in export markets. The key element of success appears to be genuine customer orientation and value, coupled with a commitment to exporting by firm's management. Such firms are well advised to identify their distinctive competencies and nourish them constantly—whether it is a unique process or product, quicker response time, intimate knowledge of the customer, etc. Synergistic partnerships with carefully selected foreign business can also take the mystery and complexity out of international business transactions. Finally, managers should also tap into formal and informal information networks in order to position themselves as proactive players in international business (Cavusgil, 1993).

"Accelerated internationalization" refers to the phenomenon of firms engaging in international business activities earlier in their organizational life cycles than they have historically. Some authors also call them born-globals. "Born-global firms" is a label coined for companies that from the outset view the world as their marketplace. Rather than viewing foreign markets as useful adjuncts to domestic ones, these firms see their domestic activities as supporting their exports. Many world champions can lay claim to the born-global designation (Simon, 1996). Modern industries such as computers, mobile phones, and hi-fi equipment are global by nature. Their products become global at birth because these are generally new industries without historical restrictions and natural standards.

The overwhelming export success of smaller, high value-added exporters discredits the conventional wisdom that firms ought to pursue export opportunities cautiously, in a series of incremental steps. Today's realities call for leapfrogging. Exploiting their unique advantages, these firms can break out of the gradual pattern of internationalization and make bolder moves.

Rapid internationalization is feasible, and desirable, for a number of reasons. First, the means of internationalization—knowledge, tools, facilitating institutions, etc.—have become readily accessible to all firms. Lack of knowledge about best export practices is less of a hindrance to firms today. Second, managers can gain valuable experience through "inward" internationalization. That is, involvement in outsourcing, transfers of technology from foreign companies, countertrade, and similar activities prepare managers for more traditional, outward internationalization. Third, successful international business today is synonymous with successful partnerships with foreign businesses—distributors, trading companies, subcontractors, etc. Inexperienced managers have a solid chance in succeeding in international business if they take the time to build mutually beneficial, long-term alliances with foreign partners. Coupled with intense competition from foreign firms in domestic markets, these conditions call for rapid internationalization (Cavusgil, 1993).

In industries where pressures to globalize are strong, managers will not be able to simply build on their company's local assets—they will need to rethink their business model. When Microsoft moved into China, for example, local software companies shifted their focus from developing Windows look-alike operating systems to developing Windows application programs tailored to the Chinese market. As Mexico has opened its markets, many manufacturing companies have reoriented themselves, becoming local component suppliers to the newly built factories of foreign multinationals. By focusing on carefully selected niches, a dodger can use its local assets to establish a viable position (Dawar and Frost, 1999).

Finding a viable niche in a global industry usually means an extended process of restructuring. Many companies may need to shed businesses that cannot be sustained on the global level. To many managers in emerging markets who are conscious of links between their businesses, that process will be difficult. However, shedding businesses, outsourcing components previously made in-house, and investing in new products and processes are the keys to repositioning contenders as focused, global producers. Indeed, the need to get smaller before getting larger is one of the major themes in the corporate restructuring process underway in Eastern Europe.

In Hungary, Raba, for example, once produced a diverse line of vehicles and components—from engines and axles to complete buses, trucks, and tractors. When markets in Eastern Europe opened, the company faced a collapse in demand. As the automotive industry rapidly consolidated globally, Raba managed to avoid Skoda's fate. It focused on the worldwide market for heavy-duty axles, a segment in which its technology was fairly close to the standards of international competitors. Restructuring has paid off, especially in the United States, where the company has captured 25 percent of the large market for heavy-duty tractor axles. Axles now account for over two-thirds of Raba's sales, and nearly all of them are exported. By contrast, the company's remaining operation in the wider engine and vehicle market, where it operates only in Eastern Europe, is facing a severe challenge from such major multinationals as Cummins and DaimlerChrysler. Despite Raba's extensive service network, the globalization pressures in that industry, throughout its value chain, may be too strong to withstand (Dawar and Frost, 1999).

CHARACTERISTIC NICHE MARKETER GROUPS

By using all available literature about niche marketing and SME marketing strategy we may point out the following groupings of those firms:

Ultrafocused Nichers (Supernichers/Ultraspecialists)

Characteristics include

- Specific product and market-oriented strategy
- Narrow product focus with broad geographic focus—single nichers
- Best performance in the areas customers care most about
- Balanced closeness to customers with deep technical knowledge
- Reliance on themselves, especially for R&D
- Close ties fostered between managers and workers (Simon, 1992, 1996)

According to Simon (1996), there is a group of companies consisting of ultraspecialists that try to build very strong positions in very small markets. He calls them supernichists. Most of the ones for which a relative market share is available are three times larger in market share than their strongest competitor. Sometimes they have no real competition, since they are the only suppliers for certain applications. An example is the Deutz Motor Industriemotoren (DMI) operating in the air-cooled diesel business. DMI wanted to abandon the air-cooled diesels due to environmental restrictions, but in the meantime, they learned that these engines are irreplaceable in certain applications and locations, such as in extremely hot or cold climates, in deserts, and in out-of-the-way places where maintenance is difficult. They were the only manufacturer in the world that could make these motors in substantial quantities. Another supernichist is Union Knopf, the world leader in buttons, which produces only buttons, but buttons in all conceivable varieties—250,000 altogether. Whatever kind of button one needs, it can be found at Union Knopf. Or take Aeroxon, a specialist in nonchemical devices to fight household insects. Its main product, the fly strip, has not changed in 90 years, and it holds 50 percent of the world market. A U.S. company that certainly qualifies as a supernichist is St. Jude Medical. With a world market share of 60 percent in artificial heart valves, it is about ten times larger than its strongest competitor, the Swiss company SulzerMedica (Carbomedics). St. Jude is extremely profitable, enjoying a gross return on sales of 75.7 percent and a net return of 43.4 percent. Or take Gallagher, a company from New Zealand, which has 45 percent of the world market in electric fences (Simon, 1996).

Globally Oriented Nichers

Characteristics include

- Global vision from inception
- Internationally experienced management
- Strong international business network
- Preemptive technology or marketing
- Unique intangible asset
- Linked product or service
- Tight organizational coordination, worldwide (Oviatt and Mc-Dougall, 1995)

Oviatt and McDougall (1995) list characteristics of successful global start-ups. They state that probably the most important characteristic associated with success is that the founders of a global start-up loosen the ties that bind their business thinking to a single country or culture. The founder must be able to communicate compellingly a global vision to everyone else associated with the venture.

Every global start-up Oviatt and McDougall (1995) contacted had internationally experienced founders or top managers, and every person interviewed believed that was a necessity. New ventures, being resource poor, are much more dependent than large mature multinational enterprises on a supportive network of business associates extending across national borders.

Most successful global start-ups begin by selling a unique product or service in leading markets. Start-ups are handicapped by both their inexperience and their small size. The way global start-ups overcome such disadvantages is to be first to market a distinctively valuable product or service (Oviatt and McDougall, 1995).

Success attracts imitators, especially in a global arena. Marketing a distinctively valuable product or service is preemptive only if that distinctiveness is sustained. Possessing relatively few resources, global start-ups must depend on intangible assets, such as tacit know-how, to sustain their advantage. In most cases, the founders of the companies (Oviatt and McDougall, 1995) studied and identified their competitive advantage as some bit or collection of special knowledge that the people in their venture had that no one else had. Unique knowledge seemed to be the key intangible asset. Successful global start-ups seem to follow their initial product or service with extensions that are closely linked to the unique assets from which they derived their original competitive advantage. Among Oviatt and McDougall's (1995) sample firms, more emphasis was placed on coordinating the implementation of the venture strategy than on adjusting the product and its marketing to varying local conditions.

Strong Customer-Oriented Nichers

Characteristics include the following ideas:

- As the customers change, they change.
- They compete on value through quality, technology, and product design.
- Cost competitiveness is important but it is a given.
- They have strong customer orientation and tailor products to meet customer requirements (this is more important than being technologically the best).
- They have a rich diversity of management skills, including skills in product and process innovation.
- The worldwide shift to smaller, more flexible manufacturing and a fall in the cost of communications and transport have been key factors in their growth (McKinsey, 1993).

A new breed of exporting companies has emerged in Australia recently. These "emerging exporters" and "born globals" contribute substantially to Australian exports. Their organizational profiles do not match those of traditional exporting enterprises, yet they exhibit fascinating features. Insights come largely from a new study sponsored by the Australian Manufacturing Council and conducted by McKinsey and Company and Australian Manufacturing Council in 1993. The study estimates that there are about 700 "emerging exporters" in Australia. These firms view the world as their marketplace from the outset; they do not see foreign markets as useful adjuncts to the domestic market. Some 25 percent of the emerging exporters are born global. They begin exporting within two years of establishment and export an average of 76 percent of their total sales. They are often small, with an average annual sales of A$16 million. The majority of born globals emerge as a result of a significant product or process breakthrough. Born globals may apply cutting-edge technology either to developing a unique product or to a better way of doing business. The McKinsey (1993) study estimates that the high value-added exports by emerging exporters exceed A$8 billion per year. Considering that these firms enjoy annual growth rates of 10 percent, their future contribution to Australian exporters is likely to rise rapidly.

The emergence of small, high value-added exporters is not unique to the Australian economy. They are visible in other mature, post-industrial economies. They are also not confined to a few industries; they are spread across all manufacturing industries. They point to two fundamental phenomena in the 1990s, however. First, small and medium-sized companies can successfully develop substantial export business, often capitalizing on their relative strengths—strong customer orientation and competing on value. Second, gradual, incremental internationalization is obsolete. Today, companies can, and should, make bolder attempts at international expansion. These two developments require elaboration ventures (Cavusgil, 1993).

In the Australian study, the export success of smaller firms was attributed to a deliberate attempt at capitalizing on their strengths. They have a strong customer orientation and tailor their products to meet particular customer requirements. They come to know their customers well and are familiar with how these customers use and value their products. They also compete on value, particularly in quality technology and product design. Although cost competitiveness is important, it is not the key determinant of their export success.

Ethnic Nichers

Characteristics include the following:

- They are the third force where the first force is "national firms" and the second force is "multinational firms."
- They are small SMEs who are niche based on ethnicity and focused on culture in more than one market.
- They serve a narrow market.
- Ethnicity and culture are the basic differentiation factors.
- Products are based on unique ethnic and national consumption patterns
  —food,
  —dress code,
  —entertainment (music, movies), etc.,
  —school organizations (e.g., driving school for Indians), and
  —TV and radio channels.

Some examples of the target market of these nichers are

- Asian population in Europe (which is the biggest population in the United Kingdom and also present in Germany, France, the Netherlands, and Belgium)
- Italian, Turkish, and Spanish population in Germany, France, and the United Kingdom
- Moroccans in the Netherlands, Germany, France, and Belgium (Dalgic, 1998)

One example of an ethnic nicher is a New York-based marketing company: Intercultural Niche Strategies (INS). Using data from the Immigration and Naturalization Service, a multilanguage staff, and a network of ethnic media and retail outlets, INS is working with major music labels to help drive incremental U.S. sales for such world artists as Japanese jazz pianist Akiko Yano, Native American artist Buffy Sainte-Marie, and Spanish-Galician bagpiper Carlos Nunez. The company joins a growing number of firms working within the music industry to help labels get their product into the hands of specialist audiences via targeted marketing, promotion, and/or distribution.

A full-service marketer, INS' own market niche is that it brings retail, radio, and promotion services under one roof and helps labels tap the often-overlooked music-buying potential of hundreds of immigrant populations residing in the United States. Taking a grassroots approach, INS cofounders Anita Daly and Holly Poirier search out and place music into immigrant pockets in cities across the country, targeting everything from preferred radio stations to well-trod retail outlets, however nontraditional. The company employs four full-time staffers: one who speaks Russian, one who speaks Spanish, one who speaks French, and one who is an Irish-American. When necessary, the company will bring in hired guns of various backgrounds to work specific projects. To reach, for example, the Irish market, INS is sending copies of the album to specialist "old-time" Irish radio shows on such stations as WPPA Pottsville, Pennsylvania. Those are the types of programs and AM stations that are never serviced by labels, Daly says, but that speak directly and forcefully to the desired demographic. They also need to understand how each ethnic group conducts business (Fitzpatrick, 1997).

Another ethnic nicher is from the Philippines. Jollibee Foods, a family-owned fast-food company, has extended its reach by focusing on Filipinos in other countries. The company first overcame an onslaught from McDonald's in its home market, partly by upgrading service and delivery standards but also by developing rival menus customized to local tastes. Along with noodle and rice meals made with fish, Jollibee created a hamburger seasoned with garlic and soy sauce—allowing it to capture 75 percent of the burger market and 56 percent of the fast-food business in the Philippines. Having learned what it takes to compete with multinationals, Jollibee had the confidence to go elsewhere. Using its battle-tested recipes, the company has now established dozens of restaurants near large expatriate populations in Hong Kong, the Middle East, and California (Dawar and Frost, 1999).

Similarly, managers can look for countries with a common cultural or linguistic heritage. Televisa, Mexico's largest media company, used that approach to become the world's most prolific producer of Spanish-language soap operas. Recognizing that its programs would have considerable value in the many Spanish-speaking markets outside Mexico, the company targeted export markets in Latin America, Spain, the U.S. border states, and Florida. Recently, Televisa has begun its own news broadcasts, teaming up with Rupert Murdoch's News Corporation for distribution to Spanish-language markets worldwide. The concept of analogous markets can be stretched far indeed (Dawar and Frost, 1999).

During the early twentieth century, the ethnic neighborhoods of large northern cities supposedly created conditions that promoted the concentration of European ethnic groups in niches in the retail trade. However, this popular assertion is based mainly on studies of one group in one location (e.g., Jews in New York). Following the "interactionist approach" to ethnic business, Boyd (2001) used a multigroup/multilocality research strategy to show that in 1900 the groups most heavily concentrated in niches in the retail trade (Russians, Italians, and Poles) had their highest rates of retail enterprise in cities far removed from the sizable ethnic communities and large populations of major urban centers. The results suggest that (1) past studies have overstated the importance of ethnic communities and big cities for the formation of ethnic niches in retailing, and (2) the extraordinary concentration of entrepreneurial groups in such niches during the early twentieth century is best explained by a theoretical and analytic approach that takes account of both ethnicity and location (Boyd, 2001).

Vocal Local Nicher

Characteristics include the following:

- They create a global image and appeal to bring in the customers.
- Differentiation is based on
  —local amusements,
  —local culture/lifestyle,
  —natural endowments,
  —historic monuments,
  —products, services, etc.
- They establish local identity based on geographic differentiation.

- They market themselves by
  —contacting the tourism agents,
  —organizing music, folk, dance, food, etc. festivals.

Examples

- Cannes, France, as the host of world famous film festivals
- Davos, Switzerland, as a conference city
- Geneva, Switzerland, as the European center of the UN
- New York, as the biggest city and metropolis on earth
- Rotterdam, the Netherlands, as the biggest port on earth
- Boston, Massachusetts, as the city of the marathon

REFERENCES

Attiyeh, R. S. and S. L. Wenner (1981). "Critical Mass: Key to Export Profit." *McKinsey Quarterly,* November, pp. 73-87.

Ayal, Igal and Jehiel Zif (1979). "Competitive Market Choice Strategies in Multinational Marketing." *Journal of Marketing,* 43 (Spring), pp. 84-94.

Baird, S. I., A. M. Lyles, and J. B. Orris (1994). "The Choice of International Strategies by Small Businesses." *Journal of Small Business Management,* January, pp. 48-59.

Bantel, Karen A. (1997). "High Tech, High Performance: The Synergy of Niche Strategy and Planning Focus in Technological Entrepreneurial Firms." Washington, DC: RISEbusiness, Working Paper Series 97-02.

Bartlett, Christopher A. and Sumantra Ghoshal (2000). "Going Global: Lessons from Late Movers." *Harvard Business Review,* March-April, pp. 132-142.

Biggadike, Ralph (1997). *Entering New Markets: Strategies and Performance.* Cambridge, MA: Marketing Science Institute.

Blackwell, Roger and Kristina Stephan (2001). *Customers Rule! Why the E-Commerce Honeymoon Is Over and Where Winning Businesses Go from Here.* New York: Crown.

Boyd, Robert L. (2001). "Ethnicity, Niches, and Retail Enterprise in Northern Cities 1900." *Social Perspectives,* 44(1) (Spring), pp. 89-111.

Cavusgil, S. Tamer (1993). Globalization of Markets and Its Impact. Unpublished working paper, Michigan State University.

Clifford, Donald K. Jr. and Richard E. Cavanagh (1985). *The Winning Performance: How America's High Growth Midsize Companies Succeed.* London: Sidgwick and Jackson.

Cosset, Jean-Claude and Jean Roy (1991). "The Determinants of Country Risk Ratings." *Journal of International Business Studies,* Vol. 22, Nr.1, 135-142.

Dalgic, Tevfik (1992). "Euromarketing: Charting the Map for Globalization." *International Marketing Review,* 9(5), pp. 21-42.

Dalgic, Tevfik (1998). "Niche Marketing Principles: Guerrillas versus Gorillas." *Journal of Segmentation in Marketing,* 2(1), pp. 5-18.

Dalgic, Tevfik and Maarten Leeuw (1994). "Niche Marketing Revisited: Concept, Applications and Some European Cases." *European Journal of Marketing,* 28 (4), pp. 39-55.

Dawar, Niraj and Tony Frost (1999). "Competing with Giants." *Harvard Business Review,* 77(2) (March-April), p. 119.

Delaney, John (1995). "Minding Your Own Niche Business." *Nation's Business,* 83(5) (May), pp. 56-58.

Doole, Isobel and Robin Lowe (1999). *International Marketing Strategy.* London: Pearson Higher Education.

Dunning, John (1993). *The Globalization of Business.* London: Routledge.

Fitzpatrick, Eileen (1997). "Marketer Takes Music to U.S. Ethnic Groups." *Billboard,* 109(14), pp. 1-4.

Fujita, Masataka (1998). *The Transnational Activities of Small and Medium-Sized Enterprises.* Dordrecht, the Netherlands: Kluwer Academic Publishers.

Ghoshal, S. (1987). "Global Strategy: An Organizing Framework." *Strategic Management Journal,* 8, pp. 425-440.

Glascoff, David W. (2000). "Survival of the Niches." *Marketing Health Services,* 20(4) (Winter).

Grant, Robert M. (1995). *Contemporary Strategy Analysis.* Oxford: Blackwell.

Hill, Charles W. and Gareth R. Jones (1998). *Strategic Management—An Integrated Approach.* Boston: Houghton Mifflin.

Hitt, Michael A., R. Duane Ireland, and Robert E. Hoskisson (1999). *Strategic Management: Competitiveness and Globalization,* Third Edition. Cincinnati: South-Western College Publishing.

Hunter, David (1997). "Benckiser Cleans Up with its Niche Strategy." *Chemical Week,* 159(47), p. 37.

Johanson, Jan and Jan-Eric Vahlne (1990). "The Mechanism of Internationalization." *International Marketing Review,* 7(4), p. 11.

Johnson, Gerry and Kevan Scholes (1993). *Exploring Corporate Strategy,* Third Edition. Hertfordshire: Prentice Hall Europe.

Karagozoglu, Necmi and Martin Lindell (1998). "Internationalization of Small and Medium-Sized Technology-Based Firms: An Exploratory Study." *Journal of Small Business Management,* 36(1), pp. 44-60.

Keogh, William, Sarah L. Jack, D. Jane Bower, and Elisabeth Crabtree (1998). "Small, Technology-Based Firms in the UK Oil and Gas Industry: Innovation and Internationalisation Strategies." *International Small Business Journal,* 17(1), p. 57.

Klebnikov, Paul (1997). "Mercedes-Benz's Bold Niche Strategy." *Forbes,* 160(5), pp. 68-74.

Knight, A. Gary (1997). "Emerging Paradigm for International Marketing: The Born Global Firm." Unpublished doctoral dissertation, Michigan State University.

Kotler, Philip (1991). "From Mass Marketing to Mass Customization." *Planning Review,* September/October, pp. 11-47.

Kotler, Philip (2003). *Marketing Management,* Eleventh Edition. Englewood Cliffs, NJ: Prentice Hall.

Labich, Kenneth (1994). "Class in America." *Fortune,* 129(3) (February 7), p. 114.

Leduc, Bob (1998). "Target a Niche Market to Increase Your Sales and Profits." Available online at http://www.smithfam.com/news/aug98j.html.

Leontiades, J. (1986). "Going to Global-Global Strategies vs. National Strategies." *Long Range Planning,* 19(6).

Lewis, Ivor (1998). "Niche Marketing for Beginners." *Ceramics Monthly,* 96(6) (June-August), p. 6.

Littleton, Cynthia (1996). "Cable Targets Global 'Niche' Brand; Executives Say International Recognition Can Help Polish Domestic Image." *Broadcasting & Cable,* 126(28) (July 1), p. 56.

Litvak, Isaiah A. (1992). "Winning Strategies for Small Technology-Based Companies." *Business Quarterly,* 57(2) (Autumn), p. 47.

Maynard, Roberta (1993). "Riche Niches." *Nation's Business,* 81(11) (November), pp. 39-41.

McKenna, Regis (1991). "Marketing Is Everything." *Harvard Business Review,* 69(1), pp. 65-79.

McKinsey and Company and Australian Manufacturing Council (1993). *Emerging Exporters—Australia's High Value-Added Manufacturing Exporters.* Melbourne: Australian Manufacturing Council.

OECD Report (1997). Global Information Infrastructure—Global Information Society: Policy Recommendations for Action. Paris: OECD.

Oviatt, Benjamin M. and Patricia Phillips McDougall (1994). "Toward a Theory of International New Ventures." *Journal of International Business Studies,* 25(1) (Spring), p. 45.

Oviatt, Benjamin M. and Patricia Phillips McDougall (1995). "Global Start-Ups: Entrepreneurs on a Worldwide Stage." *Academy of Management,* 9(2), pp. 30-44.

Pitts, R. A. and D. Lei (2000). *Strategic Management.* Cincinnati: South-Western College Publishing.

Porter, Michael E. (1985). *Competitive Advantage.* New York: Free Press.

Reynolds, Don (1993). *Crackerjack Positioning.* Tulsa, OK: Atwood Publishing.

Shani, David and Shujana Chalasani (1992). "Exploiting Niches Using Relationship Marketing." *The Journal of Consumer Marketing,* 9(3), pp. 33-42.

Shrader, Rodney C., Benjamin Oviatt, and Patricia Phillips McDougall (2000). "How New Ventures Exploit Trade-Offs Among International Risk Factors: Lessons for the Accelerated Internationalization of the 21st Century." *Academy of Management,* 43(16) (December), pp. 1227-1247.

Shubart, Ellen (1998). "Retailers Open Up Niche Markets." *The Wall Street Journal Europe,* December 3, p. 15.

Simon, Hermann (1992). "Lessons from Germany's Midsize Giants." *Harvard Business Review,* 70 (March-April), pp. 115-123.

Simon, Hermann (1996). *Hidden Champions: Lessons from 500 of the World's Best Unknown Companies.* Boston, MA: Harvard Business School Press.

Stanton, John L. and Robert E. Linneman (1991). *Making Niche Marketing Work.* New York: McGraw-Hill Inc.

Stanton, William J., Michael J. Etzel, and Bruce J. Walker (1991). *Fundamentals of Marketing.* New York: McGraw-Hill.

PART II:
EMPIRICAL RESEARCH
IN NICHE MARKETING

Chapter 3

An Approach for Identifying Cannibalization Within Product Line Extensions and Multibrand Strategies

Charlotte H. Mason
George R. Milne

ABSTRACT

For decades, a common strategy of firms has been to offer multiple brands and/or brand variants which compete within the same product category. In many categories, dozens or even hundreds of brands are produced by a few dominant firms. Recently, however, manufacturers, retailers, and consumers are increasingly concerned about product proliferation and parity products. Constraints on retail shelf space and manufacturing considerations are examples of pressures leading firms to prune items from their product lines. When reviewing strategy and performance, a critical issue is cannibalization, or the extent to which one product's customers are at the expense of other products offered by the same firm. With the exception of new product models, there is little research on cannibalization. In this paper, we propose an approach for identifying cannibalization in mature markets. We empirically illustrate our approach for the cigarette market with 188 brands and brand variants.

Reprinted with permission from *Journal of Business Research,* Vol. 31, Charlotte H. Mason and George R. Milne, "An Approach for Identifying Cannibalization Within Product Line Extensions and Multibrand Strategies," pp. 163-170, copyright 1994, with permission from Elsevier.

The authors gratefully acknowledge Simmons Market Research Bureau for providing the data for the study discussed in this chapter.

INTRODUCTION

For decades, many consumer products firms have followed the strategy of producing multiple brands which compete in the same product category. This strategy is perhaps best exemplified by the brand management philosophy of packaged goods firms such as Procter & Gamble, widely regarded as the pioneer of this strategy (Solomon and Hymowitz, 1987; Schiller, 1988). The underlying rationale is that it is better for a consumer to choose between several of your products than to choose between one of yours and those of other firms. This multibrand strategy is not limited to packaged goods firms. Durables manufacturers of such products as tires (Goodyear also makes Kelly Springfield and Lee tires) and automobiles (General Motors produces Chevrolets, Buicks, Oldsmobiles, Cadillacs, and Pontiacs) follow this strategy. In addition, service firms have implemented this strategy such as the multibrand approach of the Fairfield, Courtyard, and Marriott hotel chains.

In recent years, the multiple-brand strategy has taken a new turn. Driven by the high costs of introducing and building an identity for a new brand, firms have increasingly turned to line extensions. Cheer detergent now comes in powder and liquid, scented or unscented, with or without Colorguard. Cheerios are now available in Apple Cinnamon, Honey Nut, and MultiGrain, as a good way to leverage a brand's "equity" and to better satisfy the diverse needs of the "splintering" mass market (*BusinessWeek,* 1983, p. 96). Micromarketing is a related trend encompassing a number of strategic directives, including offering more product variants (McKenna, 1988; Schiller, 1989; Hapoineu, 1990).

Yet, there is growing concern about brand proliferation, "me too" or parity products, and the dizzying array of alternatives consumers face (e.g., *Advertising Age,* 1993). It is not unusual to find dozens or even hundreds of alternatives within a single product category. For example, Simmons Market Research collects information about 200 different cigarettes—and this list is not exhaustive. These 200 cigarettes represent 41 brands, meaning that, on average, each brand has five variants or line extensions. Furthermore, these 200 cigarettes are produced by just six manufacturers. Other product categories present a similar picture. The majority of the numerous brands in cereals, detergents, and carbonated beverages are produced by three or four dominant manufacturers.

When reviewing their strategy and performance, a critical issue for firms that offer multiple brands or variants within a single brand is cannibalization, or the extent to which one product's customers are at the expense of other products offered by the same firm (Copulsky, 1976). The ideal situation is when a second brand or line extension draws all its customers from products offered by competing firms. At the other extreme is 100 percent cannibalization when all the customers are drawn from the firm's existing products. In practice, most rates of cannibalization fall somewhere in between. The issue of cannibalization is one of several forces which have led to a growing emphasis on category management where category managers "oversee an entire group of related products and emphasize cooperation, not competition, among brands" (Solomon and Hymowitz, 1987). Concurrent with the shift toward category management is a movement to streamline product lines by deleting slower moving or less profitable items (Schiller, 1993). Limits on available shelf space of retailers are forcing brand and category managers to decide which items to promote to both the trade and consumers. In all these situations, the issue of cannibalization is an important consideration in determining which items should be dropped.

Although the amount of cannibalization is routinely considered by new product testing models including ASSESSOR (Silk and Urban, 1978) and COMP (Burger, Gundee, and Lavidge, 1981), there is surprisingly little research which offers guidance for identifying cannibalization on an ongoing basis. Furthermore, relaunches, repositionings, changes in advertising copy or packaging, or product reformulations can shift brands' marketplace positions over time, which can impact cannibalization with other brands.

The objective of this paper is to offer a framework for identifying cannibalization among variants within a brand and/or among brands offered by the same firm. In this paper, we do not address if the effects of cannibalization have positive or negative effects on performance. As we discuss later, assessing the fiscal and competitive effects of cannibalization is not clear-cut and needs further research. What we offer, however, is a first step in identifying patterns of cannibalization for mature markets. To this end, we begin by reviewing approaches suggested in the published literature for identifying cannibalization. Next, we present our approach and illustrate it with a small-scale hypothetical example. The following section presents results from a large-scale empirical application of our approach in which we report intrabrand and intramanufacturer cannibalization rates for the U.S. cigarette market based on nearly 5,500 smokers surveyed by Simmons Market Research in 1991. We conclude with a discussion of the contributions and limitations of the proposed approach, and with suggestions for future research.

Previous Research

Although cannibalization is a familiar concept for marketers, there is surprisingly little research in this area. One exception is for new product introductions where cannibalization is clearly important for assessing the sales and profitability potential. As a result, a number of new product testing models assess cannibalization effects. Looking at cannibalization from a different perspective, Moorthy and Png (1992) use a modeling approach to demonstrate that the amount of cannibalization affects the optimal timing of new product introductions; however, because their focus is on normative recommendations (e.g., if cannibalization is high, then . . .), they do not address how cannibalization might be measured. In the remainder of this section, we briefly review previous approaches for evaluating the amount of cannibalization.

In the 1970s conjoint analysis emerged as a new tool for evaluating new product concepts (Green and Wind, 1975; Shocker and Srinivasan, 1979). If a product can be described as a collection of attributes, then conjoint analysis can be used to estimate individual-level utility, or part-worth functions for the various levels of the attributes. Using these part-worth functions, the total utility of any product concept can be computed for each individual. Assuming some choice model (e.g., that the most preferred alternative is chosen, or some probabilistic model), it is possible to simulate various market scenarios and estimate what market shares would be given different assortments of products for consumers to choose from. By systematically evaluating different scenarios, it is also possible to estimate cannibalization. For example, by comparing the market shares with and without a specific new alternative, the source of the new alternative's share can be evaluated. Page and Rosenbaum (1987) report this type of scenario analysis for a redesign of a food processor product line. A number of pre-test-market new product forecasting models routinely estimate cannibalization. For example, the objectives of the ASSESSOR model are to (1) predict equilibrium market share, (2) estimate the sources of the share, both "cannibalization" and "draw," (3) provide diagnostics for product improvements and advertising copy, and (4) allow low-cost screening of alternative marketing plans (Silk and Urban, 1978). The approach for determining cannibalization and draw is similar to the conjoint-based simulation approach. In the ASSESSOR model, consumer responses are combined with the proposed marketing plan for the new product in a preference model which is used to estimate market shares. By comparing estimated market shares with the new product to the prior market shares, one can evaluate the source of the new product's share. Other pre-test-market models such as BASES Source of Volume Analysis (SOVA), COMP (Burger, Gundee, and Lavidge, 1981) and LTM (Yankelovich, Skelly, and White, Inc., 1981) follow a similar approach, although some specific data-collection procedures, underlying model equations, and parameters are unique to the particular model.

Market simulations based on conjoint-derived utility functions and pre-test-market models are well-suited for assessing cannibalization for new product concepts and prototypes; however, these approaches require specialized (and possibly expensive) data collection. Thus, these methods are not appropriate for assessing cannibalization on an ongoing basis following their introduction. Furthermore, following the market introduction, changes in advertising copy, product modifications by competitors, and other marketplace changes can impact consumers' perceptions of brands, and hence, cannibalization.

AN ECOLOGICAL APPROACH TO CANNIBALIZATION

In this section we propose an approach for identifying cannibalization between variants within a brand or between the brands of a common manufacturer. The conceptual basis for our approach is found in the ecology literature. After introducing some terminology, we present our approach via a small-scale graphical example. In the next section, we follow up with empirical results based on a large-scale survey. The ecology literature has been suggested by many as an appropriate theory base for marketing applications (Alderson, 1957; Thorelli, 1967; Henderson, 1981, 1983, 1989; Tellis and Crawford, 1981; Weitz, 1985; Lambkin and Day, 1989; Lockshin, 1993).

To date, most of the applications in the marketing literature have been conceptual in nature, focusing on drawing parallels between ecological competition and marketplace competition (e.g., Alderson, 1957; Henderson, 1981, 1983, 1989). In addition, several researchers have developed measures for specific constructs and reported empirical results (Lambkin and Day, 1989; Milne and Mason, 1990).

A critical concept in the ecological framework as applied to marketing is the niche. In ecology, species compete with each other for scarce resources. Applied to marketing, brands compete within the marketplace for customers. Each brand has a niche which describes the customers the brand is competing for. For example, the Hyundai Excel's niche may be young, single consumers with limited incomes, whereas the Dodge minivan's niche may be the "thirtysomething," middle-to-upper income, married consumers with children. The dimensions of the niche are relevant customer characteristics that may include demographics, psychographics, value and lifestyle data, benefits sought, and/or usage data. In general, the niche dimensions will vary from one product category to another. For example, income may be an important variable in describing the niches of various automobiles, but not for brands of chewing gum. To identify cannibalization between brands, assume for now that each brand's niche has been specified (in the empirical illustration in the following section, we describe explicitly how this is done).

Figure 3.1 shows a hypothetical market with three brands—A, B, and C—in a two-dimensional niche space. Suppose that Brands A and B are produced by the same manufacturer, and C by a competing manufacturer. The circles in Figure 3.1 represent the niche boundaries. Each lowercase letter represents a consumer—the letter indicating the brand actually purchased or consumed. Note that some of the consumers in Brand A's niche purchased Brand A, but other consumers in A's niche purchased B or C. The same is true for Brands B

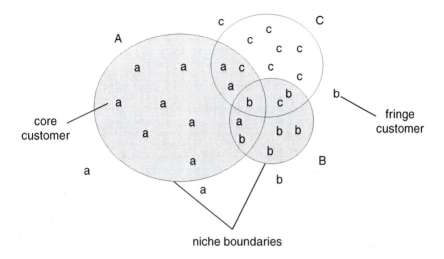

FIGURE 3.1. Niche Space

and C. Note also that some of the consumers who bought A are out-side of A's niche. We use the term core customer to refer to consum-ers of a brand who are within the brand's niche; all other consumers are fringe customers. For example, although Dodge minivans are tar-geted toward reasonably affluent families with children, it is conceiv-able that other types of consumers—young singles or retired cou-ples—may purchase a minivan. The more prototypical consumers are the core customers, and the atypical consumers for a brand constitute the fringe customers.

The total number of consumers within the niche boundary of a brand are the brand's niche potential. A brand's niche share is the pro-portion of the niche potential that actually bought the brand, and is computed as the number of core customers divided by the niche po-tential. The amount of overlap between two brands is a pairwise mea-sure of brand competition (Milne and Mason, 1990).

Cannibalization, however, may involve just two brands or many brands. As an example, consider the recent introduction of Procter & Gamble's Lemon Dawn liquid dishwashing detergent. The brand manager for Dawn is concerned about possible cannibalization of the sales of regular Dawn and Mountain Scent Dawn. From the perspective of the category manager at Procter & Gamble, the new Lemon Dawn dishwashing detergent may cannibalize the other Dawn products, Lemon Joy, or even Ivory. There is potential cannibalization for every consumer who falls within the niche of two brands or two variants within a brand produced by the same manufacturer. In Figure 3.1, consider the area where the niches of Brands A and B overlap. Two customers within this area purchased Brand B. These customers were potentially cannibalized from Brand A, because they also are within A's niche. Similarly, Brand A has potentially cannibalized one customer from Brand B. Note that from Brand C's perspective, there is no cannibalization, because C is produced by a different manufacturer. It is also possible to identify the "draw" or the amount of a brand's customers that are drawn from a competitor's niche. Looking at the overlap between the niches of Brands A and C, we see that A has drawn two of Brand C's potential customers. Table 3.1 summarizes the relevant statistics for this simple example.

Generalizing to more complex situations with many brands, we can look at the pairwise cannibalization of one brand from a second brand, or the total cannibalization of one brand from multiple other brands. Specifically, we compute the total cannibalization rate for a brand (or variant within a brand) by summing the number of purchasers of that brand who also fall within the niche boundary of any other brand produced by the same manufacturer (or another variant of that same brand). If we now assume that all three brands in Figure 3.1 are produced by a common manufacturer, Brand A has cannibalized three

TABLE 3.1. Niche Statistics for Hypothetical Example

	Brand A*	Brand B	Brand C
Total core customers	10	6	8
% Cannibalized	1/10–10%	2/6–33%	0%
% Draw	2/10–20%	2/6–33%	2/8–25%
Niche potential	13	8	12
Niche share	10/13–77%	6/8–75%	8/12–67%

*Assumes Brands A and B are produced by the same firm, whereas C is offered by a competing firm.

customers from B and C, and Brands B and C have cannibalized three and two customers, respectively.

EMPIRICAL ILLUSTRATION

Method

To illustrate our approach, we use data collected by the Simmons Market Research 1991 Study of Media and Markets. Our total sample consists of 9,659 observations from 5,474 respondents. If a respondent smokes more than one type of cigarette, a separate observation was created for each brand smoked. After eliminating brands with too few observations to provide reasonable estimates, there are 188 different cigarettes, representing 37 brands and six manufacturers.

The first step is to define the niche boundaries for each of the 188 cigarettes. The customer dimensions available to us from Simmons were the average number of cigarettes smoked per day, household income, hours worked per week, gender, race, number of years married, whether the respondent buys cigarettes by the pack or the carton, and whether the respondent prefers softpack or box. It is important to note that our intent is to illustrate our approach using a large dataset, and, for this purpose, these dimensions are adequate, if not ideal. However, if our goal was to draw substantive conclusions about the cigarette market it would be imperative to have a more complete set of relevant dimensions.

The niche boundary separates the core and fringe customers. Because these are relative terms with no absolute boundary, some criteria are needed to select an appropriate cutoff. We want the niche boundaries to reflect the brands' realized target markets. If all purchasers of a brand are included in the niche, the niches will seem too broad. This is the result of those "fringe" customers who don't fit the typical profile of the brand.

We follow the general approach of previous empirical research by McPherson (1983) and Milne and Mason (1990) that quantified niche boundaries. In these studies, the niche boundaries were set so that the clear majority, but not all, of purchasers were within the core niche. For our illustration, we define the niche to be the 75 percent of purchasers who are closest to the average consumer of that brand (as defined by the centroid of the standardized variables). Thus, each cigarette's niche can be thought of as a hypersphere in the niche space defined by the variables which have been standardized to eliminate scaling differences (in addition, we should note that in doing the calculations it is necessary to treat the nonmetric variables differently than the metric variables). The center of the hypersphere is the centroid of the variables for that cigarette. The radius of the hypersphere is the distance from the centroid to that consumer (i.e., observation) who, when all consumers are ranked in terms of distance from the centroid, is at the seventy-fifth percentile. In other words, the hypersphere encloses 75 percent of a brand's customers.

Once the niche boundaries are determined, the remaining calculations are straightforward. In particular, the number of core customers, the niche potential, niche share, and potential cannibalization can be computed. For each brand, the number of core customers is equal to the number of respondents who smoke that brand and are within the niche boundary. The niche potential for a cigarette is the number of observations within the niche boundary, regardless of the cigarette chosen. Niche share is the number of core customers divided by the niche potential.

We identify cannibalization at three levels. First, for each of the 188 cigarettes, we can identify the cannibalization from other cigarettes within the same brand, both pairwise and overall. For example, for Lucky Strike nonfilter, we identify pairwise cannibalization from Lucky Strike Lights-Kings and 100s, and Lucky Strike Low Tar-Kings and 100s. Next, we look at cannibalization between Lucky Strike nonfilter and all other Lucky Strike cigarettes. Finally, for each of the 37 brands, we identify the cannibalization from other brands produced by the same manufacturer.

Results: Pairwise Cannibalization Between Variants Within a Brand

For any given brand, it is possible to examine each variant or line extension within the brand for cannibalization effects. For illustration, Table 3.2 reports the pairwise cannibalization results for the five Lucky Strike brand variants. Looking across a row, high numbers in-

TABLE 3.2. Pairwise Cannibalization for Lucky Strike Cigarettes*

	Non-Filter	Lights-King	Lights-100s	Low-Tar King	Low-Tar 100s
Non-Filter	—	0.378	0.135	0.135	0.108
Lights-King	0.353	—	0.294	0.235	0.294
Lights-100s	0.667	0.733	—	0.733	0.267
Low-Tar King	0.545	0.455	0.455	—	0.364
Low-Tar 100s	0.267	0.333	0.200	0.267	—

*The values given are the proportion of the row brand's core customers that are cannibalized from the column brand's core niche.

dicate potential cannibalization problems with other cigarettes. From the third row of Table 3.2, we see that the Lights-l00s seems to have cannibalized its core customers from other Lucky Strike variants. In particular, 66.7 percent of the Lights-l00s core customers are also in the core niche of Lucky Strike nonfilter; 73.3 percent of the Lights-l00s core customers are in the core niche of Lights-Kings, etc. In contrast, the Low Tar-l00s line extension has lower pairwise cannibalization rates.

Results: Total Cannibalization at Brand Level

The total cannibalization rates for a brand indicates the total number of core customers of any variant within the brand that are also within the core niche of any other variant in the same brand. The theoretical range is from 0 percent to 100 percent. For this data, we found zero cannibalization only for single product line brands such as Belair where, by definition, the cannibalization will be zero. The lowest cannibalization rates for brands with multiple items was 0.1143. As one would expect, the average amount of cannibalization increases with the number of line extensions in the brand. Figure 3.2 shows the nature of this relationship for the 37 cigarette brands.

Although cannibalization tends to increase with the number of extensions in a brand, there is quite a bit of variation. For example, Table 3.3 shows the cannibalization results for the Camel and Magna brands, which both have five variants. The average cannibalization

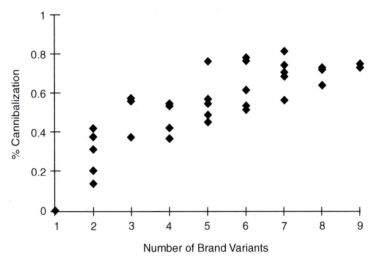

FIGURE 3.2. Average % Cannibalization by Number of Variants per Brand

TABLE 3.3. Cannibalization for Winston and Richland Brands

Camel		Magna	
Non-filter	0.8111	King, regular	0.2308
Filter	0.7273	King, menthol	0.6250
Filter, 100s	0.7879	100s, regular	0.3750
Lights, king	0.7273	100s, menthol	0.5556
Lights, 100s	0.7500	Lights, king, regular	0.4706
Average	0.7607	*Average*	0.4514

for the Camel cigarettes is 0.7607 compared with 0.4514 for Magna. An interesting observation is that all five Camel cigarettes are regular (i.e., non-menthol), whereas the Magna brand offers both regular and menthol.

Results: Total Cannibalization at Manufacturer Level

Table 3.4 reports cannibalization for the 37 brands grouped by manufacturer. The lowest cannibalization is 0.3000 for Eve, which is interpreted that 30 percent of Eve's core customers are also in the

TABLE 3.4. Cannibalization Grouped by Manufacturer

Phillip Morris		*RJR*	
Alpine	0.8621	Camel	0.9206
Benson & Hedges	0.9227	Century	0.9157
Cambridge	0.9596	Coral	0.9167
Marlboro	0.8952	Magna	0.8406
Merit	0.9549	More	0.8889
Parliament	0.9322	Now	0.9186
Players	0.9619	Salem	0.8716
Virginia Slims	0.9468	Vantage	0.9365
		Winston	0.9116
American		*Brown-Williams*	
American	0.7294	Barclay	0.9394
Carlton	0.8504	Belair	0.9024
Lucky Strike	0.9239	Capri	0.8906
Malibu	0.8837	Kool	0.6884
Pall Mall	0.7613	Raleigh	0.8791
Tareyton	0.8621	Richland	0.8624
		Viceroy	0.7750
Lorillard		*Liggett*	
Kent	0.8027	Chesterfield	0.5383
Newport	0.5455	Eve	0.3000
True	0.8333	L&M	0.5172

core niches of at least one other Liggett brand. The highest result is for Players, with potential cannibalization of 0.9619, meaning that 96 percent of Players' core customers are also in the core niche of one or more other Liggett brands.

These results, though high, shouldn't be that surprising. Most of the 37 brands are comprised of between two and nine brand variants.

Thus, for many brands a smoker can choose between menthol and regular, different lengths, light, ultra-lights, and low-tar options. As Ries and Jack Trout observed over a decade ago, "Nearly all major cigarette brands have been line-extended to death" (1981, p. 110).

Given this, it is not surprising to see so much overlap between niches, and resulting cannibalization. Furthermore, for the cigarette market, it is likely that many brands have added line extensions which deliberately cannibalize other cigarettes within the brand. In particular, with increased attention to the hazards of smoking, some smokers are moving to lower tar and lower nicotine cigarettes. To keep those customers, product managers may introduce light and low-tar variants, rather than see those customers switch to another brand.

There are several cautions or limitations. First, we have used the terms "cannibalization" and "potential cannibalization" somewhat interchangeably. Because our approach relies on purchase data, we know only what brand(s) a customer purchased. There is no way to determine if that purchase cannibalized another brand without knowing what the customer would have done if the brand purchased had not been available. Thus, from a managerial perspective our approach is conservative in the sense that we identify the worst-case, or upper limit, of the potential cannibalization.

A second caveat is that validity of the results depends upon accurately characterizing each product's niche. If important dimensions are omitted when describing the niche space, then the overlap between niches and cannibalization will be overstated.

For example, assume that the number of cigarettes smoked was not included as a dimension—although certain cigarettes (e.g., brands A and B) appeal to light smokers, and others (e.g., brands X and Y) to heavy smokers with otherwise similar characteristics. Then, by excluding this dimension, the niches of brands A, B, C, and D will appear more similar than they in fact are. Careful consideration of possible niche dimensions should help avoid this.

Finally, from the Simmons survey data, we know which brands a consumer purchases, but we do not know the amounts of each brand consumed. Thus, if a smoker indicates that he purchases two different cigarettes, we cannot determine if equal amounts of each are purchased, or if one accounts for a larger share than the other. If available, this information could be easily incorporated in the analysis in the form of weights. For other data sources, such as panel data, this information may be readily available.

Discussion

The empirical study demonstrates an approach for measuring cannibalization for multiple levels of analysis. We define cannibalization from an ecological perspective as the proportion of a product's sales that were drawn from product(s) carrying the same brand or were made by the same manufacturer. At the manufacturer or brand level, these techniques can be used to identify products with relatively high and low cannibalization rates. For a specific product, individual customers can be classified as being cannibalized out of a related product's niche or drawn from a competitor's niche. Identification of levels of cannibalization or the source of draw for individual customers can help in evaluating the fiscal and competitive effects of the cannibalization.

The literature has recommended that cannibalization analysis be included as part of the new product development process (Kerin, Harvey, and Rothe, 1978). Cannibalism can lead to fiscal problems if the result of offering multiple products is that sales are redistributed to a lower profit margin offering (Moorthy and Png, 1992). While the negative aspects of cannibalism are obvious, there are also positive aspects related to cannibalism (Kerin, Harvey, and Rothe, 1978). A product that has high cannibalization can fill out a brand's line and can inhibit competitors from gaining incremental sales.

Thus, in highly fragmented markets, much of the cannibalism is the result of an effort to preempt or to challenge the competition. Measures of cannibalism can provide managers with additional insights and evaluation tools beyond the new product development stage. Besides relaunches and repositioning—that involve changes in the marketing mix or product reformulations—measures of cannibalization could be central to line pruning and to brand image studies.

LINE PRUNING

There has been little discussion in the academic literature concerning product-line pruning despite the fact that many companies are now faced with these decisions (Schiller, 1993). The drive for market share, with firms extending brands to try to fill their product lines and to maintain parity with the array of competitor offerings, has resulted in some brands extending themselves too far. The result has been poor performance with many new product failures. An example of this is Campbell's approach for identifying cannibalization among existing brands who launched numerous new products and brand extensions that can be applied in an ongoing basis using panel or survey in the 1980s. With sagging markets, and poor performance of extensions, they have decided to "stick to the knitting" and to only sell to customers and to markets they currently serve (Power et al., 1993).

When pruning lines, a key issue to consider is where will the sales from the eliminated product go? Measures of cannibalization can help address this question. The approach presented in this article for identifying cannibalization levels for existing customers is a first step in making decisions about product line pruning.

By analyzing the patterns of sales in the niche structure, the manager can evaluate the financial and competitive impact of line pruning. For example, in evaluating the fiscal implications of pruning a brand variant, the question becomes—where would this sale go if the investigated variant is eliminated? The location of the purchase observation in niche space provides an indication of where the individual may switch. The switching options are (1) to a different variant of the same brand, (2) to another brand of the same firm, or (3) to a competing firm's brand. By analyzing the other purchases for the same customer, it would be possible to compare the relative probabilities. A fiscal assessment can be then made by using the derived switching probabilities to reassign purchasers and to re-estimate the levels of profit. Similarly, a competitive assessment can be determined by estimating the changes in share suggested by the switching probabilities.

BRAND IMAGE

Besides using cannibalization for pruning decisions, cannibalization can also provide insight to the cohesiveness of a brand and the strength of an image. A brand whose variants have large cannibalization rates indicates that each of the variants is selling to relatively similar customers—in other words, the brand seems to have established a typical customer profile or image. For example, in our dataset, Marlboro has seven variants that have high cannibalization rates among them (the average is 0.8118). Perhaps the "macho" image of Marlboro is expected. The similarity in type of smokers of the brand is reflected by the high levels of brand variant cannibalization rates. In contrast, our data suggest that the Magna brand with five variants has relatively low cannibalization rates (the average is 0.4515). By targeting its variant toward more differentiated customer groups, the Magna brand might have minimized cannibalization, but not have as cohesive an image.

CONCLUSION

Cannibalization is an often-discussed, but under-researched topic. Most research in this area has focused on the role of cannibalization in new product introductions; however, in many mature markets, the need for understanding cannibalization assumes a different, yet important, role. This study provided an approach for identifying cannibalization among existing brands that can be applied on an ongoing basis using panel or survey data. In managing mature products lines, identifying levels of high and low cannibalization rates is central to making good strategic decisions. To use this study's measures should prove beneficial to managers managing a line of products.

REFERENCES

Alderson, Wroe (1957). *Marketing Behavior and Executive Action*. Homewood, IL: Richard D. Irwin, Inc.

Brand Proliferation Attacked: Food Marketing Institute Study Urges Big Cuts in "Duplication" (1993). *Advertising Age* (May 10): 1, 49.

Burger, P. C., Gundee, H., and Lavidge, R. (1981). COMP: A Comprehensive System for the Evaluation of New Products. In Y. Wind, V. Mahajan, and R.N. Cardozo (eds.), *New Product Forecasting* (pp. 269-284). Lexington, MA: Lexington Books.

Copulsky, W. (1976). Cannibalism in the Marketplace. *Journal of Marketing* 40 (October): 103-105.

Green, P. and Wind, Y. (1975). New Way to Measure Consumer's Judgments. *Harvard Business Review* 53 (July-August): 107-117.

Hapoineu, Spencer L. (1990). The Rise of Micromarketing. *Journal of Business Strategy* 11 (November/December): 37-43.

Henderson, B. (1981). Understanding the Forces of Strategic and Natural Competition. *Journal of Business Strategy* 1 (Winter): 11-15.

Henderson, B. (1983). The Anatomy of Competition. *Marketing* 47 (Spring): 7-11.

Henderson, B. (1989). The Origin of Strategy. *Harvard Business Review* 67 (November-December): 139-143.

Kerin, R. A., Harvey, M. G., and Rothe, J. T. (1978). Cannibalism and New Product Development. *Business Horizons* 21 (October): 25-31.

Lambkin, M. and Day, G. S. (1989). Evolutionary Processes in Competitive Markets: Beyond the Product Life Cycle. *Journal of Marketing* 53 (July): 4-20.

Lockshin, L. S. (1993). The Role of the Biological Model in Marketing Strategy. In R. Varadarajan and B. Jaworski (eds.), *Marketing Theory and Applications* (pp. 226-233). Chicago: American Marketing Association.

Marketing: The New Priority, A Splintered Mass Market Forces Companies to Target Their Products (1983). *BusinessWeek* (November 21): 96-106.

McKenna, R. (1988). Marketing in the Age of Diversity. *Harvard Business Review* 66 (September-October): 88-95.

McPherson, M. (1983). An Ecology of Affiliation. *American Sociological Review* 48: 519-532.

Milne, G. R. and Mason, C. H. (1990). An Ecological Niche Theory Approach to the Measurement of Brand Competion. *Marketing Letters* 1(3) (November): 267-281.

Moorthy, K. Sridhar and Png, I. P. L. (1992). Market Segmentation, Cannibalization and the Timing of Product Introductions. *Manage. SCI.* 38(3) (March): 345-359.

Page, A. L. and Rosenbaum, H. F. (1987). Redesigning Product Lines with ConJoint Analysis: How Sunbeam Does It. *Journal of Product Innovation Management* 4 (June): 120-137.

Power, C., Kerwin, K., Grover, R., Alexander, K., and Hof, R. (1993). Flops: Too Many New Products Fail. Here's Why—and How to Do Better. *BusinessWeek* (August 16): 76-82.

Ries, A. and Trout, J. (1981). *Positioning: The Battle for Your Mind.* New York: Warner Books.

Schiller, Z. (1988). The Marketing Revolution at Procter and Gamble. *BusinessWeek* (July 25): 72-76.

Schiller, Z. (1989). Stalking the New Consumer: As Markets Fracture, Procter & Gamble and Others Sharpen "Micro Marketing." *BusinessWeek* (August 18): 54-58, 62.

Schiller, Z. (1993). Procter & Gamble Hits Back. *Business Week* (July 19): 20-22.

Shocker, A. B. and Srinivasan, V. (1979). Multiattribute Approaches for Product Concept Evaluation and Generation: A Critical Review. *Journal of Marketing Research* 16 (May): 159-180.

Silk, A. J. and Urban, G. L. (1978). Pre-Test-Market Evaluation of New Packaged Goods: A Model and Measurement Methodology. *Journal of Marketing Research* 15 (May): 171-191.

Solomon, J. and Hymowitz, C. (1987). Procter and Gamble Makes Changes in the Way It Develops and Sells Its Products. *The Wall Street Journal* (August 11), p. 12.

Tellis, G. and Crawford, M. (1981). An Evolutionary Approach to Product Growth Theory. *Journal of Marketing* 45 (Fall): 125-132.

Thorelli, H. (1967). Ecology in Marketing. *Southern Journal of Business* (October): 19-25.

Weitz, B. A. (1985). Introduction to Special Issue on Competition in Marketing. *Journal of Marketing Research* 22 (August): 229-236.

Yankelovich, Skelly, and White, Inc. (1981). LTM Estimating Procedures. In Y. Wind, V. Mahajan, and R. N. Cardozo (eds.), *New Product Forecasting* (pp. 249-267). Lexington, MA: Lexington Books.

Chapter 4

An Ecological Niche Theory Approach to the Measurement of Brand Competition

George R. Milne
Charlotte H. Mason

ABSTRACT

Marketers have long advocated the use of ecological theory to study markets, but the abstract definitions of key constructs have hampered empirical applications. We take a first step in applying ecological theory to product markets by quantifying concepts such as niches, niche breadth, and niche overlap. We propose a new approach for measuring competitive intensity and identifying competitive submarkets. This measure defines competition between brands as the extent to which brands compete for the same customers. The approach is suitable for both durable and nondurable goods, for markets with many brands, and it can be used to assess competition between existing and hypothetical brands. We illustrate our approach using data on the magazine market and offer suggestions for future research.

INTRODUCTION

Understanding the nature and extent of competition is fundamental for marketing planning and strategy. Such an understanding is critical for identifying both opportunities and threats as well as developing

This chapter was originally published in *Marketing Letters* (1989), 1(3), pp. 267-281. Reprinted with permission.

effective marketing programs (Weitz, 1985). Ultimately, understanding competitive structure is important, as competitors' actions have a direct impact on firm and brand performance (Abell, 1980; Day, 1981; Frazier and Howell, 1983; Porter, 1980). Trends of increasing brand proliferation and market fragmentation make this an increasingly difficult task. At the same time, slow growth in many markets makes assessing competitive structure an increasingly important task.

This research focuses on the question of measuring competitive intensity and then using such measures to understand market structure. We report results from our research program that investigates competitive measures based on ecological niche theory. Competition at its most basic level is natural or ecological competition (Henderson, 1989). Ecology theory offers an approach useful for describing, explaining, and measuring competition among many competitors. The potential of this theory base has been recognized by many marketing researchers (Alderson, 1957; Henderson, 1980, 1983, 1989; Lambkin and Day, 1989; Tellis and Crawford, 1981; Thorelli, 1967; Weitz, 1985). Despite this base of support surprisingly little has been done, especially empirically.

In the following section we briefly review measures of competition traditionally used in marketing and then offer an ecological perspective. Next we describe a niche overlap measure proposed by McPherson (1983) and discuss how this approach[1] can be used to estimate competitive relationships in a brand marketing context where we define competitors to be brands which target similar customer types. This is followed by a discussion of the properties of the proposed measure. We conclude by outlining future research opportunities which build on an ecological niche theory.

MEASURING COMPETITION

As with all research on competition and strategy, market definition is a fundamental first step. However, identifying market boundaries is

---

[1]This approach assumes unimodal distributions on each dimension for each brand. Bimodal distributions can be handled several ways. One is to replace a single dimension (e.g., age) with two dimensions (e.g., under 30, over 30). A second approach is to allow the range on a dimension to consist of two noncontiguous sections (e.g., 15 to 25 years old and 45 to 60 years old).

a difficult task. Since competition among brands is a matter of degree, identifying market boundaries and the brands competing within those boundaries is inevitably arbitrary (Day, Shocker, Srivastava, 1979; Weitz, 1985). The specific situation and objectives will influence the determination of the set of competitors. In this research we assume that a relevant product market has been identified using an approach such as customer judgments of substitutability (Day, Shocker, and Srivastava, 1979), substitution-in-use (Srivastava, Leone, and Shocker, 1981), or managerial judgment. Within the defined product market—which may be quite broad and contain many brands—our approach helps to identify submarkets of competing brands.

A variety of measures of competition have been proposed in the marketing literature. In general, measures can be classified by whether they are based on judgmental or behavioral data (Day, Shocker, Srivastava, 1979). Examples of judgmental measures include perceived similarity and perceived substitutability. Commonly used behavioral measures include brand switching and cross-elasticities. Each of these approaches has proven useful in a variety of situations, but all have limitations as well as strengths. For example, lack of available data with sufficient variation in prices (or other variables) can pose difficulties in estimating cross-elasticities. Analysis of brand switching is often more appropriate for frequently purchased goods than for durables, although recent work by Colombo and Morrison (1989) demonstrates the usefulness of brand-switching data for durables. Judgmental measures assume the consumer is familiar with and knowledgeable about the brands—which may be particularly problematic in product markets with many brands.

In this paper, we offer an ecological view of competition which complements previous approaches by offering a new perspective for measuring competitive intensity and identifying competitive submarkets. Our approach is suitable for both durable and nondurable goods and for markets with many brands, and it can be used to assess the competition between existing and hypothetical brands. It uses input data that are often readily available or that can be obtained without prohibitive expense. The results of this approach have intuitive appeal and offer strategic insights.

An Ecological Perspective of Competition

In ecology, competition is the struggle over scarce resources. The intensity of competition is determined by the extent to which two species compete for the same scarce resources. Central to the theory of ecological competition is the concept of the niche (Whittaker and Levin, 1975). An ecological niche is defined as the n-dimensional space which describes the characteristics of the resources a species needs for survival (Hutchinson, 1957). The niche is important for the study of competition because it provides a description of the scarce resources for which species compete. Niche breadth (or width) measures the range of resource characteristics across which a species exists. Comparing niche breadth indicates the extent that species utilize different types of resources. Species with a wide niche breadth (humans, for example) are referred to as generalists. Species with a narrow niche breadth (koalas, for example) are considered specialists. In addition to differences in niche breadth across species, there generally will be both similarities and differences in the resources needed. For example, humans and hummingbirds both require water, but humans also consume meat whereas hummingbirds do not. This commonality, or sharing of niche space, is the essence of competition. The larger the overlap, the more intense the competition.

When using this perspective to describe brand competition, it is useful to think of brands as competing species. Brands need a variety of resources to survive, including raw materials, production facilities, skilled management, exposure in the marketplace, and customers. Of these, customers are typically the critical resource and one which is nearly always limited. To be competitors, two brands must target similar customers to a significant degree. Niches are n-dimensional descriptions of customers. Niche breadth reflects the variance in the types of customers a brand is able to attract. Each brand's niche is formed through interactions with other brands. The presence or absence of competitors will affect the location and breadth of a brand's niche.

Ecologists distinguish between fundamental and realized niches. The fundamental niche is what the species/brand could exploit in the absence of competitors. The realized niche reflects a brand's position given the existing competition. Throughout, we are referring to the realized niche. On a continuum, brands with a relatively homogeneous set of customers would be specialists, whereas brands with a more heterogeneous set of customers would be generalists. Figure 4.1 displays a hypothetical brand market in two-dimensional resource space that has both specialists and generalists (the darker the shading the more specialist). The point of pairwise competition between two brands is the overlap of their niches. The extent of overlap is determined by the niches' proximity and respective niche breadths.

MEASURING NICHE OVERLAP

A recognized problem with the ecological model is that concepts such as resource spaces, niches, etc., are typically discussed at very abstract levels with little consideration of measurement issues (Lambkin and Day, 1989). We propose a measure of pairwise brand competition suitable for measuring competition in a variety of market structures, including fragmented markets. This pairwise measure serves as the input to subsequent analyses, including multidimensional scaling to map the market. In addition, several summary measures are proposed which are useful for assessing market and submarket competition among more than two brands.

In the ecology literature, niche overlap has often been used as a measure of potential competition between species (cf. Levins, 1968; Pianka, 1973). There is an extensive literature on measurement tech-

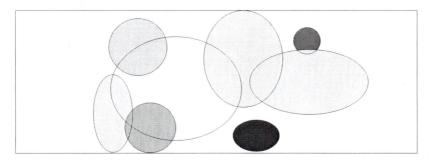

FIGURE 4.1. Hypothetical Competitive Market with Specialist and Generalist Brands

niques to calculate niche overlap. Reviews can be found in Abrams (1980), Hurlbert (1978), and Lawlor (1980). The approach we propose is based on research in the "population ecology of organizations" literature. The paradigm of population ecology (Hannan and Freeman, 1977) is an adaptation of ecology for the study of organizations. McPherson (1983) extended the concepts of niche overlap in ecology and developed a method for measuring competition among nonprofit organizations that are competing for members. Applying McPherson's approach in a brand marketing context involves the following steps:

1. Identify the dimensions of the resource space.
2. Determine the niche boundaries along each dimension for each brand.
3. Compute niche breadth for each brand.
4. Compute the size of the niche overlap between each pair of brands.
5. Compute an index of competitive resource overlap that brand Y faces from brand X, CROxy, which is defined as the ratio of niche overlap between X and Y and the niche breadth of Y.

Each of these steps is discussed next.

A Measure of Competitive Resource Overlap Between Brands

Determining the dimensions of the resource space requires identifying the relevant attributes of the customers. Possible customer dimensions may include demographics, psychographics, value and lifestyle data, benefits sought, usage, and/or situation data. For many markets, the complex nature of consumer decision making may mean that a large number of dimensions are needed. Past studies and variables previously used in segmentation studies should provide guidelines for identifying relevant dimensions.

The second step is to determine the niche boundaries for each dimension and each brand—that is, which customers are buying each brand? This is done by calculating the mean (or other measure of central tendency) on each dimension for each brand. A measure of the range of customers that buy each brand is the standard deviation (or other measure of variability). With these two measures, we can calculate the range (or breadth) on each customer dimension—which is the mean plus the standard deviation times a scaling factor. Selecting this scaling factor and the impact this selection has on the results will be discussed next.

A brand's total niche breadth, or the volume of the niche, is the product of all these ranges. The units of niche breadth depend on the dimensions selected (e.g., age, income, consumption rate, etc.) and have little meaning in an absolute sense. However, comparisons of relative niche breadth across brands are possible since each brand's niche breadth is measured in the same units. Note that, for now, we assume a uniform distribution of customers across each range and thus across the entire niche breadth (volume). That is, we are assuming that all points within a brand's niche are equally filled with customers. A more realistic approach would incorporate nonuniform customer distributions. This extension, while complicating the mathematics significantly, doesn't alter the general approach.

Niche overlap is the intersection of two brands' niches in n-dimensional space and is measured by the volume of the intersection. The first step in calculating the total overlap is to measure the overlap between any two brands on each dimension. Total overlap between any two brands is the product of the overlaps across dimensions.

An index of competitive resource overlap that brand Y faces from brand X (CROxy) is found by dividing the niche overlap between X and Y by the niche breadth of Y. Alternatively, to find the competitive resource overlap that brand X faces from Y (CROyx), the overlap is divided by the niche breadth of X. Thus, competitive resource overlap is measured as the proportion of a brand's niche space that is shared with a competitor. More formally:

$$CRO_{XY} = \frac{\prod_{i=1}^{n} Overlap_{XY}(i)}{\prod_{i=1}^{n}(Upperbound_{Y}(i) - Lowerbound_{Y}(i))}$$

$$= \prod_{i=1}^{n} \frac{Overlap_{XY(i)}}{Niche\ Breadth_{Y(i)}}$$

where $i = 1. \ldots . n$ (number of dimensions).

For example, consider two brands, Brand A and Brand B, in a two-dimensional resource space as shown in Figure 4.2. The customers that these brands are competing for are described by age and income. The boundaries of Brand A's niche are from 30 to 60 years old and from $10,000 to $40,000 in annual income. Similarly, Brand B's niche boundaries are from 20 to 40 years old and $30,000 to $50,000 in income. The niche breadth for Brand A is 900,000 units (30 × 30,000) and for Brand B is 400,000 units (20 × 20,000). The volume of overlap between the brands is 100,000 units. Thus, CROAB is .25 and CROBA is .11. The CRO indices for the total product-market comprise a square, asymmetric matrix.

Properties of the Competitive Resource Overlap Index

The measure CROxy has several interesting properties. First, CROxy is a dimensionless index bounded between 0 and 1. If two brands are exact competitors, the index is 1. In contrast, if two brands do not compete at all, the index is 0. Note that the brands need only be disjoint on one dimension for CROxy to be zero. For example, two brands might attract customers that are identical in terms of age and

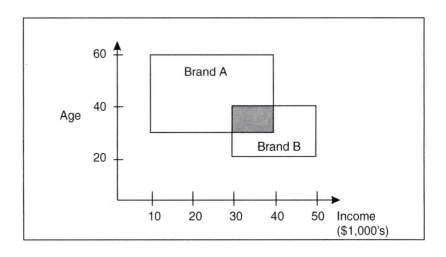

FIGURE 4.2. Niche Overlap Example

income. But if one brand is used exclusively by males and the other by females, the brands do not compete for the same customer groups.

The type and number of variables that are used can produce different results. Either omitted or redundant variables can be problematic. Omitted variables can lead to overestimates of the "true" competition, whereas redundant variables (such as multiple measures of essentially the same dimension) can underestimate competition. For example, two brands might appear to be competitors when, in fact, they might be disjoint (on the omitted variable). On the other hand, mistakenly adding a redundant variable has the effect of multiplying CRO by a factor which is, by definition, less than one (since the overlap on the redundant variable must be less than the range). Careful consideration of all possible variables should help avoid these problems. In applications where there are many (and potentially redundant) variables to choose from, factor analysis may be used to derive orthogonal factors. An advantage of our proposed approach is its ability to incorporate all different types of variables including both judgmental (e.g., benefits sought) and behavioral (e.g., usage rates) data. Note that the measurement scales of the variables needn't be comparable. In fact, linear transformations of the measurement units have no effect on CROxy. For example, rescaling age from years to months simply multiplies the numerator and denominator by 12—and the effect cancels out.

One of the factors that determine the CRO coefficient is the scaling factor used to calculate the niche boundaries. McPherson (1983) suggested a scaling factor of .75 to produce a total range 1.5 times the standard deviation. This scaling factor was derived through experimentation so that the maximum amount of discrimination is achieved, while keeping a reasonable amount of overlap. This factor is similar to what was found in the ecology literature.

There are some strategic analyses that can be made by varying the scaling factor. Different "levels" of competition can be assessed. Choosing a smaller scaling factor will yield measures of competition that involve just the "core" customers of each niche. Alternatively, a broader measure of competition that includes "fringe" customers is obtained by using a larger scaling factor.

Another interesting property is the asymmetric nature of the CRO index. Since brands, in general, will have different niche breadths, CROxy will not equal CROyx. Several researchers, including Blatt-

berg and Wisniewski (1989) and Cooper (1988), have argued that
competition is asymmetric. Information regarding asymmetries can
be valuable for repositioning and determining against whom a tactical marketing strike could be made. Closely related to this is the concept of market power, which reflects the difference in asymmetrical
competition between brands.

So far we have focused on pairwise competition between brands as
measured by the extent to which they attract similar customers. However, in markets with numerous brands, it is useful to be able to sum-
marize a brand's competitive position with respect to the whole market or some submarket of interest. Measures of a brand's competitive
clout and vulnerability (or receptivity) have been proposed to sum-
marize brand competition (Cooper 1988; Kamakura and Russell,
1989). We use the computed CRO matrix and define for each brand i,
$i = I, \ldots, K$

$$\text{Competitive clout}_i = \frac{I}{K-I} \sum_{j \neq i} \text{CRO}_{ij}$$

$$\text{Vulnerability}_i = \frac{I}{K-I} \sum_{j \neq i} \text{CRO}_{ji}$$

The row average (excluding the diagonal) reflects the competitive
overlap that other brands face from brand i (competitive clout). In
contrast, the column average (excluding the diagonal) reflects the
amount of competition that brand i faces from other brands (vulnerability). Thus, if the vulnerability for brand i is found to be .25, this
means that on average, the other brands each overlap onto 25 percent
of brand i's niche. Another possible measure of vulnerability would
compute the proportion of a brand's niche which is overlapped by any
of the other brands' niches.

Finally, measures of competitive resource overlap can also be used
to describe market level competition. Summary measures for a group
of competing brands are useful for assessing the overall level of competitive intensity in a market or submarket. The mean competitive resource overlap provides a measure of overall competitive intensity. In
addition, the pairwise CRO measures can serve as input to techniques
for revealing market structure. For example, the CRO index can be
used in multidimensional scaling or clustering algorithms. In addi-

tion, the CRO index can serve as input to dynamic ecological growth models.

EMPIRICAL DEMONSTRATION

To illustrate this measure, a small-scale analysis was done using data from eight national magazines. The groups of magazines were selected to contain both "known competitors as well as magazines which were believed a priori not to be particularly competitive with each other." The niche calculations were based upon demographic and usage variables from a national probability sample as reported by Simmons Market Research Bureau (1986). The Simmons data provide a comprehensive set of variables useful for describing magazine audiences (Fletcher and Bowers, 1979). From this set, variables were selected using a two-step approach. First, variables were screened to eliminate those with no plausible basis for distinguishing among the readers of the various magazines. Second, the variability of the remaining variables across magazines was examined. In the extreme, if all the magazines have the same range for a dimension, then the overlaps on that dimension will be equal to the range, and including that dimension has the effect of multiplying all the CRO indices by one. If the ranges are almost the same for all magazines, the impact of that dimension is to multiply the CRO indices by a factor very close to one. Thus, in the interest of parsimony, those dimensions that showed very small differences across the magazines were not considered further. The dimensions used are age, household income, years of education, social class, sex, race, occupation, whether the magazine is read at work or at home, marital status, urban/suburban/rural location, and number of children.

Table 4.1 summarizes the niche breadths, niche overlaps, and indices of competitive resource overlap for the set of eight magazines. Table 4.1 reports all pairwise indices of CRO and normalized niche breadth measures for each magazine. When examining Table 4.1, first note the niche breadths for each magazine. *Discover* (5) has a niche breadth that is 250 times as large as *Car Craft* (4). This indicates there is wider variance in the type of people that read *Discover* magazine than there is in the group of people who read *Car Craft*.

TABLE 4.1. Niche Breadth and Competitive Resource Overlap Among Eight Magazines*

Magazines	Niche breadth	CRO								Competitive clout
		(1)	(2)	(3)	(4)	(5)	(6)	(7)	(8)	
Better Homes & Gardens	0.042	–	0.06	0.00	0.00	0.01	0.66	0.00	0.01	.106
Bon Appetit	0.043	0.06	–	0.01	0.00	0.01	0.08	0.01	0.07	.034
BusinessWeek	0.287	0.02	0.09	–	0.00	0.04	0.01	0.30	0.05	.073
Car Craft	0.004	0.00	0.00	0.00	–	0.00	0.00	0.00	0.00	.000
Discover	1.000	0.12	0.31	0.13	0.02	–	0.11	0.11	0.26	.143
Family Circle	0.010	0.16	0.02	0.00	0.00	0.00	–	0.00	0.00	.026
Fortune	0.160	0.01	0.05	0.17	0.00	0.02	0.00	–	0.04	.041
Gourmet	0.230	0.07	0.40	0.04	0.00	0.06	0.11	0.05	–	.104
Competitive Vulnerability:	–	0.063	0.133	0.050	0.003	0.020	0.139	0.067	0.061	–

*Niche breadths are scaled so that the maximum is one.

Thus, we would label *Discover* a generalist and *Car Craft* a specialist. Note that niche breadth does not necessarily lead to predictions about sales volume or readership. In this small sample of magazines, the correlation between niche breadth and readership is –0.403.

The indices of CRO vary substantially from 0.0 to 0.66. In addition, several asymmetries are apparent in the pairwise measures. For example, consider the resource overlap between *Family Circle* and *Better Homes & Gardens*. These results indicate that 66 percent of *Family Circle*'s niche space is shared by *Better Homes & Gardens*. In contrast, only 16 percent of *Better Homes & Gardens'* niche is shared by *Family Circle*. Clearly, *Better Homes & Gardens* has the upper hand in that competitive relationship.

The pairwise competitive relationships indicated by Table 4.1 are graphically highlighted in a MDS representation of the competitive market as shown in Figure 4.3. The locations of the magazines in the *xy* plane in Figure 4.3a is the result of a two-dimensional MDS solution using the averaged values of CROxy and CROyx as input. Magazine proximity in the MDS solution space reflects competitive intensity between magazines. Figure 4.3b incorporates the asymmetries in the CRO matrix which are reflected in the *z* coordinates. The value of the *z* coordinate for each magazine is calculated as the difference between its competitive clout and vulnerability. Thus, the *z* axis may be thought of as a measure of market power, as positive *z* values reflect more clout than vulnerability.

The pattern in Figure 4.3 is intuitive and provides some face validity for the proposed approach. The locations of the magazines (on the *xy* plane) indicate that *BusinessWeek* and *Fortune* are competing; *Family Circle, Better Homes & Gardens,* and *Discover* are competing; *Bon Appetit* and *Gourmet* are competing; and *Car Craft* is not directly competing with any of these magazines. Further, by looking at the *z* axis, we can get an indication of the relative niche breadth of each magazine and the asymmetric power the magazine wields. *Discover* is a magazine that appeals to a wide range of readers and this is reflected by the large positive *z* value. Also, recall the relationship between *Family Circle* and *Better Homes & Gardens*. Since *Better Homes & Gardens* has a larger niche breadth, it has an advantage over *Family Circle* because the competitive interaction between the two magazines affects *Better Homes & Gardens* less.

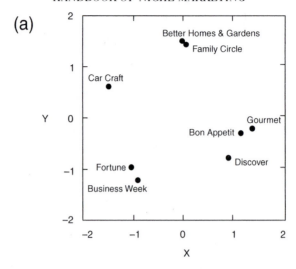

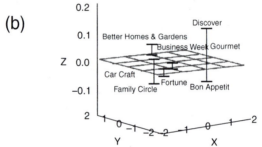

FIGURE 4.3. (a) Two-Dimensional MDS Representation of Magazine Market and (b) Three-Dimensional Representation of Magazine Market

Finally, to aid in interpreting the MDS solution, Figure 4.4 shows the same two-dimensional solution along with some of the original variables shown as vectors. The direction of the vectors indicates the dimension (of the MDS solution) with which each variable is associated, and the length of the vector indicates the strength of the association. For clarity, the figure shows the vectors for just seven of the original variables, which have relatively strong associations. By including the original variables in the competitive space we highlight the linkages between niche definition and competition. We are able to better see which customer types brands compete for.

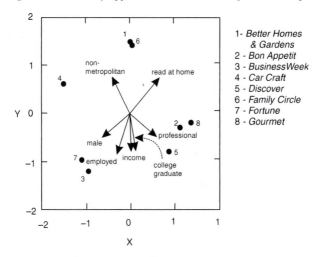

FIGURE 4.4. MDS of Magazine Market

CONCLUSIONS AND EXTENSIONS

Marketers have long advocated the use of ecological theory to study markets, but the abstract definitions of key constructs have hampered empirical applications. In this research, we take a critical first step in applying ecological theory to product markets by quantifying such concepts as niches, niche breadth, niche overlap, and competition between brands. We demonstrated the proposed measures for a small group of magazines. The empirical results are intuitive, thus providing some face validity for our approach, and we suggest that future research should be pursued. Our proposed approach has several appealing features. First, the data required are the attributes of the customers purchasing each brand. Although our empirical illustration relied heavily on demographic variables, the approach can use all types of variables including usage data, psychographics, or benefits sought such as conjoint results. These data, if not already available, can be relatively easily obtained by surveying a representative sample of customers. Second, this type of data is equally appropriate for frequently purchased and durable goods. Third, the approach is suitable for markets containing dozens or even hundreds of brands, which is likely when dealing with fragmented markets or broadly defined markets.

The CRO index is useful for repositioning and marketing mix decisions. It reveals asymmetric competitive relationships and measures competition in terms of niche overlap along multiple fronts. In addition, since niches are defined in terms of customer attributes, it is possible to understand which types of customers are being fought over among brands. For example, a brand may face competition over one type of customer from one brand and face competition over another type of customer from another brand. Such knowledge can be useful for planning advertising messages and promotions. In addition, the CRO index can play a role in evaluating potential new products. Although the realized niche for a hypothetical product is unknown until it's marketed, it can be approximated by estimating the boundaries of the customer type it is targeted toward. Using this estimate, potential overlaps with existing products can be examined.

There are many directions that future research can take. Work is in progress to develop summary measures of market level or submarket competitive intensity. Such measures are particularly useful when dealing with large numbers of brands, in which case the matrix of CRO indices becomes unwieldy. Work is also under way to rigorously assess the reliability and validity of the proposed measure. In general, validation of measures of competition has not been adequately addressed in the literature (Shocker, Stewart, and Zahorik, 1990). In this initial research, an implicit assumption is that the distribution of customers across the niche space is uniform. Violations of this assumption may either overstate or understate "true" competitive overlap, depending upon the situation. Thus, the impact is difficult to assess a priori. More realistic approaches could either assume a nonuniform customer distribution, or use more detailed data to determine the empirical distribution.

Developing a measure of the intensity of pairwise competition is a necessary first step to be able to explore the possibilities that ecological theory holds for helping to understand markets and competition. For example, with such a measure, dynamic ecological models can be applied to describe and predict sales over time. We believe that the proposed ecological-based measure of competitive resource overlap is the beginning of a research stream which can further our understanding and models of competition.

REFERENCES

Abell, Derek (1980). *Defining the Business.* Englewood Cliffs, NJ: Prentice Hall, Inc.

Abrams, Peter (1980). "Some Comments on Measuring Niche Overlap." *Ecology* 61 (11), 44-49.

Alderson, Wroe (1957). *Marketing Behavior and Executive Action.* Homewood, IL: Richard D. Irwin, Inc.

Blattberg, Robert C. and Ken Wisniewski (1989). "Price-Induced Patterns of Competition." *Marketing Science* 4 (Fall), 291-309.

Colombo, Richard A. and Donald G. Morrison (1989). "A Brand Switching Model with Implications for Marketing Strategies." *Marketing Science* 8 (Winter), 89-99.

Cooper, Lee G. (1988). "Competitive Maps: The Structure Underlying Asymmetric Cross-Elasticities." *Management Science* 34 (June), 707-723.

Day, George (1981). "Strategic Market Analysis and Definition: An Integrated Approach." *Strategic Management Journal* (May), 281-299.

Day, George S., Allan D. Shocker, and Rajendra K. Srivastava (1979). "Customer-Oriented Approaches to Identifying Product-Markets." *Journal of Marketing* 43 (Fall), 8-19.

Fletcher, Alan D. and Thomas A. Bowers (1979). *Fundamentals of Advertising Research.* Columbus, OH: Grid.

Frazier, Gary and Roy Howell (1983). "Business Definition and Performance." *Journal of Marketing* 47 (Spring), 59-67.

Hannan, Michael T. and John Freeman (1977). "The Population Ecology of Organizations." *American Journal of Sociology* 82, 929-996.

Henderson, Bruce (1980). "Understanding the Forces of Strategic and Natural Competition." *Journal of Business Strategy,* 11-15.

Henderson, Bruce (1983). "The Anatomy of Competition." *Journal of Marketing* (Spring), 7-11.

Henderson, Bruce (1989). "The Origin of Strategy." *Harvard Business Review* (November-December), 139-143.

Hurlbert, S. H. (1978). "The Measurement of Niche Overlap and Some Relatives." *Ecology* 59(1), 168-174.

Hutchinson, G. Evelyn (1957). "Concluding Remarks." *Cold Spring Harbor Symposium of Quantitative Biology* 22, 415-427.

Kamakura, Wagner A. and Gary J. Russell (1989). "A Probabilistic Choice Model for Market Segmentation and Elasticity Structure." *Journal of Marketing Research* 26 (November), 379-390.

Lambkin, Mary and George S. Day (1989). "Evolutionary Processes in Competitive Markets: Beyond the Product Life Cycle." *Journal of Marketing* 53(3) (July), 4-20.

Lawlor, Lawrence R. (1980). "Overlap, Similarity, and Competition Coefficients." *Ecology* 61(2), 245-251.

Levins, R. (1968). *Evolution in Changing Environments: Some Theoretical Explorations.* Princeton, NJ: Princeton University Press.

McPherson, Miller (1983). "An Ecology of Affiliation." *American Sociological Review* 48 (August), 519-532.

Pianka, Eric R. (1973). "The Structure of Lizard Communities." *Annual Review of Ecology and Systematics* 4, 53-74.

Porter, Michael (1980). *Competitive Strategy.* New York: The Free Press.

Shocker, Allan D., David W. Stewart, and Anthony J. Zahorik (1990). "Mapping Customer Perceptions of Markets." *Journal of Managerial Issues* (Summer), 127-159.

Simmons Market Research Bureau, Inc. (1986). Study of Media and Markets: Total audiences-(M-I)-Annual Research. New York and Chicago: Simmons Market Research Bureau.

Srivastava, Rajendra K., Robert P. Leone, and Allan D. Shocker (1981). "Market Structure Analysis: Hierarchical Clustering of Products Based on Substitution-in-Use." *Journal of Marketing* 45 (Summer), 38-48.

Tellis, G. and M. Crawford (1981). "An Evolutionary Approach to Product Growth Theory." *Journal of Marketing* 45 (Fall), 125-132.

Thorelli, Hans (1967). "Ecology in Marketing." *Southern Journal of Business,* 19-25.

Weitz, Barton A. (1985). "Introduction to Special Issue on Competition in Marketing." *Journal of Marketing Research* 22 (August), 229-236.

Whittaker, Robert H. and Simon A. Levin (1975). *Niche: Theory and Application.* Stroudsburg, PA: Dowden, Hutchinson & Ross, Inc.

Chapter 5

A Visual Approach for Identifying Consumer Satisfaction Niches

Hooman Estelami
Peter De Maeyer

ABSTRACT

Much of today's consumer satisfaction research relies on ratings obtained through the administration of consumer surveys. A key item of interest to the researcher is the existence of underlying segments in the marketplace. Such information can be uncovered by studying the shape of the distribution of the obtained consumer satisfaction measure. The shape of this distribution can, for example, provide insights on the number and size of the underlying segments in the marketplace. This chapter discusses various approaches available for graphing the distribution of consumer satisfaction responses and demonstrates the use and benefits of a proposed nonparametric method.

INTRODUCTION

Marketing managers often rely on ratings obtained through surveys to assess the degree of satisfaction experienced by consumers. The use of surveys in consumer satisfaction research has, in fact, witnessed a dramatic growth in the past two decades, and corporate use of customer satisfaction research has contributed billions of dollars to the market research industry (e.g., *Advertising Age,* 1993; Gengler and Popkowski, 1997). Survey-based studies of consumer satisfaction span the business horizon from small local retailers to large multinationals and cover industries ranging from insurance and financial services to the automotive and home appliance industries. Customer satisfaction measurement has therefore become a standard part of corporate performance assessment in many organizations (Parasuraman et al., 1991; Rapert and Babakus, 1996).

Once a customer satisfaction survey has been administered, one typically relies on the emerging basic statistics such as the mean and the variance to make the necessary managerial judgments. For example, year-to-year comparisons can be conducted and comparisons to specific baselines and benchmarks can be made. However, in addition to the mean and the variance, managers can often rely on an equally vital measure: the distribution of the satisfaction ratings. The shape of the distribution of the satisfaction ratings provides one with a better understanding of the customer base. For example, the existence of a multimodal distribution of satisfaction ratings may signal the potential existence of multiple consumer segments. Such information may prompt additional managerial attention, and could initiate a more focused and segment-based marketing program.

As will be demonstrated in this chapter, using the existing approaches for obtaining the shape of the distribution of consumer satisfaction ratings often results in ambiguous and unreliable interpretations of the data. Therefore, in this chapter, a new approach for estimating the shape of the distribution of consumer satisfaction ratings will be introduced. The proposed approach, based on an established nonparametric method in econometrics, is shown to have superior properties to existing approaches used for graphing consumer satisfaction response distributions. Benefits of the proposed approach are demonstrated and replicated in two different consumer satisfaction settings.

IMPORTANCE OF CONSUMER SATISFACTION DISTRIBUTIONS

From an applied survey research point of view, the appropriate understanding of the shape of the distribution of consumer satisfaction responses is a valuable undertaking for three key reasons:

1. The distribution of consumer satisfaction responses in a satisfaction survey can reveal information about underlying consumer

segments. The estimation of consumer satisfaction distributions is useful to any survey-based consumer satisfaction study. The knowledge of the shape of this distribution is critical in assessments made regarding the existence of multiple consumer segments. A highly dense area in the distribution of the satisfaction ratings would represent a high concentration of consumers. For example, if the distribution of the consumer satisfaction measure is multimodal or highly dense in certain regions of the response scale, multiple consumer segments may potentially exist. Such graphical inspections can aid one in identifying the relevant market segments. A study by Kumar and Rust (1989) on managers' preferences for various segment identification methods has, in fact, shown that practicing managers find the graphical approach of inspecting response distributions to be the most convenient way of assessing the existence of underlying segments in the marketplace. The authors argue for the preferred use of graphic methods since alternative segment identification methods, such as cluster analysis and AID (Automatic Interaction Detection), rely to a large extent on the technical sophistication of the manager.

2. Survey methods are popular in consumer satisfaction research. Academics and practitioners have for a long time relied on survey methods in collecting consumer satisfaction data. In academia, from the earlier works of Oliver (1980) to the more recent ones (e.g., Fornell, 1992; Anderson and Sullivan, 1994), consumer surveys have served as a primary source of consumer satisfaction information. Industry's use of surveys in consumer satisfaction research has especially witnessed a growth in recent years (*Advertising Age,* 1993), and many corporations are now developing employee compensation schemes based on factors related to customer satisfaction. For example, between 1992 and 1995 alone, the number of companies using customer satisfaction as a basis of employee compensation grew fivefold (Romano, 1995).

3. A better understanding of segment-based differences in consumer satisfaction is needed. Understanding the shape of the distribution of consumer satisfaction ratings also facilitates the study of the largely ignored notion of heterogeneity in consumer satisfaction research. As both Yi (1991) and Iacobbuci et al. (1992) assert, consumer satisfaction research needs to place more focus on the varying satisfaction dynamics across consumer segments. As Iacobbuci et al.

(1992) suggest, "to account for a richer variety of phenomena, reasonable models of evaluations (quality and/or satisfaction) should also explicitly incorporate some rather fundamental concepts—like segmentation" (p. 22).

A DEMONSTRATION
OF THE PROBLEM AT HAND

Using an example, we will now proceed with a demonstration of the typical problem one faces when attempting to estimate the distribution of consumer satisfaction responses. The consumer satisfaction data utilized for this example were obtained through a survey of 315 graduate business students at an East Coast educational institution. The survey, which was conducted as part of a standard annual satisfaction study, yielded a response rate of 63 percent and covered various questions about the services provided at the institution. Five satisfaction-related questions, rated on a scale of 1 to 10 (with 10 being the positive end), were obtained and utilized:

Item 1:   My overall assessment of the school is (very negative . . . very positive).

Item 2:   Considering all the services and facilities provided by the school, I am (very dissatisfied . . . very satisfied).

Item 3:   Considering the cost of attending this school, it is (not a good value . . . a very good value).

Item 4:   My decision to attend this school has left me (very dissatisfied . . . very satisfied).

Item 5:   The time spent at this school has left me (unhappy . . . happy).

These five variables were input into factor analysis, which yielded one factor based on the eigenvalue > 1 criterion. The satisfaction scale was therefore constructed by taking an average of the previous measures for each respondent. The resulting scale yielded a high degree of measurement reliability, as reflected by a coefficient alpha of 0.92.

Once the satisfaction data have been gathered, one needs to assess the shape of the distribution of the satisfaction measure. The most common way of estimating distributions is the histogram (Silverman, 1986). A histogram is defined by an origin and a bin width. Given the origin and the bin width, a series of bins are then defined by consecutive intervals, and the histogram is constructed by graphing the percentage of responses that fall into the bins. The histogram provides an estimate of the distribution by presenting the percentage of observations that fall into each bin. In constructing a histogram one needs to make two choices: (1) a choice of the origin and (2) a choice of the bin width. The shape of the histogram therefore primarily depends on these two decisions.

While the choice of bin width determines the degree of smoothness in the histogram, the choice of the origin determines the reference point, based on which consecutive bins are defined. As a result, depending on one's chosen value for the origin and the bin width, drastically different distributions may result. The choice of one bin width or origin over another may therefore significantly influence one's assessment of the shape of the distribution of the satisfaction ratings. Figure 5.1 provides a histogram of the consumer satisfaction measure. With its origin at 5, and a bin width of 1 unit, Figure 5.1 suggests that the consumer satisfaction measure's distribution is unimodal and slightly skewed to the right. However, a simple change of the bin width from 1 to 0.75 produces Figure 5.2, which suggests that the consumer satisfaction distribution is actually multimodal. Figure 5.3 shows a similar effect resulting from a bin width of 0.5. At this point, one is left with contradicting interpretations of identical data, one suggesting the potential of multiple consumer segments, and the others refuting it.

An alternative approach to histogram building is the parametric approach. In this approach, one assumes that the sample data are drawn from a population with a particular distribution function. The sample data are then used to estimate the parameters of that distribution function. Although the parametric approach to density estimation is computationally convenient, as we will see shortly, its main drawback is that it constrains the shape of the estimated distribution to the one as-

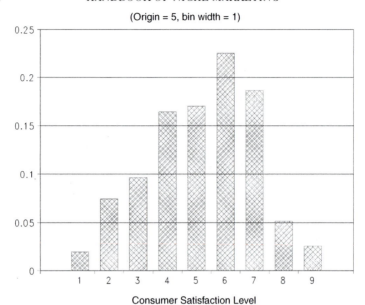

FIGURE 5.1. Consumer Satisfaction Histogram

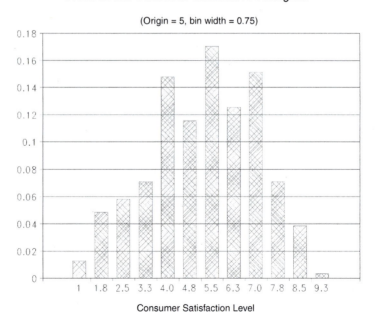

FIGURE 5.2. Consumer Satisfaction Histogram

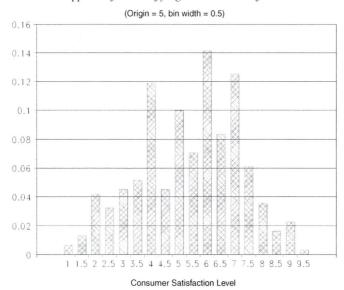

FIGURE 5.3. Consumer Satisfaction Histogram

sumed by the researcher. Meanwhile, unless sufficient prior information exists, forcing a particular functional form on the distribution of satisfaction measures is both conceptually flawed and practically inappropriate.

Two commonly used distribution functions are the normal and the beta. As can be seen in the Appendix, both of these distributions are two-parameter distributions. Figure 5.4 shows the estimated normal distribution for the consumer satisfaction data mentioned in the previous section. As can be seen, much of the details of the data seem to have vanished. Specifically, due to the unimodal nature of the normal distribution, the suggested high-density area in the 6 to 7 range of Figure 5.1 has disappeared. Also, due to the symmetric nature of the normal distribution, skewness in the data can no longer be observed. In order to assess the appropriateness of using the normal distribution on the consumer satisfaction data, the Shapiro-Wilk test was conducted. The results of the test rejected the null hypothesis of normality at the $p < 0.0001$ level, thereby confirming that the data are not drawn from a normal distribution. Therefore, the normal approximation seems to be an inappropriate representation for the distribution

Normal Distribution

Consumer Satisfaction Level

FIGURE 5.4. Consumer Satisfaction Density Estimate

of consumer satisfaction data. This observation is consistent with observations made by Peterson and Wilson (1992), that most consumer satisfaction data have significant deviations from normality.

An alternative distribution function is the beta distribution. The advantage of the beta distribution over the normal distribution is that it can take on many different forms, such as a U or an inverted U, and can also be nonsymmetric. As a result, it is a convenient distribution function for many marketing and social science applications (e.g., Morrison, 1981; Heckman and Willis, 1977; Sabavala and Morrison, 1981). However, as in the case of the normal distribution, the beta distribution is also constrained in its shape in that, with the exception of a U or J shape, it is unable to reflect other cases of multimodality in the data. It too is therefore limited in its application to consumer satisfaction data, where multimodality in consumer responses is likely. Figure 5.5 shows the estimated beta distribution using the consumer satisfaction data mentioned earlier. Again, as in the case of the normal distribution estimate, much of the detail has disappeared due to

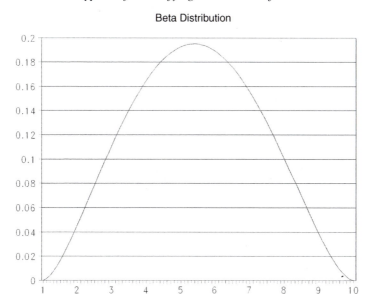

Beta Distribution

Consumer Satisfaction Level

FIGURE 5.5. Consumer Satisfaction Density Estimate

the shape of the distribution function enforced by the beta distribution.

THE PROPOSED METHOD: KERNEL ESTIMATION

Because the existing methods are unable to reflect subtle fluctuations in consumer satisfaction responses, a more flexible method for estimating consumer satisfaction distributions is needed. In this section, the kernel estimation method is introduced as an approach to obtaining estimates of the underlying distribution of the consumer satisfaction measures. Kernel estimation is a well-established nonparametric approach to estimating distributions. It is the most commonly used nonparametric distribution estimation method and has been widely used in a variety of applications in economics. Among its many advantages is that it relaxes the restrictive assumption that the observed data are drawn from a given parametric distribution. The relaxation of the parametric assumptions is especially appealing in applications involving consumer satisfaction data, as prior assumptions about the shape of the distribution of consumer responses can often significantly restrict the shape of the estimated distribution. In addition, kernel estimation provides much more stable results than those obtained through histograms (Silverman, 1986).

Prior applications of kernel estimation in the marketing literature are limited. Rust (1988) introduced the concept of flexible regression to the marketing literature, using the kernel method as a means for relaxing many of the restrictive assumptions of classical regression. Abe (1991) further advanced Rust's work by introducing the moving ellipsoid estimation method. Donthu and Rust (1989), in an interesting application of the method, used the kernel method to estimate the geographic distribution of a city's population. Having determined the shape of the distribution, they then identify the optimal location for a new retail outlet. In a later work, Donthu (1991) applied kernel density estimation to estimate market area densities, and Abe (1995) applied the method for studying consumers' brand choice behavior.

Conceptually, the kernel estimation method is actually quite simple. The kernel density estimate at a particular point x is simply the sum of n individual "kernel" functions. The value of each of these n kernel functions depends on the distance between x and the observations around it. If x is close to many observations, the kernel functions are set up such that the value of the individual kernel functions is large, and therefore their sum is large. As a result, if x is located in a densely populated portion of the scale, the distribution would end up being "bumped up." In contrast, if x is far from most sample observations, the individual kernel function values are small, resulting in a low distribution estimate at x. Figure 5.6 graphically demonstrates the basic concept, and the Appendix presents the technical details. The horizontal axis in Figure 5.6 shows the satisfaction response scale. Each point on the horizontal axis represents a single observation from a respondent. Therefore, all the dots on the horizontal axis reflect the entire sample of consumer satisfaction responses in the survey. For example, the point "a" is the observation for one respondent (having a response of 5) and point "b" is another observation for another respondent (having a response of 6). The vertical axis repre-

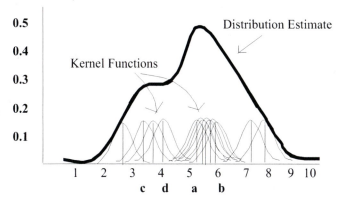

FIGURE 5.6. Demonstration of the Kernel Method

sents the density of the distribution of observations. For example, the area between points a and b has a large bump because many observations are in this area. On the other hand, the area between c and d has a drop in the distribution, because very few observations are in this region of the scale.

What makes kernel estimation such a useful technique is some of its attractive statistical properties. Specifically, given a sufficiently large sample size, we are guaranteed to obtain a distribution estimate that closely resembles the true distribution of the measure in the population, as the kernel estimate has also been shown to be both consistent and unbiased (Rosenblatt, 1956; Parzen, 1962).

Estimation

Kernel estimation of the distribution of the satisfaction ratings in the survey was achieved using the Gauss programming language. Total estimation time with an Intel 486-33 processor was under 45 seconds. Figure 5.7 graphically presents the kernel estimate of the satisfaction measure. Contrasted against Figures 5.1 and 5.2, visual inspection of Figure 5.7 shows the existence of two highly dense regions, one centered at 4.3, and the other at 6.5. Moreover, contrasted against Figures 5.4 and 5.5, the kernel estimate suggests that the estimated distribution does not look anything like a beta or a normal distribution.

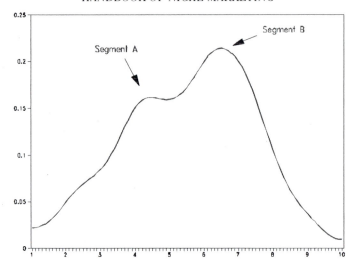

FIGURE 5.7. Consumer Satisfaction Distribution Using Kernel Estimation

In the following subsections, the merits of the kernel method will be discussed on three grounds: (1) the ability of the kernel estimate to fit the original data, (2) the ability of the method to identify consumer segments, and (3) the managerial implications of the findings.

Superior Fit

To assess the relative fit of the various approaches, the consumers' responses were randomly split into two samples. An estimation sample of 150 respondents was used to estimate the consumer satisfaction distribution using the various methods. The remaining 165 respondents' data were then used as a holdout sample. The cumulative distribution of the resulting estimates were then compared to the cumulative density of the holdout sample using the goodness of fit index (GFI) described in the Appendix. Table 5.1 shows the results of the fit test. As can be seen from the table, and as expected, the kernel density estimate produced the best fit to the holdout sample data. This was followed by the two parametric estimates. The worst fit was obtained using the histogram.

TABLE 5.1. Results of the Fit Test

Estimation Method	Goodness of Fit Index (GFI)
Kernel	18.52
Normal	11.41
Beta	3.03
Histogram (origin = 5, bin width = 1)	2.10

Segment Identification Ability

Because the kernel distribution estimate is an unbiased and consistent estimator of the underlying distribution (Silverman, 1986), one can reasonably conclude that the fluctuations observed in the distribution graph are likely to be due to the underlying distribution of consumer satisfaction. Visual inspection of the resulting kernel estimate indicates two consumer segments, one with satisfaction levels centered at 4.3 (referred to as segment A), and another with satisfaction levels centered at 6.5 (referred to as segment B), with the midpoint separating the two segments. To further establish the existence of these segments, the two identified segments should be demonstrated to be conceptually different from each other in some managerially meaningful way. This may therefore help guide further managerial actions. It may also help address the largely ignored notion of consumer heterogeneity in consumer satisfaction research and the possibility that consumer satisfaction dynamics might vary from one consumer segment to another (Yi, 1991).

In order to do so, in addition to the satisfaction measures, the survey also obtained measures of the performance of the institution on individual aspects of its services. These include performance perceptions of the student service offices, the physical facilities, the administration, and teaching quality. These measures were obtained to assist the management in identifying areas where quality improvement initiatives can be directed. The items in the scales were developed based on management input, followed by a set of pretests, and are outlined in Exhibit 5.1. As can be seen from the chart, the multi-item scales all provide highly reliable measures, reflected by coefficient alpha values of 0.74 and and higher. One possible way in which the

EXHIBIT 5.1. Multi-Item Scales Used in the Survey

(All Items on a 1-10 Scale)

Physical Facilities: Coefficient alpha = 0.74
　Room availability for group projects and meetings (low . . . high)
　My desire to spend more time in the building (low . . . high)
　The cleanliness of the building (low . . . high)
　The overall quality of the building's facilities (low . . . high)

Student Services: Coefficient alpha = 0.80
　The usefulness of the Career Resource Center in my job search (low . . . high)
　The professionalism and courtesy of the Placement Office (low . . . high)
　The ability of the Placement Office in bringing in a variety of companies (low . . . high)
　The ability of the Placement Office in bringing in a large number of companies (low . . . high)
　Overall quality of the school's student services (low . . . high)

Administrative Offices: Coefficient alpha = 0.89
　The dean's office's effort in improving the quality of student life (low . . . high)
　The honesty and openness of the administration (low . . . high)
　The availability of the administration to discuss student issues with students (low . . . high)
　The administration's follow-up of issues that are presented by students (low . . . high)
　The Admissions Office's ability to present a true picture of the school to prospective students (low . . . high)

Teaching Quality: Coefficient alpha = 0.87
　The level of quality of the teaching by professors is (low . . . high)
　The accessibility of professors for questions outside of class (low . . . high)
　Overall level of satisfaction with the teaching approach (low . . . high)

two identified segments might vary is in the way the dynamics of the satisfaction process function. In other words, the way consumers form their satisfaction evaluations, based on the individual components of the service, may vary between the two segments. In order to test this assertion, a standardized regression analysis was conducted on the obtained measures. Specifically, the satisfaction measure was regressed on the component level performance measures outlined in Exhibit 5.1 (i.e., physical facilities, student services, administration, and teaching quality). The analysis was conducted separately for each segment, and the standardized coefficients were then used to gain insights on the varying satisfaction dynamics between the two segments. Table 5.2 presents the results of this analysis.

As can be seen from the results, the two segments vary in their satisfaction dynamics. For segment A respondents, teaching quality and the physical facilities are the strongest driver of satisfaction, reflected by the high t-values. Student services and administration do not seem to have any significant influence on the satisfaction ratings of this segment. For segment B, on the other hand, the effect of teaching quality on satisfaction is considerably lower, and the effect of the physical facilities is negligible. In contrast to segment A, for segment B respondents, the perceptions of the administration are a significant driver of satisfaction.

TABLE 5.2. Segment-Level Estimates of the Consumer Satisfaction Model

Service Component	Standardized Betas	
	Segment A	Segment B
Physical Facilities[a]	0.187[b]	0.088
	(0.079)	(0.076)
Student Services[a]	0.128	0.002
	(0.085)	(0.079)
Administration[c]	0.141	0.162[d]
	(0.084)	(0.079)
Teaching Quality[a]	0.341[b]	0.256[b]
	(0.078)	(0.076)

[a] Segment differences significant at the $p < 0.01$ level.

[b] Coefficient significant at the $p < 0.01$ level.

[c] Segment differences significant at the $p < 0.05$ level.

[d] Coefficient significant at the $p < 0.05$ level.

Note: Numbers in parentheses are standard errors.

Managerial Implications of the Findings

From a marketing management perspective, the previous findings suggest that in order to improve consumer satisfaction levels, the management may need to consider addressing the two segments in different ways. Moreover, the management can prioritize and focus quality improvement efforts based on which consumer segment is considered to be more important to serve. For example, addressing segment A consumers would clearly require improvements to the physical facilities and improved teaching quality. On the other hand, while improvements in teaching quality would also improve segment B's satisfaction level, addressing the needs of this segment would also require improvements in the perceptions of the administration. Physical facility improvements would not significantly improve this segment's satisfaction ratings. Based on the expected costs and benefits of each of these improvements, the management can therefore proceed to develop an optimal quality improvement program.

Replication

In order to further test the proposed method, a replication of the previous analysis was done on consumer satisfaction survey data obtained from a very different service setting: a retail outlet.

The retail outlet is part of a regional chain of fast-food convenience stores, which sell grocery items, beverages, and fast food. The consumer satisfaction data utilized were obtained from a standardized survey done to assess consumer perceptions of service quality at the retail outlet. A total of 242 customers were administered the consumer satisfaction questionnaire, which assessed their perceptions of various aspects of the service, such as its cleanliness, employee responsiveness, and food quality.

As in the previous example, a multi-item scale was developed in order to obtain reliable measures of consumer satisfaction. The satisfaction scale was constructed by averaging six survey questions, each on a scale of 1 to 5 (with 5 being the positive end). The six questions were regarding (1) the cleanliness of the food area, (2) the cleanliness of the cash register area, (3) the freshness of the food, (4) the speed of preparation of the food, (5) the friendliness of the employees, and

(6) the speed of service by the employees. The coefficient alpha for the scale was 0.85, and the mean satisfaction rating was 4.39.

As in the previous case, kernel estimation was done using the Gauss programming language. Figure 5.8 shows the resulting kernel distribution estimate. A split sample analysis found the kernel estimate to provide a fit to the holdout data superior to the alternative methods. The goodness of fit index (GFI) for the kernel was 21.29, as compared to 13.34 for the normal, 11.72 for the beta, and 14.92 for the histogram. Moreover, as can be seen, multiple consumer segments can be identified on the basis of the peaks exhibited in the distribution of the satisfaction measure. A highly satisfied group of consumers can be observed in the 4.2 to 5.0 portion of the response scale (Segment B), as indicated by the peaks. Moreover, a low satisfaction segment can be found in the sub-4.2 region of the scale (Segment A).

To assess the difference between the two segments, standardized regression was conducted to examine the relative impact of the various service attributes on consumer behavior. To do so, data obtained from scales assessing the rating of employees, the quality of the food,

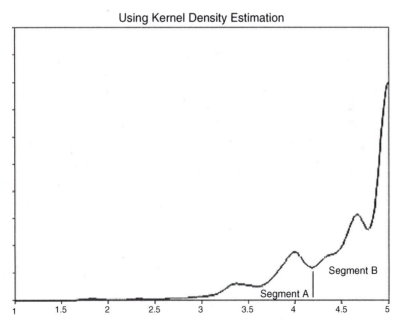

FIGURE 5.8. Consumer Satisfaction Density for Retail Outlet

**EXHIBIT 5.2. Multi-Item Scales
for Service Quality Components**

Cleanliness (Coefficient Alpha = 0.90)
Cleanliness of the Sidewalk
Cleanliness of the Parking
Cleanliness of the Coffee Area
Cleanliness of the Fountain
Cleanliness of MTO
Cleanliness of Cash Register
Cleanliness of the Rest Room

Employees (Coefficient Alpha = 0.86)
Employee Friendliness
Employee Speed
Employee Appearance

Freshness of the Food (Coefficient Alpha = 0.80)
Speed of Food Preparation
Cleanliness of Food Preparation Employees
Freshness of the Coffee

and the cleanliness of the retail outlet were used. Exhibit 5.2 outlines the items used to develop these scales. A standardized regression analysis for each segment was conducted. The dependent variable used was consumers' self-reported level of frequency of visiting the retail outlet. Table 5.3 shows the resulting standardized beta coefficients for the two segments.

As can be seen, Segment B's behavior seems to be mostly affected by perceived food quality. On the other hand, Segment A seems to be less sensitive to food quality. For this segment, the cleanliness of the outlet and employee responsiveness seem to be more important. The two segments are further differentiated based on their demographics. The high satisfaction segment, Segment B, is mostly made of males. Males account for 60.8 percent of respondents in this segment. On the other hand, the low satisfaction segment is equally represented by the two sexes. The gender difference between the two segments is signif-

TABLE 5.3. Replication: Segment-Level Estimates of the Consumer Satisfaction Model

	Standardized Betas	
Service Component	Segment A	Segment B
Employees[a]	0.21	0.17
	(.11)	(.21)
Food Quality[b]	−0.02	.27[c]
	(.15)	(.13)
Cleanliness[b]	0.19	−0.30
	(0.13)	(.14)

[a] Segment differences significant at the $p < 0.05$ level.
[b] Segment differences significant at the $p < 0.01$ level.
[c] Coefficient significant at the $p < 0.05$ level.
Note: Numbers in parentheses are standard errors.

icant at the $p < 0.1$ level. No other significant demographic differences were found between the two segments. From a managerial perspective, these results suggest that each of these segments needs to have different marketing programs tailored to them. Improving consumer satisfaction in Segment A requires improvements in the cleanliness of the outlet while Segment B may benefit from improvements in the quality of the food. Moreover, since the high satisfaction segment (Segment B) has a higher proportion of males, further research on the needs of female consumers may facilitate additional service quality improvements.

PROS AND CONS OF THE METHOD

Despite its favorable statistical properties and ease of use, the kernel estimation method does have some minor drawbacks. It has, for example, been shown that when applied to data from long-tailed distributions, the distribution estimate in the tails may become unreliable. An alternative estimation method, called the nearest-neighbor method, needs to be used in such cases (Silverman, 1986). In addition, although the kernel technique is easy to program, it is a data-intensive procedure. As a result with very large samples (i.e., 1,000 or more), the estimation procedure may become considerably slow. In such cases fast Fourier transforms can be applied to speed up the process (Hardle, 1993). Moreover, with small sample sizes (i.e., less than 100), the reliability of the obtained estimates tends to be low, as shown by the simulation work of Donthu and Rust (1994). In such cases, the histogram approach is likely to be preferable.

Fortunately, such concerns typically do not apply to most consumer satisfaction data, as consumer satisfaction response scales are limited in their range of possible values, and many consumer satisfaction surveys utilize moderate sample sizes. The proposed method is especially relevant since many consumer satisfaction studies utilize survey methods to gauge consumer satisfaction. Moreover, as shown by Kumar and Rust's (1989) study, a visual approach for detecting segments such as the one proposed here is the most preferred approach by practicing managers. As the authors argue, to utilize alternative approaches for segment identification, such as cluster analysis and AID, "a great deal of sophistication is required to accurately interpret the results" (p. 24). On the other hand, with a method such as kernel estimation, the resulting distribution graph can easily be inspected, analyzed, and communicated, making it a useful tool for both applied and academic research in consumer satisfaction.

CONCLUSION

In this chapter, we reviewed various popular methods for estimating the shape of the distribution of consumer satisfaction ratings obtained from consumer surveys. We further offered the kernel estimation method as a tool for improving our ability to assess the shape of this distribution. In doing so, we demonstrated that kernel estimation enables us to better visualize and interpret the distribution of consumer satisfaction measures. The method is superior to the traditional approach of building histograms, which is highly sensitive to one's choice of the origin or the bin width. In addition, unlike parametric estimation methods, kernel estimation does not constrain the form of the estimated distribution to a particular shape. Therefore, the kernel method allows the consumer response data to "speak for itself" in determining the shape of the distribution of consumer responses.

The application of the method on consumer satisfaction data in two separate scenarios helped identify underlying consumer segments. These segments were further differentiated based on the dynamics by which satisfaction is arrived at. As a result, the proposed method facilitates the study of heterogeneity in consumer satisfaction data, an issue of equal concern to academics and practitioners. Moreover, it facilitates the development of segment-based and focused quality improvement programs in consumer services.

APPENDIX: DISTRIBUTION ESTIMATION AND COMPARISON APPROACHES

Normal Distribution

Formally, the normal distribution at a point x is defined by

$$f(x) = \frac{1}{\sigma\sqrt{2\pi}} e^{-\frac{1}{2}[\frac{x-\mu}{\sigma}]^2} \tag{5.1}$$

where μ and σ are the population mean and standard deviation, respectively. The normal distribution has a symmetric and unimodal shape. Moreover, it ranges from minus infinity to positive infinity.

Beta Distribution

The beta distribution, on the other hand, can take on a variety of shapes. The beta distribution at a point x is defined by

$$f(x) = \frac{\Gamma(\alpha + \beta)}{\Gamma(\alpha).\Gamma(\beta)} x^{\alpha-1}(1-x)^{\beta-1} \quad \text{for} \quad 0 < x < 1 \tag{5.2}$$

where α and β are the distribution parameters. Depending on the values of α and β a variety of distribution shapes, including U, inverted U, J, and inverted J can be produced. Moreover, in contrast to the normal distribution, the range of values that x can hold is bounded.

Estimation of Distribution Parameters

For both the normal and beta distributions, parameter estimation can be achieved through maximum likelihood estimation or the method of moments. In this chapter, the method of moments was used due to its computational convenience (Freund and Walpole, 1980). Using the method of moments, the first and second moments of the sample are set equal to those of the distribution, and the pair of equations is solved in order to determine the distribution parameter values.

Kernel Density Estimation

Formally, the kernel density estimate at a point x is defined by

$$f(x) = \frac{1}{nh} \sum_{t=1}^{n} K(\frac{x - x_i}{h}), \qquad (5.3)$$

where n is the sample size, h is the smoothing parameter, K is the kernel function, and the x_i are the data points. In order to conduct kernel estimation, one needs to choose both a kernel function K, and a smoothing parameter h. Often the kernel function is chosen such that it is nonnegative, symmetric, and integrable to 1. Many choices of the kernel function, such as the normal, the Epanechnikov, and the uniform exist. Interestingly, the choice of the kernel function, even with small sample sizes, does not greatly affect the resulting kernel estimate (Silverman, 1978).

The smoothing parameter h is also chosen such that as n approaches infinity, h approaches 0. The correct value of the smoothing parameter is predetermined such that it minimizes the expected error in the distribution estimate and is approximated by (Silverman, 1986)

$$h_{opt} = (\frac{4}{3})^{1/5} sn^{-\frac{1}{5}} \qquad (5.4)$$

where s is the standard deviation of the measure in the sample, and n is the sample size.

Goodness of Fit Comparisons

In order to compare the performance of the various distribution estimates (e.g., normal, beta, histogram, and kernel), a goodness of fit index expressed by

$$GFI = \frac{1}{\displaystyle\int_{L}^{U} [F_{estimate}(x) - F_{sample}(x)]^2 \, dx} \tag{5.5}$$

was used, where $F_{estimate}(x)$ and $F_{sample}(x)$ are the cumulative distribution functions at point x of the distribution estimate and the sample, respectively, and L and U represent the lower and upper bounds of the scale. The higher the index, the better the fit. The intuition behind this fit measure is that a good fit would result in a cumulative distribution estimate which closely follows the actual distribution of the holdout sample. As a result, the better the fit, the smaller the denominator, and the higher the GFI.

REFERENCES

Abe, M. (1991). "A Moving Ellipsoid Method for Nonparametric Regression and Its Application to Logit Diagnostics with Scanner Data." *Journal of Marketing Research,* August, 339-346.

Abe, M. (1995). "A Nonparametric Density Estimation Method for Brand Choice Using Scanner Data." *Marketing Science,* 14(3), 300-325.

Anderson, E. and M. Sullivan (1994). "The Antecedents and Consequences of Customer Satisfaction." *Marketing Science,* 12(2), 125-143.

"Customer Satisfaction Blooms: Rivalry at Top Grows" (1993). *Advertising Age,* 64(44) (October 18), S-1, S-44.

Donthu, N. (1991). "Comparing Market Areas Using Kernel Density Estimation." *Journal of Academy of Marketing Science,* Fall, 323-332.

Donthu, N. and R. Rust (1989). "Estimating Geographic Customer Densities Using Kernel Density Estimation." *Marketing Science,* Spring, 191-203.

Donthu, N. and R. Rust (1994). "Seeing the Forest Instead of the Trees: A Comparison of Approaches to Capture Consumer Heterogeneity in Perceptual Maps." 1994 AMA Educators' Proceedings, 84-90.

Fornell, C. (1992). "A National Customer Satisfaction Barometer: The Swedish Experience." *Journal of Marketing,* 56, 6-21.

Freund, J. E. and R. E. Walpole (1980). *Mathematical Statistics.* Englewood Cliffs, NJ: Prentice Hall.

Gengler, C. and P. Popkowski (1997). "Using Customer Satisfaction Research for Relationship Marketing: A Direct Marketing Approach." *Journal of Direct Marketing,* 11(1), 23-29.

Hardle, W. (1993). Applied Nonparametric Regression. Econometric Society Monographs No. 19, Cambridge University Press.

Heckman, J. and R. Willis (1997). "A Beta-logistic Model for the Analysis of Sequential Labor Force Participation by Married Women." *Journal of Political Economy*, 85, 27-58.

Iacobbuci, D., K. Grayson, and A. Ostrom (1992). "The Calculus of Service Quality and Customer Satisfaction: Theoretical and Empirical Differentiation and Integration." Working paper, Kellog Graduate School of Management, Northwestern University.

Kumar, V. and R. Rust (1989). "Market Segmentation by Visual Inspection." *Journal of Advertising Research*, August/September, 23-29.

Morrison, D. (1981). "Triangle Taste Tests: Are the Subjects Who Respond Correctly Lucky or Good?" *Journal of Marketing*, Summer, 111-119.

Oliver, R. (1980). "A Cognitive Model of the Antecedents and Consequences of Satisfaction Decisions." *Journal of Marketing Research*, November, 460-469.

Parasuraman, A., L. Berry, and V. Zeithaml (1991). "Perceived Service Quality As a Customer-Based Performance Measure." *Human Resource Management*, 30(3), 335-364.

Parzen, E. (1962). "On Estimation of Probability Density Function and Mode." *Annals of Mathematical Statistics*, 33(3), 1065-1076.

Peterson, R. and W. Wilson (1992). "Measuring Customer Satisfaction: Fact and Artifact." *Journal of the Academy of Marketing Science*, 10(Winter), 61-71.

Rapert, M. and E. Babakus (1996). "Linking Quality and Performance." *Journal of Health Care Marketing*, 16(3), 39-43.

Romano, C. (1995). "Pay for Satisfaction." *Management Review*, 84(12), 16.

Rosenblatt, M. (1956). "Remarks on Some Nonparametric Estimates of Density Function." *Annals of Mathematical Statistics*, 27(3), 832-837.

Rust, R. (1988). "Flexible Regression." *Journal of Marketing Research*, February, 10-24.

Sabavala, D. and D. Morrison (1981). "A Nonstationary Model of Binary Choice Applied to Media Exposure." *Management Science*, June, 637-657.

Silverman, B.W. (1978). "Choosing the Window Width When Estimating a Density." *Biometrika*, 65, 1-11.

Silverman, B.W. (1986). *Density Estimation for Statistics and Analysis*. New York: Chapman and Hill.

Yi, Y. (1991). "A Critical Review of Consumer Satisfaction." In V. Zeithmal (ed.), *Review of Marketing*. Chicago, IL: American Marketing Association.

Chapter 6

High Tech, High Performance: The Synergy of Niche Strategy and Planning Focus in Technological Entrepreneurial Firms

Karen Bantel

INTRODUCTION

At the core of strategic management is the notion that strategy should create an alignment between the firm's strengths and weaknesses and the opportunities and threats in its environment (Andrews, 1971); this is critical for long-term competitive viability. While the literature is extensive on the importance of an appropriate strategy for long-term success in mature businesses, recent work on strategy for entrepreneurial firms draws similar conclusions (e.g., Feeser & Willard, 1990; Sandberg & Hofer, 1987).

The importance of an appropriate strategy is difficult to dispute. The essential uniqueness of firms in their resources, history, and knowledge suggests that a range of strategies is potentially compatible with a firm's long-term viability. A resource-based view of the firm argues that firms are a bundle of unique, rare, and inimitable resources (Barney, 1991; Dierickx & Cool, 1989), implying that firms are likely to develop different strategic responses to environmental and competitive pressures, based on their capabilities and resources.

This material was originally printed by RISEbusiness (Research Institute for Small & Emerging Business, Inc.). Working Paper Series 97-02. ©1997 by Karen A. Bantel.

A further argument of the resource-based view is that firms gradually accumulate the capabilities necessary to support and implement their chosen strategic direction; skills for implementing strategy must be specific to the particular strategies being implemented (Werner-felt, 1984). Thus, implementation capabilities are systematically and deliberately developed as resources to provide a sustainable competitive advantage (Amit & Shoemaker, 1993; Hamel & Prahalad, 1993). A key implication of this view is that synergies can develop between strategy type and implementation capabilities and can have important influences on the firm's success.

This chapter explores the influence on a technological entrepreneurial firm's performance of a specific product/market strategy, the quality/service niche, and one aspect of strategic implementation capabilities: breadth or focus in strategic-planning processes. Further, reflecting the resource-based view of firms (i.e., that there are synergies between strategy and implementation characteristics), the effect of the interaction of these variables will be examined. Because the strategic benefit of implementation skills can be understood only in reference to the firm's competitive context (Barney & Zajac, 1994), the contextual influences of the environment (instability and munificence) and the product stage of development will also be examined, as will the organizational context of age and size.

Technological entrepreneurial firms are the subject of this study because they are an increasingly important segment of international economies (although little is known about them) and achieving strategic success is particularly challenging for them. Technology-based industries, with their rapidly changing environment, require that firms make highly flexible and rapid strategic moves which can be difficult for young firms with few slack resources. Entrepreneurial firms also have the difficulty of the "liability of adolescence" (Bruderl & Schussler, 1990) in which failure is high during the firm's early years. Insight into strategic success for such firms has potential business and public-policy value.

SCOPE OF ENTRY: NICHE STRATEGY

When a new firm enters a market, an entry strategy defined as initial commitments to markets and technologies (Carter, Stearns, Reynolds, & Miller, 1994) is central to its business and functional strategies and performance. Key to a young firm's entry strategy is the scope defined as the choices of which customer groups and how to serve them (Teplensky, Kimberly, Hillman, & Schwartz, 1993). In their analysis of MRI manufacturers' entry strategies, Teplensky et al. (1993) identified three different kinds of scope of entry: niche, portfolio, and full-line. Portfolio and full-line strategies are somewhat broad in scope; a niche strategy is more narrowly focused on a particular product or market segment.

An important debate in the literature on new ventures, pertinent to the adolescent firms studied here, is whether new firms should pursue a niche strategy, avoiding direct competition with large firms, or compete broadly (Carter et al., 1994). The rationale for a niche strategy is that specialized, high-quality products targeted to overlooked market segments avoid competing on price (Cohn & Lindberg, 1974; Deeks, 1976), where large, established firms have an advantage. The niche firm develops specialized expertise and knowledge, enabling it to serve the narrow market better than its competitors and achieve high market share, leading to high performance (Porter, 1980). Competitors often ignore a narrow segment in which a highly specialized competitor is satisfying its customers, particularly when other growth opportunities are plentiful, such as early in the industry's evolution.

By establishing a clear, consistent vision of the firm, a niche approach implies a precise definition of what is in and what is out of the firm's scope of activities. In the early stages, the pursuit of a single-minded vision is often critical to the firm's long-term viability (Churchill & Lewis, 1983). As such, a niche strategy can lead to highly efficient use of resources, which is crucial for entrepreneurial, resource-constrained firms. Specialization involves a narrow product line and distribution system and a customized production capacity (Hannan & Freeman, 1977; Lambkin, 1988). Advertising publicizes a highly targeted image and message as the firm's reputation becomes clearly aligned with specific product/market areas (Teplensky et al., 1993). Management complexity remains low, facilitating relatively simple and quick decision making (Bray, Kerr, & Atkin, 1978) and internal coordination; duplication of effort is minimized. These characteristics can improve performance. Hambrick, MacMillan, and Day

(1982) found that successful market-share firms tended to have narrower domains.

Although there are clear advantages to a narrow-niche strategy for small entrepreneurial firms, there are also risks. One argument in favor of a broad approach is if it does not enter aggressively and broadly, it risks lacking the wide appeal of its competitors (Biggadike, 1976; Cooper, Willard, & Woo, 1986; MacMillan & Day, 1987). Formidable competitors might decide to pursue a previously ignored market segment (Porter, 1980), offering product advantages the niche firm cannot match, such as lower price. Shifts in technology or buyer preferences in the niche might decrease sales and profit potential, threatening viability. The niche firm's basis for differentiation might erode, leading to insufficient value for the customer. Specialization also makes the firm unable to withdraw easily or rapidly from one market segment and enter a new one.

The tradeoffs between a narrow and a broad entry approach are best understood when considering the large, more established firm. A broad approach often makes sense for such firms with their deeper and more diverse resources. Porter (1980) and Ghemawat (1986) argue in favor of achieving product and market breadth, indicating that competitive advantage based on multiple sources is more sustainable. Hannan and Freeman (1977) make a similar point in distinguishing between generalist and specialist firms.

A generalist firm tries to satisfy a diverse market's needs through a wide product line, extensive distribution network, and large, flexible production capacity (Hannan & Freeman, 1977; Lambkin, 1988). Generalist firms are less vulnerable if one of the products or markets fails, as they are able to react more flexibly.

A broad strategy has risks, even for large, established firms. Strategic breadth requires high resource use to develop and sustain the requisite internal capabilities. High product variety increases costs in manufacturing (Stalk, 1988), product development, and advertising. Broad firms struggle to establish a more diffuse image and reputation to encompass their myriad activities; lack of consistency or distinctiveness can be a critical shortcoming (Teplensky et al., 1993). Decision making becomes more complex because a variety of actions must be considered, reducing decision speed (Bray, Kerr, & Atkin, 1978). Performing a variety of simultaneous actions can result in increased coordination needs and duplication of effort. Spreading resources too thin and achieving insufficient depth in any area are always concerns. These risks must be clearly identified and addressed to ensure maximum performance from a broad strategic approach.

In summary, while the wisdom of a niche strategy for large firms is equivocal, its high degree of focus, specialization, and efficiency facilitates performance in the early, resource-constrained stages of an entrepreneurial, technology-based firm's life.

DIFFERENTIATION: QUALITY/SERVICE

Porter (1980) argues that firms pursuing a niche strategy must be able to achieve either differentiation or cost leadership within the targeted market. This is consistent with Wernerfelt's (1984) development of the resource-based perspective of the firm, where he emphasizes the need for firms to create unique, specialized resources—such as skilled personnel and in-house knowledge of technology—in establishing differentiation. Empirical support for the competitive advantage of differentiation by new ventures pursuing a narrow scope was found by Sandberg and Hofer (1987).

Differentiation achieved through a strong emphasis on quality and service is the strategy of interest. Woo and Cooper (1981, 1982) have established that a selective focus on quality is an effective strategy for small, low-share firms. Similarly, a number of researchers have emphasized service as a key component of competitive strategy for a variety of types of firms, including new ventures (Carter et al., 1994; Vesper, 1990). Further, service differentiation is a viable option for technology-based firms. For example, Mosakowski (1993) found that entrepreneurial firms in the computer software industry, because of product complexity and specialization, often differentiate on service customized to specific needs. Such service differentiation predicted performance in her sample. Similarly, in their examination of the range and types of strategies pursued by new ventures in the information processing industry, McDougall and Robinson (1990) found that a subset of their sample had a dual emphasis on high quality and service.

Technology Timing

The timing of introductions of new technology to the marketplace is a key issue. The goal for firms differentiating on technology is to achieve such "first mover" advantages (Lieberman & Montgomery, 1988) as the stimulant for market demand, rapid market growth, and locking up key market segments by creating industry standards. These advantages must be weighed against such potential risks as early investments in production leading to overcapacity (Wernerfelt & Karnani, 1987). Follower firms can benefit by observing where the product leader went wrong (Bleakley, 1991), and then achieving a viable competitive position through such methods as marketing expertise or low-cost manufacturing.

Technology timing meets the specific needs of targeted customers for firms pursuing a quality/service niche strategy. The firm might be "cutting edge" in a highly focused technology area and not achieve such a reputation in the broader market. Conversely, the niche firm might be a deliberate technology follower if the customer requires an emphasis on other characteristics, such as serviceability and reliability.

In summary, the entire spectrum of technology timing might occur for firms pursuing a quality/service niche strategy.

Hypothesis 1: Technological entrepreneurial firms with a quality/service niche strategy will have high performance.

STRATEGIC IMPLEMENTATION: THE PLANNING PROCESS

Breadth Planning

A main concern of firms in technology-intensive industries is the need to be continually engaged in adaptive thinking and action. Hage (1986) argues that organic organizational structures, defined as decentralized, informal, flexible, and with open communication, lead to the most effective adaptation. Covin, Prescott, and Slevin (1990) confirm that firms in high-tech industries do have more organic organization structures. Similarly, Maidique and Hayes (1984) believe an entrepreneurial culture that encompasses elements of an organic structure is one of the most important characteristics of firms in high-tech environments.

Small, entrepreneurial firms in particular must adapt to overcome their vulnerability (Aram & Cowen, 1990), a liability of their small size (Bruderl & Schussler, 1990). This is particularly true in technology-based industries, where all firms are vulnerable to changes in technology and/or buyer preferences (Meyer & Roberts, 1985), and entrepreneurial firms are at particular risk. To manage such risk, firms must be highly vigilant about sensing and responding to change, which could easily reduce or eliminate their targeted market or competitive advantage (Dertouzos, Lester, & Solow, 1989; Levitt, 1960).

This need for vigilance is seen in Hart's (1992) transactive strategy-making process, described as participative and iterative in nature. A central tenet of this process is the firm's ongoing adaptation, which is consistent with a variety of other researchers (e.g., Chaffee, 1985; Shrivastava & Grant, 1985). Hart's concept emphasizes the importance of feedback from a firm's stakeholders, suggesting that the transactive approach is appropriate and effective for firms faced with a highly complex and heterogeneous business environment (Dess & Beard, 1984). Similarly, Rhyne (1985) develops the notion of strategic-planning openness, defined as the ongoing collection and use of environmental information from a variety of stakeholders to establish proactivity, flexibility, creativity, and receptivity to new ideas. Planning openness suggests that the firm is open and flexible. Rhyne found that environmental complexity positively predicted the level of a firm's planning openness.

While Dess and Beard (1984) and others define complexity and heterogeneity by the number of inputs and outputs related to product/market scope, complexity also arises from the very nature of technology-based industries. Khandwalla (1976) describes technological sophistication as a fundamental environmental dimension and suggests that high sophistication implies products and processes arising from complex operations technologies with a high degree of R&D involvement. Rapid change inherent in technology-based industries also increases environmental complexity. Anderson and Tushman (1990) describe periods of discontinuous technological change in which variations within a product class (including a range of designs) increase substantially, resulting from experimentation and shifts in competition. An environment of simultaneous development and evaluation of multiple technologies is highly complex.

Both Hart's transactive strategy making and Rhyne's planning openness are captured here in the "breadth" label for the planning process. Breadth planning reflects the firm's ongoing adaptation based on continual dialogue with and feedback from a variety of key stakeholders. Although higher costs are incurred in PR efforts, market testing, more highly personalized sales-force efforts, and slower decisions to assimilate and integrate a wide variety of input, such resources are used well if breadth planning leads the firm to adapt rapidly and in a timely fashion. When considered independent of the firm's strategic approach, breadth planning is expected to facilitate the performance of entrepreneurial firms in technology-based industries.

Hypothesis 2: Technological entrepreneurial firms with a breadth planning process will have high performance.

STRATEGY-PLANNING PROCESS

Synergy

Consistent with the resource-based view, developing a tight connection between strategy and supportive implementation capabilities reflects a well-managed and successful firm. As discussed previously, both a quality/service niche strategy and a breadth planning process, considered independently, should facilitate success for technological entrepreneurial firms. However, when considering the potential synergy between a strategy and the planning process, consistent with the resource-based view (Wernerfelt, 1984), synergy is expected to develop between a niche strategy and focused planning—the opposite of breadth planning. As indicated earlier, Hart (1992) asserts that the transactive strategy-making process is best suited for firms facing complex and heterogeneous environments, characterized by a variety and range of stakeholders from whom wide participation is critical for legitimacy. Although environmental complexity and heterogeneity arise out of the nature of technology-based industries (Khandwalla, 1976), much of it is associated with the breadth of the product market scope (Dess & Beard, 1984). The niche firm, with its narrower product/market scope, deliberately minimizes this aspect of complexity and heterogeneity and thus the number and variety of its stakeholders. Therefore, the highly time-consuming and expensive breadth strategy-making process is unwarranted. Simple, focused strategic planning saves time and expense for the resource-constrained niche firm, resulting in competitive advantage. Further, many inputs from various stakeholders distract the niche firm from its clear mission. High stakeholder involvement suggests that the firm's strategic domain is fluid and changing (Rhyne, 1985), which is inconsistent with the niche firm's strength in its clear, simple, well-defined, and consistent domain.

This argument in favor of a synergy between a quality/service niche strategy and a focused strategic-planning process, resulting in higher performance, is conceptually similar to one made by Lumpkin and Dess (1995). They assert that simplicity in strategy-making processes, defined as decisions on a set of "highly constrained values and strategies" (Miller, 1993, p. 123), is consistent with the strategic objectives of single-minded, specialized firms. Their empirical findings are supportive: in firms with narrow strategies, they found a positive association between performance and simplistic strategy making.

Hypothesis 3: Technological entrepreneurial firms with a high quality/service niche strategy, combined with a focused planning process, will achieve synergies resulting in high performance.

CONTEXTUAL INFLUENCES ON PERFORMANCE

Barney and Zajac (1994) point out that the resource-based view of the firm recognizes that the competitive value of internal implementation capabilities must be understood within the context of both the firm's strategy and the competitive arena it operates in. Variables in the organizational context are also important. The competitive context is examined here with three variables: environmental instability, environmental munificence, and product stage of development. The organizational context is analyzed with two variables: firm age and size.

Competitive Context

Environment

Managers' environmental perceptions are among the most critical inputs into the strategic planning process (Bourgeois, 1980). Instability and munificence are two of the most important aspects of the environment in their effects on strategy (Bourgeois, 1980; Hambrick & Finkelstein, 1987). Environmental instability refers to the rate of unpredictable change in those environmental factors pertinent to strategic decision making (Duncan, 1972). Unpredictable shifts in consumer demands, competitor actions, and rapid product obsolescence increase risk and yet can also create opportunities. Environmental instability is thus expected to influence all aspects of performance. Environmental munificence refers to the extent to which the environment supports sustained growth (Starbuck, 1976) and decreases interorganizational hostility (Porter, 1980). Munificent environments provide substantial latitude for managers to choose among a variety of strategic choices (Hambrick & Finkelstein, 1987).

Stage of Product Development

Product development has often been thought of as consisting of four stages: introduction, growth, maturity, and decline (Covin & Slevin, 1988). The developmental stage of its main products is thought to influence a firm's performance. Porter (1980) points out that profits tend to be greater for firms in emerging industries with a high degree of technological uncertainty; firms with most of their products in introductory or growth stages might achieve higher profitability. Sales and growth are also expected to be higher for firms with products in earlier developmental stages. This is particularly true of the growth stage, defined as growing at a rate of at least 100/0. On the other hand, financial stability might be enhanced by the predictable nature of more mature markets.

Organizational Context

Firm Size and Age

Following Grant, Jammine, and Thomas (1988) and a variety of other researchers (e.g., Chen & Hambrick, 1995), firm size is expected to have an influence on firm performance. Given the relatively young age of these firms, and their vulnerability in the early years (Bruderl & Schussler, 1990), age is also expected to affect performance.

Sample

The sample consists of 998 firms competing in technology-based industries represented by 35 SIC industry codes in the states of Michigan and Ohio. The selection of industries followed Shanklin and Ryan's (1987) definition of "high technology" and was made due to the rapidly changing nature of their base technology. These include semiconductors, magnetic media, measuring and controlling devices, and optical instruments. Such industries represent an excellent opportunity for young firms to position themselves strategically for long-term competitive advantage. At the same time, the volatile and unpredictable nature of these industries leads to a high failure rate among them. A relatively broad range of industries was selected to gain a more generalizable understanding of the relationships analyzed here. Addresses were obtained from Dun & Bradstreet (D&B).

The companies in this study are between eight and sixteen years old (founded between 1980 and 1988). They are considered "adolescent" in that they have survived the initial critical years during which many firms fail and have not yet reached the mature phase in which they resemble all other firms. These firms are still highly vulnerable to the "liability of adolescence," described by Bruderl and Schussler (1990) as an inverted U risk pattern in which firm mortality peaks between one and fifteen years, depending on initial resource endowments. Adolescent firms were selected to increase the likelihood that their strategies have demonstrated at least some potential for long-term viability. Analyses of firms highly unstable in competitive methods and performance are often difficult to interpret, decreasing potential insight.

Methods

The location of the participants was limited to the states of Michigan and Ohio to allow a better understanding of the dynamics of competition in a segment of the Midwest that has traditionally been highly dependent on manufacturing and has had a net loss of jobs in recent years.

Questionnaires, validated by pretesting, were sent to the CEO, president, or chairman of the board of each of the 998 firms in the sample. About 70 of these firms were no longer in business. Of the remaining 928 firms, a total of 208 surveys were returned and useable (22 percent response rate). Chi-square tests to assess response bias revealed no significant differences based on firm location (Michigan or Ohio) or on SIC code. The number of cases reported here is 166, reflecting cases deleted for missing data.

Measures

Environment. The environmental measures of turbulence and munificence are those of Khandwalla (1977; see Appendix), used extensively by a number of strategy researchers. The coefficient alphas for these turbulence and munificence measures are .71 and .79, respectively. For each, the mean score on all questions was used as the measure.

Product stage of development. Product stage of development is a categorical measure based on the work of Covin and Slevin (1988; see Appendix). The CEO was asked to indicate the percentage of total firm sales accounted for by each of the four stages of development; a mean was calculated for each firm based on a weighted average of the responses across all four stages.

Organizational context. Two measures of organizational size—the number of full-time employees and sales revenue—were provided by the CEO on the questionnaire; the log transformation was taken for each. Organizational age is the CEO's response to a questionnaire item.

Quality/service niche. This research is a component of a larger study that included 32 measures of strategy (Bantel, 1996). The "quality/service niche" strategy emerged from a factor analysis of the 32 items; six items loaded .40 or higher, with an eigenvalue of 1.67 and a coefficient alpha of .49, considered adequate for exploratory work (Nunnally, 1978). The average of each firm's response on the six items is the measure. This operationalization is consistent with the view of a variety of researchers that strategy consists of a set of elements that are internally consistent, interdependent, and interactive (Galbraith & Schendel, 1983; Porter, 1980).

Planning breadth/focus. This variable was measured with three items developed here to reflect Hart's (1992) conceptual work on "transactive" strategy making (see Appendix). These items had an alpha coefficient of .52.

Performance. The measurement of performance for small, relatively young firms is more complex and difficult than for large, established firms for two reasons. First, a greater variety of performance issues is highly pertinent as the young firm struggles with establishment depending on the individual firms (position and goals being variables). A standard ROA measure might be relatively meaningless when compared to such outputs as sales growth and market development. Second, objective data are not the most accurate portrayal of actual performance for such reasons as wide swings in performance from year to year (Cooper, 1993) and revenue received from such sources as government grants. For the same reason, calculating an average over several years is also often meaningless. Perceptions of current performance often have the strongest relationship with the firm's actual actions. Maximizing the meaningfulness of the performance measures, each firm's CEO was asked to rate the firm on a variety of performance areas: operational efficiency, market development, sales growth, profitability, and future prospects. Industry effects were controlled through the CEOs' evaluations of sales growth and profitability, relative to other firms in their industry.

VALIDATION OF "NICHE"
OPERATIONALIZATION

Further analyses were conducted to assess the validity of the quality/service niche operationalization and interpretation. The sample was divided into high versus low at the median on the niche variable. Using data from the larger study (Bantel, 1996), tests for significant differences were conducted on five additional strategy dimensions (also resulting from the Bantel, 1996, factor analysis), four top team variables, and four organizational descriptive variables (see Table 6.1). A significant difference (at the .10 level) between high and low niche firms exists on product, market breadth, and aggressiveness, with high niche firms significantly lower on this dimension. This is consistent with and validates the niche interpretation, as well as confirms that the niche firms studied tend to have lower environmental complexity as measured by product/market scope (Dess & Beard, 1984). Two additional strategy dimensions shown in Table 6.1, customer alliances and customization/specialization, are reflective of a niche strategy. While not achieving significance, high-niche firms are notably higher on both dimensions, consistent with and validating the niche interpretation.

Further tests for significant differences among the organizational descriptive variables indicate that high quality/service niche firms tend to be notably larger in number of employees (not significant due to skewness) and sales revenue, and are in somewhat more mature product areas but are not significantly older than firms low on quality/service niche. High-niche firms tend to have less experience in the top team in R&D/engineering/software development and production, but are higher on sales/marketing and accounting/control.

Descriptive and Correlation Matrix

Table 6.2 presents the means, standard deviations, and correlations among the variables, including the interaction term. Significant positive correlations exist between quality/service niche and the following four performance measures: market development, sales growth, profitability, and future prospects. Planning breadth is positively correlated with the same four performance measures. Neither age nor

TABLE 6.1. Profile of Firms Based on Median Split on Quality/Service Niche

	Low Niche (< = 5.08)	High Niche (> 5.08) Mean	Sig.	Sample
Number of Full-Time Employees	22.71	34.31	n.s.	28.55
Age of Firm	7.90	8.19	n.s.	8.05
Stage of Product Development	2.39	2.41	*	2.40
Sales Revenue	$20.68 mil.	$79.98 mil.	*	$14.20
Top Team Experience in:[a]				
R&D, Engineering, Software Dev.	4.59	4.50	*	4.55
Sales/Marketing	3.93	4.33	n.s.	4.13
Production	4.73	4.57	*	4.65
Accounting/Control	3.88	4.06	n.s.	3.97
Other Strategy Dimensions:[a]				
Technology Product Leader	4.13	4.60	n.s.	4.36
Product/Market Breadth/ Aggressive	3.39	2.84	+	3.12
Marketing/Sales Expertise	5.04	5.55	n.s.	5.29
Customer Alliances	3.67	4.03	n.s.	3.85
Customization/Specialization	4.91	5.27	n.s.	5.09

[a]Scale: 1 = Low, 7 = High
Note: p. = + = .10,* = .05;
n = 166

size (the control variables) is significantly correlated with any of the performance measures. Munificence is positively correlated with operational efficiency, sales growth, profitability, and future prospects; instability is negatively correlated with operational efficiency and profitability; and stage of development is negatively correlated with future prospects.

Hierarchical Regression Analyses

The data were analyzed using five hierarchical regressions (Pedhazur, 1982), one for performance measure, presented in Table 6.3.

TABLE 6.2. Descriptive Statistics and Correlation Matrix

Variables	Mean	Standard Deviation	2	3	4	5	6	7	8	9	10	11	12
1. Size—# Employees	28.55	89.02	0.10	0.09	0.09	0.08	-0.01	0.03	-0.08	-0.01	0.04	-0.04	0.00
2. Organization Age	8.05	2.66		0.00	-0.07	-0.02	0.09	0.03	0.09	-0.02	0.03	0.07	0.00
3. Instability	3.97	1.19			-0.36	0.02	0.18	0.12	-0.15	-0.07	-0.05	-0.17	-0.08
4. Munificence	2.84	1.37				-0.02	-0.03	-0.08	0.15	0.11	0.19	0.26	0.31
5. Stage[a]	2.39	0.77					-0.03	0.08	0.08	-0.02	-0.05	0.00	-0.20
6. Quality/Service Niche	5.00	0.75						0.17	0.11	0.35	0.30	0.19	0.31
7. Planning Breadth	4.35	1.37							0.13	0.15	0.20	0.19	0.22
8. Operational Efficiency[b]	4.70	1.24								0.30	0.14	0.33	0.20
9. Market Development	4.03	1.43									0.42	0.30	0.43
10. Sales Growth[c]	3.58	1.24										0.48	0.47
11. Profitability[d]	4.23	1.57											0.36
12. Future Prospects	5.56	1.36											

N=166

Note: For coefficients 0.15 and above, *p* < .05 (two-tailed)

[a] 1 = introduction, 2 = growth, 3 = maturity, 4 = decline

[b] For operational efficiency, market development, and future prospects (1 = poor and 7 = excellent)

[c] 1 = shrinking, 6 = over 50 percent

[d] 1 = negative, 6 = 15+ percent return on sales

144

TABLE 6.3. Hierarchical Regression Analysis

	Operational Efficiency	Market Development	Sales Growth	Profitability	Future Prospects
Controls					
Org-size—#emp.(Log)	–0.10	0.07	0.20*	–0.01	0.13+
	(0.07)	(0.08)	(0.06)	(0.06)	(0.07)
Org. Age	0.11	–0.06	–0.06	0.04	–0.06
	(0.04)	(0.04)	(0.03)	(0.03)	(0.03)
Instability	–0.15+	–0.09	–0.02	–0.12	0.01
	(0.02)	(0.02)	(0.01)	(0.01)	(0.02)
Munificence	0.08	–0.09	0.23**	0.23**	0.35**
	(0.03)	(0.03)	(0.02)	(0.02)	(0.02)
Stage	0.10	–0.04	–0.12	–0.05	–0.20**
	(0.13)	(0.14)	(0.10)	(0.11)	(0.12)
Quality/Service Niche	0.49*	0.87***	0.74**	0.81**	0.57*
	(0.42)	(0.47)	(0.33)	(0.34)	(0.38)
Planning Breadth	0.94+	1.17*	1.04*	1.43**	0.79+
	(0.15)	0.17)	(0.12)	(0.12)	(0.14)
Niche × Focus	0.99+	1.33*	1.13*	1.55**	0.76
	(0.03)	(0.03)	(0.02)	(0.02)	(0.03)
Constant	2.11	2.34	1.67	1.70	1.92
R2	0.10	0.16	0.21	0.19	0.27
F	2.11*	3.57***	4.95***	4.24***	6.97***

Note: Standardized regression coefficients are reported. Standard errors in parentheses. + = $p < 0.10$; * = $p < 0.05$; ** = $p < 0.10$; *** = $p < 0.001$.

Strong and consistent support exists for Hypotheses 1 and 2. For all five performance measures, quality/service niche was a significant predictor; for planning breadth, however, the prediction was significant at only the .10 level for operational efficiency and future prospects. The support for Hypothesis 3 is also strong: the interaction between niche and planning focus was significant and positive for all performance measures (at the .10 level for operational efficiency), with the exception of future prospects. An examination of the change in R2 resulting from the addition of the interaction term indicated the following: for operational efficiency, 2 percent of variance explained; for market development, 3 percent; for sales growth, 2 percent; for profitability, 4 percent; and for future prospects, 1 percent.

Regarding contextual influences, organizational size had a positive influence on both sales growth and future prospects (.10 significance), while age had no significant effect. Environmental instability had a marginally negative influence (.10 significance) on operational efficiency. Munificence had a very strong positive influence on three of the performance measures: sales growth, profitability, and future prospects. Product stage of development had a negative influence on future prospects

CONCLUSIONS

This research provides strong support for the resource-based perspective of the firm. Clear evidence is provided that firms perform well if they accumulate the necessary capabilities to support and implement their chosen strategic direction, and strategy implementation skills are tailored (Wernerfelt, 1984). This is well illustrated by implementation characteristic being evaluated, and the breadth or focus of the strategic-planning process (one that is positively related to performance when considered in the context of rapidly changing, technology-based environments). Firms that choose to reduce the complexity of their technology-based industries by becoming highly focused on a narrow niche, a focused planning process (the opposite of breadth), create a synergy with strategy that facilitates performance. Apparently, focused planning supports the high degree of strategic focus implied by the niche strategy, leading to an efficient use of resources and rapid decision making.

This finding is consistent with a key argument made by Nayyar and Bantel (1994), who suggest that firms must dedicate resources to internal implementation capabilities only to the extent that such skills are warranted by their environmental context; to commit resources results in inefficiencies and decreased competitive advantage. This research extends Nayyar and Bantel's (1994) assertion to the strategic context. Firms operating in the strategic context of a niche strategy apply resources to the information, gather and process activities associated with planning breadth waste resources, and can draw the firm away from its vision and purpose. This argument is particularly compelling given that operational efficiency was predicted by the niche-focus interaction in this study. Efficent resource use is critical for the highly vulnerable firms for which reduction in both costs and management complexity can make a crucial performance difference.

This study attempts to assess a variety of performance outcomes, reflective of the complexity of the performance construct as applied to technological entrepreneurial firms, and of the presumed strategic goals of a niche strategy. Each of the five selected performance measures—operational efficiency, market development, sales growth, profitability, and future prospects—was predicted by the three independent variables. The one exception was the niche-focus interaction failing to predict future prospects. Perhaps these firms understand that their long-term prosperity will depend on a broadening of strategy and planning over time.

To underscore the importance of measuring strategically relevant performance outcomes for entrepreneurial firms of this nature, the identical analyses were conducted for three additional performance dimensions—R&D results, personnel satisfaction, and financial stability—collected for a different purpose. Because these performance goals are not particularly relevant to the quality/service niche and planning breadth/focus issues, significant prediction was not expected. Hierarchical regression analyses confirmed this expectation.

A more comprehensive understanding of the high quality/service niche firms in this sample is possible through the profile indicated in Table 6.1. High quality/service niche firms are larger in number of employees and sales revenue, have more mature products, and are not significantly older. They are also efficient in resource use, as indicated by their low number of employees compared to their sales revenue. An emphasis on service is central to their strategic thrust, and these firms are apparently able to provide it without excessive personnel. When combined with the positive performance results of high-niche firms, a profile emerges of highly disciplined top managers generally adhering to their original product/market focus and growing their firms more steadily and quickly than managers of low-niche firms. Because these managers tend to have relatively more experience in accounting/control and sales/marketing and relatively less in production and R&D/engineering/software development, the top team appears to be highly oriented to meeting the needs of a very specific customer group and is able to resist the temptation to pursue new and riskier markets, technologies, and production methods. At the same time, while these firms are not "leading edge" in technology and product development, they are not falling behind broadly focused firms. This is particularly impressive since these niche firms tend to be in more mature product segments. It would not be surprising to find a high representation of "spin-off" firms, where managers start businesses that provide an outsourcing opportunity to their previous employers. The ex-managers understand the needs of their customer, including the need for technology development, while the customer can provide steady, stable, predictable growth to the fledgling firm.

With regard to contextual influences, the strong positive influence of environmental munificence on sales growth, profitability, and future prospects is not surprising and is consistent with other studies (e.g., Weiner & Mahoney, 1981). The strong negative influence of the product stage of development on future prospects suggests that as product maturity increases, managers must continually grapple with refocusing efforts on new market and product areas to ensure future performance and growth. High uncertainty about the future and the firm's prospects would exist during the period when the maturity and concomitant declining opportunity are recognized even though new plans and strategies have not yet been formulated.

Managerial Implications

Several recommendations on the optimal approach to strategic planning for technological entrepreneurial firms emerge from this research that might provide valuable guidance to entrepreneurial managers and others concerned with the success of such firms. These insights are as follows:

- Careful attention must be paid to crafting a competitive strategy that is appropriate to the industry but also reflects the skills and resources of the firm.
- Strategic implementation characteristics of the firm, such as the nature of the strategic-planning process, must be deliberately

developed to relate to, and be supportive of, the nature of the strategy.

- Because highly efficient resource use is particularly essential to the success of resource-constrained entrepreneurial firms, the resource investment in strategic-implementation capabilities should not exceed an optimal level.
- A broad, expansive, information-gathering approach to strategic planning generally facilitates success for entrepreneurial, technology-based firms.
- A highly focused strategic-planning process, during which tangible limits to information gathering and processing are set, will facilitate performance for firms pursuing a highly targeted niche strategy.
- A focus on performance for entrepreneurial firms needs to take a broad-based perspective on the notion of "success," incorporating goals most pertinent to the firm's strategic thrust.
- A strategic profile of (1) a high degree of strategic focus, deliberately resisting temptations to broaden beyond original product market scope; (2) technology development to meet the needs of highly targeted customers and limiting expansion beyond customer applications; and (3) differentiation on quality and service can be highly successful in the early entrepreneurial years. Such firms in this sample had

  — higher revenues;
  — a higher number of employees;
  — higher productivity per employee (revenue/employees); and
  — higher performance on operational efficiency, sales growth, market development, profitability, and future prospects.

While each firm has unique competencies and opportunities, limiting the direct application of these findings, it is hoped that they provide a departure point for entrepreneurs grappling with their highly critical strategic decisions.

APPENDIX

Environment

Each of the following items consists of a pair of statements that represent the two extremes on aspects of the industry that account for the largest percentage of your firm's sales (your principal industry). Please circle the number on the scale that best approximates the actual conditions in your industry.

Instability

Our firm must rarely change its practices to keep up with the market and competitors.	1 2 3 4 5 6 7	Our firm must change its marketing practices extremely frequently (e.g., semiannually).
The rate at which products/services are getting obsolete in the industry is very slow.	1 2 3 4 5 6 7	The rate of obsolescence is very high (as in semiconductors).
Actions of competitors are quite easy to predict.	1 2 3 4 5 6 7	Actions of competitors are unpredictable.
Demand for the product and consumer tastes are fairly easy to forecast.	1 2 3 4 5 6 7	Consumer demand and tastes are unpredictable.
The production/service technology is not subject to very much change and is well-established.	1 2 3 4 5 6 7	The mode of production/service changes often and in a major way (e.g., advanced electronic components).

Munificence

How would you characterize the environment in which your firm operates?

Very safe, little threat to the survival and well-being of the firm.	1 2 3 4 5 6 7	Very risky, one false step can mean my firm's undoing.
Rich in investment and marketing opportunities.	1 2 3 4 5 6 7	Very stressful, hostile, very hard to keep afloat.
An environment that my firm can control and manipulate to its own advantage, such as a dominant firm has in an industry with little competition and few hindrances.	1 2 3 4 5 6 7	A dominating environment in which my firm's initiatives count for very little against the tremendous political, technological, or competitive forces.

Product Stage of Development

Please indicate what percentage of your firm's current total sales is accounted for by products or services in each of the following life-cycle stages.

> *Introduction stage:* Products or services are unfamiliar to many potential users, and industry-wide demand for these products or services is beginning to grow. _____%
>
> *Growth stage:* The total industry-wide demand for products or services in this stage is growing at a rate of 10% or more annually. _____%
>
> *Maturity stage:* Products or services in this stage are familiar to the vast majority of prospective users, and industry-wide demand for these products or services is relatively stable. _____%
>
> *Decline stage:* The total industry-wide demand for products or services in this stage is decreasing at a more or less steady rate. _____%

Quality/Service Niche Strategy

Each of the following items consists of a pair of statements that represent the two extremes on different methods by which businesses compete. Please circle the number in the scale that best describes the emphasis your firm has placed on each.

Strongly disagree		**Strongly agree**
Emphasis on acceptable product quality.	1 2 3 4 5 6 7	Emphasis on superior product quality.
Attempt to achieve small market share in our market segment(s).	1 2 3 4 5 6 7	Attempt to achieve high market share in our market segment(s).
Minimal advertising and promotion expense.	1 2 3 4 5 6 7	High level of advertising and promotion expense.
Provide minimal or no customer service.	1 2 3 4 5 6 7	Provide high level of customer service.
No forward integration toward consumer.	1 2 3 4 5 6 7	Extensive forward integration toward consumer.
After-sales service provided by others.	1 2 3 4 5 6 7	Do our own after-sales service.

Planning Breadth/Focus

Please indicate the extent to which each of the following descriptions characterizes your firm. Circle the number in the scale indicating the exctent to which you agree with each statement.

	Strongly disagree	**Strongly agree**
Strategy is crafted based upon an ongoing dialogue with key stakeholders (e.g., employees, suppliers, customers, government, and regulators).	1 2 3 4 5 6 7	
We actively solicit input from people outside the firm (e.g., consultants, bankers) in developing our plan.	1 2 3 4 5 6 7	
Our firm continually adapts its strategy based upon feedback from stakeholders (e.g., customers, suppliers).	1 2 3 4 5 6 7	

Performance

How would you rate the firm's performance in the following areas?

	Poor	**Excellent**
Operational Efficiency	1 2 3 4 5 6 7	
Market Development	1 2 3 4 5 6 7	
Future Prospects	1 2 3 4 5 6 7	

Compared to your competition, how would you rate your firm's current performance?

	Much worse		**About the same**		**Much better**
Sales Growth	1	2	3	4	5
Profitability	1	2	3	4	5

REFERENCES

Amit, R. & Shoemaker, P. (1993). "Strategic Assets and Organizational Rent." *Strategic Management Journal,* 14:33-46.

Anderson, P. & Tushman, M. (1990). "Technological Discontinuities and Dominant Designs: A Cyclical Model of Technological Change." *Administrative Science Quarterly,* 35:604-Q33.

Andrews, K. (1971). *The Concept of Corporate Strategy.* Homewood, IL: Dow Jones-Irwin Inc.

Aram, J.D. & Cowen, S.S. (1990). "Strategic Planning for Increased Profit in the Small Business." *Long Range Planning,* 23(6):63-70.

Bantel, K. (1996). "Technology-Based, 'Adolescent' Firm Configurations: Strategy Identification, Context, and Performance." Working paper, Detroit, MI: Wayne State University.

Barney, J. (1991). "Firm Resources and Sustained Competitive Advantage." *Journal of Management,* 17:99-120.

Barney, J.B. & Zajac, E.J. (1994). "Competitive Organizational Behavior: Toward an Organizationally Based Theory of Competitive Advantage." *Strategic Management Journal,* 15:5-9.

Biggadike, R. (1977). *Entering New Markets: Strategies and Performance.* Cambridge, MA: Marketing Science Institute.

Bleakley, F.R. (1991, April 3). "Citicorp's Folly? How a Terrific Idea for Grocery Marketing Missed Its Targets." *Wall Street Journal,* p. AI.

Bourgeois, J. (1980). "Strategy and Environment: A Conceptual Integration." *Academy of Management Review,* 1:25-39.

Bray, R.M., Kerr, N.L., & Atkin, R.S. (1978). "Effects of Group Size, Problem Difficulty, and Sex on Group Performance and Member Reactions." *Journal of Personality and Social Psychology,* 36:1224-1240.

Bruderl, J. & Schussler, R. (1990). "Organizational Mortality: The Liabilities of Newness and Adolescence." *Administrative Science Quarterly,* 35:530-547.

Carter, N.M., Stearns, T.M., Reynolds, P.D., & Miller. B.A. (1994). "New Venture Strategies: Theory Development with an Empirical Base." *Strategic Management Journal,* 15:21-41.

Chaffee, E. (1985). "Three Models of Strategy." *Academy of Management Review,* 10:89-98.

Chen, M. & Hambric, D. (1995). "Speed, Stealth, and Selective Attack: How Small Firms Differ from Large Firms in Competitive Behavior." *Academy of Management Journal,* 38(2):453-482.

Churchill, N.C. & Lewis, V.L. (1983). "The Five Stages of Small Business Growth." *Harvard Business Review,* May-June:30-51.

Cohn, T. & Lindberg, R.A. (1974). *Survival and Growth: Management Strategies for the Small Firm.* New York: AMACOM.

Cooper, A.C. (1993). "Challenges in Predicting New Firm Performance." *Journal of Business Venturing,* 8:241-253.

Cooper, A.C., Willard, G.E., & Woo, C.Y. (1986). "Strategies of High Performing New and Small Firms: A Reexamination of the Niche Concept." *Journal of Business Venturing,* 5(6):391-412.

Covin, J., Prescott, J.E., & Slevin, D. (1990). "Effect of Technological Sophistication." *Journal of Management Studies,* 27(5):485-510.

Covin, J. & Slevin, D. (1988). "New Venture Competitive Strategy: An Industry Life Cycle Analysis." *Frontiers of Entrepreneurship.*

Deeks, J. (1976). *The Small Firm Owner-Manager.* New York: Praeger.

Dertouzos, M.L., Lester, R.K., & Solow, R.M. (1989). *Made in America: Regaining the Productive Edge.* New York: Harper Perennial.

Dess, G. & Beard, D. (1984). "Dimensions of Organizational Task Environments." *Administrative Science Quarterly,* 29:52-73.

Dierickx, I. & Cool, K. (1989). "Asset Stock Accumulation and Sustainability of Competitive Advantage." *Management Science,* 35:1504-1511.

Duncan, R.B. (1972). "Characteristics of Organizational Environments and Perceived Environmental Uncertainty." *Administrative Science Quarterly,* 17:313-327.

Feeser, H. & Willard, G. (1990). "Founding Strategy and Performance: A Comparison of High and Low Growth High Tech Firms." *Strategic Management Journal,* 11:87-98.

Galbraith, J. & Schendel, D. (1983). "An Empirical Analysis of Strategy Types." *Strategic Management Journal,* 4:153-173.

Ghemawat, P. (1986). "Sustainable Competitive Advantage." *Harvard Business Review,* 61(5):53-58.

Grant, R.M., Jammine, A.P., & Thomas, H. (1988). "Diversity, Diversification, and Profitability Among British Manufacturing Companies, 1972-84." *Academy of Management Journal,* 31:771-801.

Hage, J. (1986). "Responding to Technological and Competitive Change: Organizational and Industry Factors." In D. Davis & Associates (eds.), *Managing Technological Innovation* (pp. 44-71). San Francisco: Jossey-Bass.

Hambrick, D. & Finkelstein, S. (1987). "Managerial Discretion: A Bridge Between Polar Views of Organizational Outcomes." In L.L. Cummings & B. Staw (eds.), *Research in Organizational Behavior* (Volume 9) (pp. 369-406). Greenwich, CT: JAI Press.

Hambrick, D., MacMillan, I., & Day D. (1982). "Strategic Attributes and Performance in the BCG Matrix: A PIMS-Based Analysis of Industrial Product Businesses." *Academy of Management Journal,* 25:510-531.

Hamel, G. & Prahalad, C.K. (1993). "Strategy As Stretch and Leverage." *Harvard Business Review,* 71(2):75-84.

Hannan, M.T. & Freeman, J. (1977). "The Population Ecology of Organizations." *American Journal of Sociology,* 82:929-964.

Hart, S.L. (1992). "An Integrative Framework for Strategy-Making Processes." *Academy of Management Review,* 17(2):327-351.

Khandwalla, P. (1976). "Some Top Management Styles, Their Context and Performance." *Organization and Administrative Sciences,* 7(4):21-51.

Khandwalla, P. (1977). *The Design of Organizations.* New York: Harcourt, Brace, Jovanovich.

Lambkin, M. (1988, Summer). "Order of Entry and Performance in New Markets." *Strategic Management Journal,* 9:127-140.

Levitt, T. (1960, July-August). "Marketing Myopia." *Harvard Business Review,* 26-37.

Lieberman, M.B. & Montgomery, D.B. (1988, Summer). "First-Mover Advantages." *Strategic Management Journal,* 9:41-58.

Lumpkin, G.T. & Dess, G.G. (1995). "Simplicity As a Strategy-Making Process: The Effects of Stage of Organizational Development and Environment on Performance." *Academy of Management Journal,* 38(5):1386-1407.

MacMillan, I.C. & Day, D.L. (1987). "Corporate Ventures into Industrial Markets: Dynamics of Aggressive Entry." *Journal of Business Venturing,* 2(1):29-40.

Maidique, M.A. & Hayes, R.H. (1984). "The Art of High Technology Management." *Sloan Management Review,* 25(2):17-29.

McDougall, P. & Robinson, R. (1990). "New Venture Strategies: An Empirical Identification of Eight 'Archetypes' of Competitive Strategies for Entry." *Strategic Management Journal,* 11:447-467.

Meyer, M.H. & Roberts, E.B. (1985). "New Product Strategies in Small Technology-Based Firms." *Management Science,* 32(7):806-821.

Miller, D. (1993). "The Architecture of Simplicity." *Academy of Management Review,* 18:116-138.

Miller, D. & Toulouse, J.M. (1986). "Strategy, Structure, CEO Personality and Performance in Small Firms." *American Journal of Small Business,* 10(3):47-62.

Mosakowski, E. (1993). "A Resource-Based Perspective on the Dynamic Strategy-Performance Relationship: An Empirical Examination of the Focus and Differentiation Strategies in Entrepreneurial Firms." *Journal of Management,* 19(4): 819-839.

Nayyar, P. & Bantel, K. (1994). "Competitive Agility: A Source of Competitive Advantage Based on Speed and Variety." *Advances in Strategic Management,* 10A:193-222. Greenwich, CT: JAI Press.

Nunnally, J. (1978). *Psychometric Theory.* New York: McGraw-Hill.

Pedhazur, E.J. (1982). *Multiple Regression in Behavioral Research: Explanation and Prediction.* Chicago: Holt, Rinehart & Winston.

Porter, M. (1980). *Competitive Strategy.* New York: Free Press.

Rhyne, L.C. (1985). "The Relationship of Information Usage Characteristics to Planning System Sophistication: An Empirical Examination." *Strategic Management Journal,* 6:319-337.

Sandberg, W. & Hofer, C. (1987). "Improving New Venture Performance: The Role of Strategy, Industry Structure, and the Entrepreneur." *Journal of Business Venturing,* 2:5-28.

Shanklin, W.L. & Ryan, J.K. (1987). *Essentials of Marketing High Technology.* Lexington, MA: Heath.

Shrivastava, P. & Grant, J. (1985). "Empirically Derived Models of Strategic Decision-Making Processes." *Strategic Management Journal,* 6:97-113.

Stalk, G. (1988). "Time, the Next Source of Competitive Advantage." *Harvard Business Review,* 66(4):41-51.

Starbuck, W. (1976). "Organizations and Their Environments." In Marvin Dunnette (ed.), *Handbook of Industrial and Social Psychology* (pp. 1069-1123). Chicago: Rand McNally.

Teplensky, J.D., Kimberly, R J., Hillman, A.L., & Schwartz, J.S. (1993). "Scope, Timing, and Strategic Adjustment in Emerging Markets: Manufacturer Strategies and the Case of MRI." *Strategic Management Journal,* 14:505-527.

Vesper, K.H. (1990). *New Venture Strategies.* Revised Edition. Englewood Cliffs, NJ: Prentice Hall.

Weiner, N. & Mahoney, T.A. (1981). "A Model of Corporate Performance As a Function of Environmental, Organizational, and Leadership Influences." *Academy of Management Journal,* 24(3):453-470.

Wernerfelt, B. (1984). "A Resource-Based View of the Firm." *Strategic Management Journal,* 5(2):171-180.

Wernerfelt, B. & Karnani, A. (1987). "Competitive Strategy Under Uncertainty." *Strategic Management Journal,* 8:187-194.

Woo, C. & Cooper, A. (1981). "Strategies of Effective Low Share Businesses." *Strategic Management Journal,* 2:301-318.

Woo, C. & Cooper, A. (1982). "The Surprising Case for Low Market Share. " *Harvard Business Review,* 59(6):106-113.

PART III:
NICHE MARKETING CASES

Chapter 7

Crafting a Niche in a Crowded Market: The Case of Palliser Estate Wines of Martinborough (New Zealand)

Michael Beverland
Lawrence S. Lockshin

INTRODUCTION

A constant question asked by marketing students is, "What can a small business do to establish a market position today?" Many students think that small firms are powerless in an increasingly global marketplace, characterized by large global players with significant brand power and economies of scale, powerful channel members, and fickle consumers. In this scenario, marketing is out of reach for most of these firms, as the advertising needed to create mass awareness is beyond their financial resources, and at best they can hope to develop a loyal but small following among local consumers. In this scenario,

---

Data for this chapter were gathered through a number of interviews with Palliser's co-owner and managing director Richard Riddiford. Four interviews, lasting on average one hour each, were carried out between 1998 and 2002. The authors referred to over 50 newspaper and wine magazine articles on Palliser Estate, gathered material from the company's Web site, referred to conference presentations given by Riddiford, and financial material provided by the company. Drafts of the interviews, a detailed historical case analysis, and a copy of this chapter were sent to Mr. Riddiford for review.

The authors would like to acknowledge the help of Richard Riddiford, managing director of Palliser Estate, for participating in the study, allowing us extended access to the site, commenting on drafts of this chapter, and for the odd glass of his wonderful Pinot Noir.

life for these firms consists of a day-to-day struggle to make sales, build cash flow, and make do with fewer resources. Marketing texts (e.g., Kotler, 2000) provide little guidance to these firms, being replete with examples of large global firms. The strategy literature provides little help, identifying as it does the conditions under which a general "niche strategy" is recommended (Porter, 1980), but provides little by way of practical guidance on the content of such strategy (Mintzberg, Ahlstrand, and Lampel, 1998). Finally, traditional marketing theorists have ignored small firms, despite the fact that these firms overwhelmingly make up the bulk of existing marketing organizations (Carson, 2001), and most of these are destined to remain small (Beverland and Lockshin, 2001).

However, strategy, marketing, and a market orientation remain important for small firms that have business goals (Swaminathan, 2001; Beverland and Lockshin, 2001). Research suggests that as markets become more competitive, firms of all sizes must become more focused (Swaminathan and Delacroix, 1991). Large generalist firms must focus on building mass brand awareness and economies of scale to meet the needs of global markets (Aldrich, 1999). Smaller specialist organizations must develop market niches that distance themselves from generalists (Swaminathan, 2001). As the resource base of the firm limits the strategic options available (Mintzberg et al., 1998), small firms are likely to place greater emphasis on relationship strategies with a small target market of distributors and retailers, while larger firms are likely to focus on building market share using transactional marketing approaches to build consumer awareness (Beverland et al., 2002). However, Webster (2000) suggests that all firms must build value both with end users and resellers, although how small firms can do so is unclear. Therefore, the marketing literature could benefit from rich examples of successful and unsuccessful niche strategists (Carson, 2001; Mintzberg et al., 1998).

This chapter will report on the case of Palliser Estate Wines of Martinborough, New Zealand (herein referred to as "Palliser"). This firm is an established niche producer and exporter of ultrapremium wines. The case is appropriate for several reasons. First, the world wine market is undergoing substantial change, with an increasingly clear partition emerging between large and niche players (Geene et al., 1999). Second, research suggests that wineries of all sizes will need to increase their market orientation, and focus simultaneously on building market awareness and relationships (Beverland and Lindgreen, 2001), necessitating an increased strategic focus (Beverland and Lockshin, 2001; Swaminathan, 2001). Third, this case has been developed longitudinally and as such provides one of the few longitudinal examples of strategic emergence and evolution in a field dominated by cross-sectional research (Pettigrew et al., 2001; Varadarajan and Jayachandran, 1999). Longitudinal studies are important, as competitive advantage is built over time (Porter, 1980) and is often an emergent process (Mintzberg et al., 1998; Varadarajan and Jayachandran, 1999). Finally, this case is a successful niche marketer, and as such offers insights into how such firms craft strategy in an increasingly competitive market.

THE NEW ZEALAND WINE INDUSTRY AND THE GLOBAL WINE TRADE

New Zealand wineries operate in an environment of high competition, high barriers to entry, increasing costs, and sophisticated consumers. The number of new wineries is increasing (to 385 in 2001), and they are competing for a share of a highly concentrated domestic market, with three big producers accounting for 78 percent of domestic sales. The other 382 wineries are competing for just 10 percent of the local market, with imports accounting for 12 percent. With a static domestic market and an increasingly competitive export market, these wineries face significant challenges if they are to survive. Despite this, New Zealand producers have continued to thrive and have been unable to meet growing demand. A "New Zealand Category" has been achieved in the United Kingdom, and exports continue to increase with New Zealand wines receiving the highest price per liter in the world at NZ$8.61L (in 2001). Future growth will be dependent on winning over new domestic consumers or through exports. The almost automatic growth of the late 1980s and early 1990s is being replaced by the need to become more focused and professional in a more competitive market, both at home and abroad. Lack of economies of scale (New Zealand accounts for 0.1 percent of world production) will mean that producers will need to sell where they can gain the highest prices. Development of these markets requires a heavy focus and will require increased investment in distribution channels, marketing, and branding. This presents incumbents and new entrants with a number of challenges and opportunities, requiring clear strategies and sophisticated systems.

The global wine market is experiencing both expansion and contraction at the same time (Geene et al., 1999). Demand for basic wine is in decline while consumption of quality wine is on the increase (see Table 7.1). Rabobank (Geene et al., 1999) found that the wine industry faced many challenges, including the following:

- Shifting demand: Consumers are enjoying new tastes in wine, brought about by New World production and new varietals. They are increasingly drinking wine at home and are becoming more educated about wine and cuisine.
- Increasing competition: The number of wineries is increasing dramatically. At the same time retailers are rationalizing their product lines.
- Increasing retail power: Retailers, distributors, and wholesalers are consolidating through mergers and acquisitions, and as a result are demanding closer relationships with fewer suppliers of well-branded products, with guaranteed supply and pricing.
- Creating brand value: Consumers, desiring more clarity, have moved away from traditional appellation (regional) labeled products of the Old World (e.g., Burgundy), toward varietal labeled products of the New World (e.g., Australian Chardonnay), leading to increased competition in the premium and super premium parts of the market. However, brand awareness remains low. Retailers demand more brand development from wine companies and are also demanding both horizontal brand extensions through adding more varieties and vertical brand extensions through developing more price tiers.

Changes in distribution and retail are also affecting the structure of the wine industry. Loubere (1990) found that the rise of large-scale chains forced many producers to get bigger, driving the increasing globalization of winery ownership and the development of global wine corporations. Rachman (1999) found that supply constraints

TABLE 7.1. Descriptions of Quality Segments

Segment	Icon	Ultrapremium	Super-premium	Premium	Basic
Price range	>US$50	US$14-50	US$7-14	US$5-7	<US$5
Market share	1%	5%	10%	34%	50%
Type of consumer	Connoisseur	Wine lover	Experimenting consumer	Experimenting consumer	Price-focused consumer
Purchase decision based on	Image, style	Quality, image	Brand, quality	Price, brand	Price
Retail	Winery, boutiques, food service	Specialty shop, food service	Better supermarket, specialty shop	Supermarket	Supermarket, discounter
Retail trends	Retailers hardly active; Industry structure fragmented[a]	Retailers hardly active; Industry structure fragmented[a]	Distinct market position; Specialty shops featured; Consolidation limited[b]	Key segment for retailers; High purchasing power; Scale and assortment key; Consolidation likely[c]	Key segment for retailers; Discount chains; High purchasing power; Large-volume sales; Consolidation likely[d]

TABLE 7.1 (continued)

Segment	Icon	Ultrapremium	Super-premium	Premium	Basic
Market trend (size)	Little growth	Little growth	Growing	Growing	Decreasing
Competition	Limited, "closed" segment	Gradually increasing	Increasing, based on brand, quality, price ratio	Fierce, based on brand, price	Based on price
Availability	Scarce	Scarce	Sufficient, year round	Large quantities, year round	Surplus

Source: Adapted from Geene et al., 1999, p. 16.

[a] Retailers are hardly active here. The industry structure of these wine segments will remain fragmented as this matches with the structure of the main outlets for these wines.

[b] Segment through which service retailers can create distinct market position; smaller specialty shops and foodservice are also important outlets. Consolidation in this part of the wine industry will be limited.

[c] Key segment for retail chains as these are the wines with a good quality/price ratio. The purchasing power of the retailer will manifest itself to its fullest extent in this segment. Scale and assortment are key for the suppliers. This part of the industry will likely consolidate.

[d] Key segment for retail chains, discount chains in particular. The purchasing power of the retailer will manifest itself to its fullest extent here. Retailers need large-volume sales of these low-priced wines. Scale is important, and this part of the industry will likely consolidate.

present real problems for wine companies. Successful global companies would be those that understood the needs of global wine consumers and have the necessary distribution arrangements to service those needs on a year-round basis. This would necessarily involve sourcing grapes from different regions around the world. In the superpremium/ultrapremium segment, more strategic choice is available. For example, wineries could become a significant player in one region, form alliances with other players to share distribution and marketing costs, or form global alliances or joint ventures (Swaminathan, 2001). Beverland et al. (2002) argued that as a result, wineries must target a clear niche, placing more emphasis on strategy and strategic planning than they had in the past.

Coupled with this was a need to place greater emphasis on both relationship marketing approaches and transactional approaches. Firms that placed too much emphasis on transactional (mass marketing) to the detriment of building relationships would increasingly find their products discounted by disgruntled retailers. On the other hand, firms who placed all their emphasis on relationships with retailers but did little to make consumers aware of their products would find that their "free rider position" (where the promotion of a product is left up to retailers) was untenable (Beverland and Lindgreen, 2001).

PALLISER ESTATE WINES
OF MARTINBOROUGH

Palliser Estate is co-owned and managed by Richard Riddiford. Palliser was started in 1982 by a group of six investors, with approximately 20 acres of vineyard. The first vintage for the company was in 1989. Between 1982 and 1989 not a great deal was happening as the company's vineyards took longer to establish than planned, and grapes from the vineyard were sold to another winery. This reflects the emergent nature of the company. Riddiford noted that the initial aims of the firm were unclear, and although he developed a prospectus, it bore little relation to future reality.

> I don't believe anybody really knew what we were doing, and I must admit that I invested in it for tax reasons. In 1982 a pro-

spectus was developed which would make interesting reading today, as it was totally irrelevant. . . . Personally if you talk about business plans and strategies and visions, I'm not a great fan. The world just moves so rapidly that you can write down what you're going to do this year, and on review something entirely different happened. However we're involved in a very long-term business because red grape vines take about seven years to produce with white grapes taking about four years, so you're always trying to guess what people are going to drink in seven years time, which in itself is pretty high risk. We got it reasonably right in 1982 because we just picked the four main varietals—Chardonnay, Riesling, Pinot Noir, and Sauvignon Blanc—and our mix hasn't really changed much since.

The initial impetus to start a wine-producing company came after Riddiford returned from a period of working overseas and tasted a 1989 Pinot Noir[1] which had been made by a local winemaker. "I didn't know what I'd invested in to be honest, but when I tasted that wine I thought—that is outstanding. It wasn't just good; it was outstanding!" In 1990 Palliser won a Liquorland Top 100 Gold Medal (a top local wine show) for its 1989 Estate Pinot Noir. The company became a publicly unlisted company in 1991 as in Riddiford's experience most wineries of Palliser's initial size start undercapitalized. The company did nothing to establish the brand in 1989. In effect the company produced some wine and sold it to the partners. However, as he was positioning his brand in the ultrapremium end of the market, Richard realized that with New Zealand's small population base, he needed to focus on building export markets to drive future growth. Therefore, the company started exporting to the United Kingdom in 1991 and now serves 18 different export markets. This requires a strong focus with clearly identified positioning. Richard stated,

> With my particular brand, I appeal to about 5 percent of the wine-drinking population of New Zealand, a potential market of 36,000 people. I currently export 60 percent of my production; I'll go to 80 percent over the next four years. I will do that by positioning my product in the international marketplace with restaurants and retailers who share my vision. I don't think a

company like mine, which is small and niche focused, can ever be everyman's wine. I've got no desire to be everyman's wine. I don't want to be in every restaurant in the world. I have a vision and it's very simple. It's (a) to be the best winery of my type in the world, and (b) to have my wines served at the best restaurant in every major capital city of the world.

By "best winery of our type," Palliser aims to be an ultrapremium producer with a world renown brand name. The stated aims in the previous quote were developed early on, although Richard notes that they were controversial and ran contrary to the dominant culture in New Zealand.

When I formulated this vision, my colleagues had no trouble with the "best winery of our type in New Zealand," but as for being "best in the world," when I first said that the rest of my colleagues thought I was nuts, but over three years that has changed. Now I think they genuinely share that goal. It doesn't really matter whether it happens in our lifetime—it probably won't, but if you don't have that vision, you end up with a mentality like the English rugby team who do a victory lap of honor after they've been beaten by seventeen points. To them that was the ultimate, so how do they hope to win the World Cup with that mentality? I know through experience, if you want to do something bad enough then you can do it. You've just got to set out what you want to do and go for it!

The vineyard has grown in planned stages to reach the current size of 80 hectares (all in the Martinborough area), 60 of which are currently producing fruit. The company's production and growth is heavily dependent upon weather conditions and therefore growth is financed through retained earnings rather than debt.

Marketing Strategy

Palliser has developed a number of marketing strategies over time. These can be divided into marketing mix, branding, and relationship marketing. Richard believes in the importance of developing both strong relationships with customers and an awareness of his brand among his target market. This latter aim is difficult given the company's small size and limited resources. To overcome this limitation, Palliser seeks endorsements from wine shows and wine writers, and by aligning the Palliser brand with other strong brands that reflect the company's positioning. Finally, the company also makes use of collaborative marketing approaches such as event marketing and overseas marketing networks. These are all supported by a focused marketing mix strategy and a strong culture.

For Riddiford, the future lies in branding. He regards a bottle of wine as the ultimate in branding: "Take off the label and the wine is worth nothing. To buyers the first impression is visual: the average consumer has hundreds of labels to choose from in a single outlet." Thus Palliser reflects the region's beauty and Maori history in its imagery,[2] while retaining the English connection in the name of Rear Admiral Sir Hugh Palliser, after whom nearby Palliser Bay was named.[3] "I regard Palliser's brand as its most valuable asset. We will never put out a wine that does not fit our quality parameters because you can ruin a brand with a bad vintage. If you're selling a product at NZ$35 bottle, quality has to be a given."

The brand-building strategy was not just about getting the positioning and image right. Riddiford stated, "From a production point of view we must be the best in the world for turning grapes into wine. But all the links in the production, distribution, and selling chain have to be rock solid." Richard sees this as critical, as New Zealand has high production costs, low economies of scale, long distances to market, and a fluctuating exchange rate. In 1996, with the exchange rate high, Richard spoke to exporters at an exchange rate summit:

> Our real challenge is to refocus exporters on the importance of some fundamental and strategic issues. By investing heavily in brand Palliser, we have maintained profitability in exports to Britain, despite a shift in the Sterling-$NZ exchange rate from .28 to .44 in the last four years. Currency is just one issue that needs to be managed within the business mix. Exporters of our size need to produce quality products and not worry about the end of the market where there is no price elasticity to absorb changes in currency rates. To be at this end of the market re-

quires heavy investment in your brand in order to get the right quality association to take the focus away from price.

The development of the Palliser brand has involved, and continues to involve, a number of specific marketing actions that aim to build and enhance relationships throughout the demand chain, build market awareness of the product, and build internal commitment to the firm's goals. When combined, these strategies result in a number of strong internal capabilities that enable the firm to create and deliver value, and respond to future market changes.

Endorsements

A firm of Palliser's size cannot afford to undertake mass advertising, nor does it wish to, as it does not desire to target a mass market and increase to a size to meet this level of demand. As such, Palliser seeks other ways of building the brand's reputation and awareness among its target audience. This strategy is based around gaining endorsements from a number of sources: independent journalists and wine shows, co-branding with strong complementary brands, and the use of collective events and promotion. Wine show results and awards were also important in the firm's early years. The first Pinot Noir won a gold medal in 1989 and helped put the company on the "wine consumer's map." In 1992 Palliser's wines won three gold medals. For a new winery this helps to establish the brand as it generates a level of press coverage that a small winery could never afford to pay for. For example when Palliser's 1997 Sauvignon Blanc won the Best Sauvignon Blanc Trophy at the International Wine Challenge in London,[4] the result and interviews with the winemaker and owner were broadcast on BBC and TVNZ, and noted in major wine magazines throughout the world, which equates to tens of thousands of dollars of free editorial press.

Shows must be entered with care for several reasons. Not all shows are equally regarded. They are unlikely to provide the basis for a sustainable competitive edge, since in most cases shows give awards based on whether the entered wines meet a certain level of quality (any number of wines can therefore win an award). Also, results are highly uncertain depending on the subjective views of a number of wine judges. However, wine consumers and buyers do see the results as an indicator of quality. Therefore, Palliser still enters its wines and sees endorsements as an important part of their marketing strategy.[5] Richard stated,

> Most wineries will enter shows early on in their development to establish a track record of performance. They will win a couple of gold medals and then cease entering shows. Now we have a relationship with our consumer and we owe it to them to have some outside measurement to show that our wines are still great. That's why we enter shows; 1999 was a classic example. Alan Johnson our winemaker said to me, "Perhaps we shouldn't enter," and I said, "We should." We ended up getting four gold medals, one silver, and three trophies, which is a result you dream about. To some extent they are a lottery, but over a period of time it averages out, and I think if you're an excellent producer you will get rewarded.

Another way to gather this positive coverage is to co-brand, through cooperative marketing strategies with other like-minded wineries or by aligning yourself with high-profile brands that share your desired positioning. Richard is a big supporter of co-branding and has invested much energy into gaining listings on top airlines,[6] at top restaurants, and at high-profile events such as Wimbledon. By co-branding, Richard means

> Using other brands to support my brand. That's why we had the wine at Wimbledon. Everyone in the world knows what Wimbledon is; not many people know what Palliser is. But if you combine the two, I think we add value to Wimbledon and they certainly add value to Palliser. That's why the airlines have always been a key part of this business. Ever since we began we've always had wine on Air New Zealand. I've got a very strong view on positioning products. If you're going to be at the ultrapremium end or the icon end, it's where you put your wines that is important. Another of my key aims is that I want Palliser's wine in the best restaurant in every major capital of the world, because if I say the Pinot Noir is in Aureoles in New

York, 99 percent of people will say that's fine we'll have it, because they need reassurance.

In 1996 Palliser gained listings with Harrods of London, Pride of Auckland luxury yachts, Raffles Hotel in Singapore, KLM business class, Emirates business class, Peak Café and Café Deco in Hong Kong, elite restaurant Icon in the National Museum of New Zealand, and Wharekauhau, one of New Zealand's top luxury lodges (to name a few). The company also has a relationship with Audi in New Zealand, whereby every purchaser of an Audi receives two bottles of Palliser Estate wine with their purchase. On the use of airlines, Riddiford stated,

> You're talking about a captive audience. Again it was a matter of positioning. I suppose Qantas taking the Pencarrow Chardonnay gave it some international credence and in 1999 the Pencarrow Sauvignon Blanc won a gold medal at the Air New Zealand Wine Awards and you have to have that to establish a label.

For Palliser, the brand exposure rather than sales quantity was important with the Raffles deal: "It gives us an endorsement and that's what consumers look for." Richard stated,

> It took about a year to get the wine on KLM's list and about nine months for Raffles. Success with these companies was gained through offering a quality product and a consistent level of supply. Price was less of an issue since consumers at Raffles were not that price conscious.

These deals take a long time to set up, but not all of them result from planned action. Palliser invests heavily in overseas staff travel as part of their marketing strategy, which has the benefit of keeping them in touch with the marketplace, and therefore takes advantage of emergent opportunities. For example, the Emirates contract (worth NZ$140,000) came about as a result of Richard reading in a magazine that the airline claimed to have the best wines in the world. Richard stated,

I rang them and asked how they can have the best wines in the world if they didn't have our wines. They asked me to send some wine, and a contract was signed in June 1997 and renewed in 1998. In the export business you follow a lot of leads. Eighty percent don't bear fruit, but this one did. . . . If you don't ask, you don't get.

The company also invests in networks as part of its export marketing strategy. Richard has long been a member of the Wine Institute of New Zealand, a body that works to advance the interests of the New Zealand wine industry. As part of this, Palliser was a founding member of the Wine Guild, which was a group of like-minded wineries that developed strategies for the U.K. market. In 1995, Palliser was part of a group of six winemakers who mounted a minicampaign to sell their products on the East Coast of the United States. The operation placed the six companies' wines in 60 retail outlets and restaurants. Richard noted that the campaign was based on the "New Zealand" image, which had been enhanced by the recent America's Cup victory. "It's a matter of selling New Zealand before the wine but I have no problem with that because it has a trickle-down effect. . . . I know New Zealand wine is very good and it gets wide acceptance once they taste it."

The company also became a member of The New Zealand Way, an organization that links complementary brands together and promotes them as part of a generic New Zealand promotion strategy. Richard also founded the Toast Martinborough Wine Festival (to raise the profile of the region) and was the Inaugural Chairman of the Pinot Noir 2001 Conference in Wellington (which gained worldwide coverage and helped raise the profile of New Zealand Pinot Noir around the world).[7] As well as gaining market knowledge and co-branding activities, the common theme running through these activities is that cooperation helps raise the profile of a region, country, or grape variety among consumers in a way that individual producers such as Palliser could never do, and this action ultimately benefits every network partner.

The Marketing Mix

The marketing mix consists of four factors: product, price, placement, and promotion. The original aim of the company was always to produce a quality product. This commitment to quality permeates everything the company does.

> I think that everything we do has to reflect the quality of our wines. Now obviously that takes a lot of hard work and to a degree a lot of planning. What we try and do is match every other part of our business with the quality of our wines so, for example, you have the wine being delivered on time to the right place.

For example, Richard tested a range of materials for the branded shirts sold through the cellar door, examining whether the material held its color after several washes. The company was also among the earliest to adopt screw cap enclosures (as opposed to cork) when it became clear that they could help eliminate the "corked wine" phenomena.[8] The quality of Palliser's wines is very high, and the company has been able to achieve what many of the world's famous wine estates have achieved—producing high-quality wines in poor vintage years (such as 1993 and 1995). This is reflected in the fact that on average, 80 percent of Palliser's production is Estate-quality wine, with 20 percent being Pencarrow labeled wine (a ratio unusual in the wine industry). Ongoing investment in product quality has also been coupled with increased knowledge about the company's vineyards, sites, and production techniques.

Palliser has seven varieties of wines and two price tiers. The top of the range is labeled as "Estate," while the next tier of wines is labeled "Pencarrow." The makeup of each depends on the quality of the vintage. Richard regards Pencarrow as the company's "commercial range," with the Estate label acting as a "reserve" label. The wine is labeled Pencarrow only when the quality is not up to the standards of the Estate range. However, the Pencarrow label is not a second-tier label as it is positioned as a quality label at a lower price point. Richard stated, "You can taste a Pencarrow NZ$15 dollar bottle of Chardonnay against all the other bottles of NZ$15 Chardonnay—we aim to be in the top five percent of that price point." This also gives the winery more flexibility and a wider market, as the Pencarrow range is less expensive than the Estate range. The Pencarrow range has won several awards since its launch and is often seen as an earlier drinking range when compared to the Estate.

The company is conservative when it comes to developing new products. They released a Vintage Methode Champenoise in 1998. This product has a natural synergy with the company's plantings, as it is made from Chardonnay and Pinot Noir, although sparkling wines require different production techniques and the investment required is significant. Richard stated,

> I had said in the past that we'll never produce a sparkling wine because it's expensive and the lead time is huge. I changed my mind simply because there are certain occasions when I think the only thing people want to drink is Champagne or Methode Champenoise and it was such a neat fit with our range. Then of course with our second vintage we scored big time,[9] so I changed my mind.

The company also released their first Pinot Gris in 2001 but have no plans to develop the range further. Richard believes that developing a new wine product is difficult because of the long delay between planting and harvesting.

> It is very difficult. Even two years ago the white/red wine ratio was entirely different to what it is today. That change occurred overnight; you could never have predicted that. You can sit down and call on expensive consultants and they couldn't have predicted that. I operate a lot on how my stomach feels. I think the wine industry has a lot to do with style, and style is something that is very difficult to quantify or put down in a business plan. You have a feeling that a wine style will work. That feeling comes from looking at the world, traveling the world, and talking to people—they are key in the whole mix and people generally love to try something new.

Richard argues that ensuring stability in supply is a key component of future success. Wine production is reliant on the weather, and although Martinborough will always produce small quantities of wine, the region is often affected by weather that drastically reduces the size of the harvest (even in cases where quality remains high). Building on this view, Richard committed the company to a growth program in 1997, aiming to double production to 50,000 cases per annum by 2004 (Palliser currently produces 40,000 cases). As part of this strategy Palliser undertook significant new planting in Martinborough to meet the demand for their product (the company's wines are on strict allocation and always sell out). The company aims to change their mix so that the increased production will be about 50 percent Pinot Noir[10] (Palliser exports 70 percent of its Pinot Noir), most of which is destined for export to meet the needs of Palliser's buyers.

The decision to grow was not made lightly, as Riddiford believes the market has a clear structure and that if Palliser grows too big it will have to compete with competitors that have greater scale advantages. Richard stated,

> If you produce 100,000 cases in New Zealand, you're in no-man's-land. You have to go to half a million cases and you have to change the whole operation really. We are not in the business of competing with Montana [a large local producer] or on an international basis with BRL Hardy or Southcorp [large Australian producers].

Concerns about controlling quality have caused the company to invest further in its own vineyards rather than relying heavily on contract growers (which is cheaper in the short term and would enable growth to occur more quickly). In the past Palliser did make use of contract vineyards, but Richard has changed his mind on the use of contract growers. He previously thought you could buy in fruit, but now believes you have to own your own vineyards if you are to deliver the consistency and quality necessary for the ultrapremium end of the market.

> Growers inherently have a different view than you do. We know we can produce great Pinot Noir at about two-and-a-half tons of fruit to the acre. Growers naturally want to have the tonnage at four or five per acre. If nature doesn't give us a low yield we will physically prune the vines to reduce the yield, but it is very diffi-

cult to get contract growers to cut off grapes and throw them away because to them it is money, but to us it's a liability.[11]

The company has continued to invest heavily in improving production quality. The company has invested in viticulture in order to improve quality. Winemaker Alan Johnson stated, "We are aiming for the ultrapremium end of the market so quality is extremely important. Consequently our viticulture is more expensive than the larger vineyards but the extra inputs pay off." This commitment to increased quality in the vineyard was to bear fruit with the release of their 1996-2000 award-winning Pinot Noirs that firmly established Palliser as a consistent quality Pinot Noir producer from Martinborough.[12] In 1999 Palliser spent a million dollars on new harvesters, sprayers, crushers, and a winepress, and spent an additional one-and-a-half million in 2001-2002 on extensions to its barrel room and production facilities.

> That's our livelihood. If you're going to make do with second-hand barrels and second-hand harvesters then you get a second-hand tasting product. So whilst I'm very happy to invest the money, it's got to come out the other end. I often have arguments with Alan (the winemaker) when he says the wines are getting better. The only good place to store good wine is in a bank after it has been converted into money.

Richard believes the greatest challenge for Palliser will be to maintain their margins and their quality as they double production from 30,000 cases to 50,000 cases. This, says Richard, "sounds easy, but it is a big task." The price range for Palliser's wines is shown in Table 7.1 (under "premium" [Pencarrow] and "super-premium" [Estate]). A key part of Palliser's pricing strategy is price stability. Richard stated,

> You can't have products that change price daily—it doesn't work. You have a relationship with your consumer. If I went into the Hilton in London and said "our prices had gone up 30 percent because the harvest was low," they would say "that's very interesting but there's a million other brands that we can buy

that (a) will supply us year round and (b) will have a price that is consistent."

Richard believes that protecting price points will be a large challenge for the company in light of increased competition in the marketplace; however, the lack of price increases over the years (only the Estate Pinot Noir has increased in price in response to large jump in quality from the 1996 vintage) will place the company in a much better position vis-à-vis its higher-priced competition from the region. (A number of wine magazines have commented on the fact that Palliser's wines represent tremendous value for money.)

Global distribution changes also present challenges as channels are getting bigger through mergers and acquisitions and more wine is on the market. Although stores are getting bigger, Richard believes,

> There will be a backlash against that. I think the consumer at the top end still wants to meet people. They still want to talk to people about the product they're buying. Wine is one of the few industries in the world where taste is so important. You can't go into a supermarket and eat an apple and say, "I don't like that," but you can walk into a winery and taste eight wines and make your selection based on that. Therefore, continuing to manage the relationship throughout the distribution channel, as the winery gets bigger, will remain one of the most important challenges faced by the company.

As mentioned earlier, Riddiford has clear goals when it comes to the placement of Palliser wines. In 2001-2002, 60 percent of Palliser's wines were exported. The basis of Palliser's approach to distribution lies in building relationships.

> I'll freely admit that prior to my current distribution arrangement I had two other distributors, and they didn't work out because they didn't share our vision. I don't like referring to people as agents; I like to refer to them as my partners, and to that extent I actively encourage agents to be shareholders, and two of them are. I consider each agent a partner because if you're just transferring the ownership from here to a warehouse in London or New York, it doesn't do the partner much good and

it ultimately doesn't do me very much good. It's a short-term game because we get the money and they've got the wine, but if you're not getting that pull through in the marketplace, then it doesn't work.

As part of this strategy, Richard believes in working in partnership with demand chain members in order to build mutual long-term value. This involves building up trust. For example,

> I think that you have to be completely transparent in your value chain. There's no point trying to keep the cost of production a secret. If you're going to have a relationship with one of those guys its got to be profitable for both sides; therefore, you need to be totally open about margins.

Richard's job involves creating demand, primarily offshore. To do this, you need to be prepared to travel to the key markets.

> I don't think you can do it any other way than by being there in person; that's why I've always traveled a lot. I know that in the U.K. for instance, with an outlet like the Thresher Group who owns 3,000 outlets, I can't hope to visit them all. However, I will do regional tastings and I do know that after I've done a tasting with forty shop managers, the sales of Palliser wines the following month will go up forty percent. It's never changed. We do a lot of work with restaurants because they are our ultimate salespeople. People forget that. They think "just give the wine to an agent and they will distribute it," but in retail outlets or restaurants around fifty percent of people say "what shall I buy?" If you've got wine in Singapore or Hong Kong, if you have talked to those restaurant people and said "buy Palliser," if they've tasted it and met you, they will. It's just human nature.

Richard freely admits they made mistakes with their initial distribution in the United States and in Singapore. Richard states,

> In foreign markets you often have a very small window. Maybe you're there for three days and you've got to make a decision about people, most of whom you've met only very briefly.

Sometimes as that relationship develops you find out you've made a mistake so you just get on and correct it. However, if you don't take these risks, you'll get companies that spend an enormous amount of time analyzing what they're doing and where they're going. That's fine, but if you're not constantly adding to your sales or your value all you're doing is analyzing where you've gone wrong and you're not improving the bottom line.

Although the company undertakes some limited advertising (in Australasian magazines such as *Cuisine*), most in-print exposure is gained through wine reviews and involvement in promotional events. Print exposure of this type is unpredictable (no planning could have ensured that *Wine Magazine* [United Kingdom] would have put Palliser's Sauvignon Blanc on its front cover in March 2002), and as such is seen as playing a supportive role. The company's main advertising is done via the Internet, as they believe the Internet will have a huge impact on the sale of wine. The Internet enables Palliser to disperse a lot of information very effectively and very cheaply. The company was one of the first to have a Web site (www.palliser.co.nz). The site is constantly updated and redesigned, which involves continuing investment. However, as Richard stated,

At the top end of the market you're dealing with people, and people still want to meet you. They want to understand what you're about, they want to see where Martinborough is, and they want to know what you do. You can give an impression on the Internet, but if you look at any successful business in the wine industry, you will inevitably find there is some person who is driving it.

This is why the company ensures a number of its staff travels to meet buyers and overseas customers, and why it invests heavily in its cellar door facility, as well as regional wine events such as Toast Martinborough.

People and Processes

The company has a flat management structure. The company has clear functions, but without the bureaucracy of separate functional departments. Palliser employs a winemaker, administration manager, cellar sales manager, and vineyard managers, although the winemaker is also a viticulturist as it is difficult to separate the winemaking and viticultural side of the business. The company also hires accountants. As part of having a flat structure, Palliser requires its staff to be multiskilled.

> It [functional structures] doesn't work. You get that Chinese wall mentality. People ring a place and order some wine, and someone will say, "that's not my job." If that happens to me as a customer I get annoyed, and after all, the customer ultimately pays our wages.

This culture has been difficult to establish, but the company has a low staff turnover, and a number of employees have worked for the company for long periods of time. The company started with three employees. In 1999 the company employed 30 staff, 15 of whom are casuals.

Although Palliser has a flat management structure, Richard argues that somebody needs to make the key decisions at the end of the day, because he or she can see what is happening to the whole of the business. Richard believes that you have to keep in mind what your end goal is when you are evaluating a new idea, especially when it comes from staff. They may come up with what seems like a great idea, but it was developed in isolation from the rest of the business.

> I say to staff, "That's way out of left field. Is that really going to help us achieve our end goal?" When they look at it that way, they say, "No perhaps it won't." I often will say to them, "Look, if that were your money, would you do it?" I try and get them to treat it as if they own the business.

This is also helped by the fact that 95 percent of all staff own shares in the business. Richard argues that when "people have a financial involvement they think differently."

The company also ensures that its key staff, managing director, winemaker, assistant winemaker, and the cellar sales manager get out and visit the markets that they export to. Richard stated,

You can sit in Martinborough and it's idyllic, but if they don't have a global view you can't teach them that. They've got to go there and experience London or New York. They have to understand that what happens in Martinborough isn't necessarily what happens in the rest of New Zealand and it certainly isn't what happens in the rest of the world. You have got to export; you're on an international stage. People go on about how America is booming but they forget that there are planeloads of people arriving daily in New York or L.A. with briefcases full of products to sell. It's tough out there and that's why you can't afford not to do it. You have to invest in the marketplace.

Palliser has become more systemized over time, although the systems tend to be processes that ensure the quality of the product as opposed to administrative systems. For example Palliser was the first winery in New Zealand to have ISO 9002, and in 1998 formed a group called Living Wine with four other wineries and gained ISO 14001 certification for their commitment to environmental responsibility. Riddiford believes that this last program is one of the most important decisions the company ever made. Richard stated that Palliser had always attempted to be at the forefront of change and believed that initiating better environmental protection measures would ward off regulation from the government, differentiate them in the market, and give them continued access to export markets.[13] He is certain that there will be commercial benefits gained from this program, even if it is long term, and now lists environment as the company's single most valuable asset. Following this, Palliser became part of the New Zealand Business Council for Sustainable Development, partnering with large companies such as 3M, The Warehouse, and Waste Management. This provides the company with another source of public relations activity, enabling widespread diffusion of its commitment to the environment among consumers.

Financial Results

Palliser is very clear that benchmarking wine quality against other comparable producers is not enough, because "you can say our wine is right up there, but if the financial performance is down then there is something wrong." The company did not make a profit for the three years 1989-1991, but since that time the company has always paid a dividend and made substantial profits with an appreciating share price. Palliser Estate is one of Australasia's highest performing wineries,[14] producing a net profit of NZ$930,000 in the year ended 2002. Their shares were trading at NZ$4.80 each, and had a market capitalization of NZ$19.2 million (up from NZ$4.5 million in 1997). The company increased its sales to NZ$4.5 million and profits to $1.24 million in 2003.

DISCUSSION AND CONCLUSION

The Palliser case illustrates the importance of investing in marketing activities early on in the firm's life cycle. However, Palliser's broad marketing strategy cannot be classified neatly into the usual black-and-white concepts presented in textbooks (Kotler, 2000). Rather, Palliser's approach involves the blending of many different approaches, often in novel ways, to develop a competitive advantage. This is shown in Table 7.2. The company emerged quickly from a product-oriented one, as the leaders realized that the future lay in export markets and in market segments where branding was paramount. Lack of economies of scale meant that Palliser had to either grow very large or target markets where it could effectively compete. However, this market also demands quality, meaning that quality had to be improved while investments were also made in marketing activity. As the company could not afford to undertake mass marketing, owners committed resources to networks and relationships, developing a local festival to build brand exposure locally, and entering networks of like-minded wineries to gain exposure in key international markets. At the same time, relationships were built with agents and distributors to ensure the positioning of the product. The results of product investments have helped the winery gain continual endorsements from wine writers and wine shows, which enhances the brand, increases brand awareness, and supports the company's business relationships. This also helps attract new relationship partners. For example, in 2002 Palliser signed an agreement with Champagne House Bollinger

TABLE 7.2. Palliser Marketing Strategy and Results

Marketing variable	Approach and evolution	Result
Strategy	Initial aim to produce the best quality product, evolves into a business aim of being best winery of type in New Zealand, and then the world.	Winery invests in product quality, marketing activity, and relationships and networks both in New Zealand and overseas. Long-term result is that winery becomes recognized as world leader, and thereby attracts customers and publicity.
Market orientation	Moves from simple strategy focused around leader to a values-based culture and systems to link internal firm to external environment, all the time controlled by clear sense of purpose.	Allows firm to respond in a planned and consistent way to emergent market opportunities. Identifies what opportunities are appropriate and which are not. Allows firm to control its destiny and grow without crisis.
Price	Lack of economies of scale, high distance to markets, uncertain exchange rate, and necessity of low cropping led Palliser to target markets where price was not a major motivation to purchase. However, price stability remains critical.	Targeting markets allows Palliser to increase prices when it must, but price stability is an important point of differentiation at the premium end of the market, and helps build brand equity and relationships.
Place	Target top end of market, including distributors, restaurants, airlines, and events. This helps winery gain endorsements from high-quality brands.	Endorsements generate publicity and new opportunities. As long as it is supported by marketing activity, this strategy is self-perpetuating, with customers seeking out Palliser's wines.

TABLE 7.2 (continued)

Marketing variable	Approach and evolution	Result
Product	Continual investment in product quality. Recognition that product quality is not enough to provide a source of differentiation. Development of two quality tiers to help deal with uncertainty of weather. Increase in supply to provide supply stability to partners.	Investments in product quality act as an enabler for endorsement and distribution strategy. It also helps build the brand.
Promotion	Limited promotion done in mainstream or specialist press due to cost. Promotion done through networking, events, and wine shows.	Apart from limited promotion, most promotion is a result of other marketing activity, not an input. The firm does not need to create demand through promotion; rather, high demand for its wine, created by investments elsewhere, leads to continued media coverage in mediums likely to be noticed by target market.
Networks	Form networks to gain economies of scale in promotion and develop market opportunities.	Networks generate new market opportunities and help winery gain a level of exposure that it could not otherwise obtain. This approach opens up new opportunities for publicity and promotion, as well as attracts like-minded businesses into network, all the time improving Palliser's position.
Relationships	Sees distributors and agents as partners, and actively encourages them to own shares in the company. Forms close relationships with distributors and agents as a means of improving word-of-mouth recommendations. At the same time, continual commitment to quality means relationships are reduced with contract growers.	Ownership counters power of distributors and also leads all parties to create value together. Relationships between Richard, salespeople/agents, and Palliser staff and salespeople/agents results in word-of-mouth promotion in targeted outlets

to distribute its wines in France. Richard stated that such an agreement was recognition by our peers.

These activities early in the firm's life cycle resulted in sustained financial success, which enabled further investments. However, it also enabled the company to grow larger, to take advantage of new opportunities, and to ensure supply stability with current customers. As part of this growth process, Palliser has invested further in organizational systems and people, encouraging staff to own shares in the company. This helps build commitment to the brand and the company's values, thereby ensuring the emergence of an organizational culture. This culture assists the firm to identify which opportunities are appropriate for it to take up and which to avoid. This is critical, as growing firms are prone to a loss of focus without these core goals or simple rules (Brown and Eisenhardt, 1998).

Palliser's approach cannot be captured by traditional textbook models of marketing (such as the selling approach or marketing orientation), rather it supports the view of Carson (2001) who proposed that small and medium-sized firms practice "marketing in context" whereby they pick and choose from a number of marketing models. However, Carson's model implicitly accepts that small firms do this because they must react to market changes beyond their control. This reflects the common view in much of the organizational literature that small firms are more likely to be pawns of their environments than creators of new environments or masters of their own destiny (Astley and Van de Ven, 1983). However, the Palliser approach clearly demonstrates that niche specialists can create the basis for a competitive advantage through ongoing investments in a multitude of activities at once (see Brown and Eisenhardt, 1998). As can be seen from the case, niche specialists can also create new niches, often through networks, and often as a result of earlier participation in networks.

This conflicts with the traditional view of marketing, which proposes that firms have moved through a number of eras or stages, starting with the production/product era, moving to the selling era, then the marketing orientation, and then to the relationship orientation (Fullerton, 1988; Keith, 1960). Each stage in this view is seen as being appropriate for the time, but as competition increases and demand changes, the basis of success in each stage is eroded, and firms must seek new sources of advantage (Grönroos, 1996). However, based upon this case, we propose a different view, whereby each supposed era or stage is viewed as a theoretical frame or window, which provides a useful perspective for managers interested in building firm value. This is shown in Figure 7.1.

Clearly, Palliser used each quadrant (see Figure 7.1) at different stages of its development, but equally clearly, it continues to use each quadrant as part of building and enhancing its competitiveness. For example, Palliser invests heavily in production processes and in its product. Although this helps it maintain its market position and target high-value markets, its competitors can match this level of quality. Therefore, by itself, product quality is not a source of differentiation, although it is necessary to compete in its targeted market. Improved production processes help add value to its relationship networks, and also gain a level of scale economies unusual for its niche and for the region of Martinborough. This creates a point of difference and, given the limited area of Martinborough, potentially an insurmountable one.

Second, the various marketing mix activities help position the brand, but also act more as supports to the firm's relationship activities. The investment in systems and people (staff share ownership) and the development of a culture is consistent with a marketing orientation. This helps the firm react to market changes and ensures that the firm makes decisions and investments in line with its stated goals. However, market orientation has been criticized for being too reactive (Baker and Sinkula, 1999). Clearly, Palliser has retained its emergent,

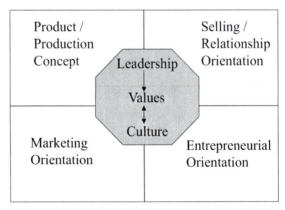

FIGURE 7.1. Multiple Perspectives to Niche Marketing Success

or entrepreneurial, spirit, enabling it to identify market opportunities and keep ahead of its competition, being careful to avoid the mistake of many other elite wineries of resting on their laurels (as Richard states, "Success is a journey, not a destination"). These four perspectives are blended effectively to create the basis of Palliser's current and future positioning. However, the entrepreneurial approach is tempered by a strong set of values around the firm's positioning, driven at first by Richard and now becoming entrenched in the firm's culture. These values help ensure that the firm takes advantage of the right opportunities while maintaining its historical activities. This approach has been identified by Collins and Porras (2000) as an essential component of long-term firm success.

The case highlights a number of key issues for niche marketers. As markets become increasingly competitive and partitioned between large and small players, firms must develop a clear focus in order to survive. They must also develop values and systems that allow them to respond to environmental changes and take advantage of emerging opportunities. This suggests that niche firms must develop both planned and emergent strategies. Planning has two roles. First, planning has a medium-term role at the tactical level, focusing on the commitment of resources to achieve goals and the timing of these commitments. An emergent strategy will involve identifying and responding to market challenges and opportunities. For niche players, the danger of relying solely on one strategic approach is that wholly planned firms are inflexible in the face of a changing environment, and wholly emergent firms have no basis by which to judge whether they should take up emergent market opportunities. This can lead them to enter niches where they have little hope of competing.

The case illustrates the importance of firms of all sizes investing in the marketplace. This involves developing a number of internal/external firm capabilities. In the case examined, investments were made at a product level, at a relationship level, at a brand awareness level, and at an internal staff level. Combined, these investments provide the basis for Palliser's continuing competitive advantage. This suggests that niche marketers must focus on developing different competencies at different times and that firms may be characterized by a number of different perspectives (product orientation, sales orientation, marketing orientation, and relationship orientation). Firms that take only one perspective will struggle in an environment of increased competition and slow growth. Finally, the role of leadership in marketing orientation needs further examination, particularly for small niche firms.

NOTES

1. Wine commentators noted how this appeared to be a onetime achievement, as the company took seven years to produce another award-winning Pinot Noir. The company owners put this down to increased vine age, poor vintages during the early 1990s, and increased understanding of the vineyards through greater investments in quality.

2. The local landscape is brought to life on the label of Palliser's Estate-labeled wines, depicting the foothills named Nga-Waka-A-Kupe after the first Maori, Kupe, to visit New Zealand. Labels can be viewed at www.palliser.co.nz.

3. Cape Palliser is at the southern tip of the North Island of New Zealand. Cape Palliser appears on the winery's Pencarrow label.

4. This is the most difficult competition to win, as it receives over 10,000 entries from around the world, and each potential medal winner is tasted twice by six experienced wine judges.

5. Since its first vintage in 1989, Palliser has won 62 national and international gold medals or trophies, numerous silver and bronze medals, and has received very high quality ratings from the likes of *Wine Spectator* (United States), *Decanter* (United Kingdom), and *Winestate* (Australia).

6. Including Cathay Pacific, Qantas, Lufthansa, Emirates, KLM, and Air New Zealand.

7. Due to the success of this venture, a second conference was held in 2004.

8. Cork taint results in around a 5 to 15 percent failure rate in wines. Although only 3 to 5 percent of wines have noticeable cork taint, 10 to 15 percent can have less discernable cork taint, which to the average consumer means the wine tastes dull or flat.

9. In 1999 Palliser Estate won the trophy for best sparkling wine at the Air New Zealand Wine Awards. In 1999 Palliser's sparkling wine was the first non-French sparkling wine to be included in business class on Air New Zealand.

10. It is currently 40 percent, with Sauvignon Blanc 40 percent, Chardonnay 10 percent, Reisling and Pinot Gris 5 percent each.

11. This is reflected in the view of winemaker Alan Johnson who believes quality wines are derived "60 percent from the vineyard and 40 percent from the winery."

12. Palliser Estate Pinot Noir is ranked as one of Martinborough's top ten wines, and one of New Zealand's top ten Pinot Noirs.

13. Palliser maintains a record of significant environmental aspects of their processes and makes this available to the public on demand.

14. Palliser benchmarks its financial performance against all publicly listed wine companies in Australia. The company's results in 2001-2002 were 35 percent EBIT percent sales, 22 percent NPAT percent sales, 14.3 percent EBIT percent funds employed, and 10.3 NPAT percent equity, placing it in the top 5 percent of wine companies in Australasia.

REFERENCES

Aldrich, H. E. (1999). *Organizations Evolving.* London: Sage Publications.

Astley, W. G. and Van de Ven, A. H. (1983). "Central Perspectives and Debates in Organization Theory." *Administrative Science Quarterly,* 28: 245-273.

Baker, W. E. and Sinkula, J. M. (1999). "The Synergistic Effect of Market Orientation and Learning Orientation on Organizational Performance." *Journal of the Academy of Marketing Science,* 27(4): 411-427.

Beverland, M. B., Bretherton, P. B., and Lindgreen, A. (2002). "The Evolution of Marketing Strategy in the New Zealand Wine Industry." The Marketing Landscape: Signposts for the Future. Proceedings of the Academy of Marketing Conference, University of Nottingham: Chartered Institute of Marketing.

Beverland, M. B. and Lindgreen, A. (2001). "The Search for Competitive Advantage: Do Relationships Hold the Key to Future Success?" *Australian and New Zealand Wine Industry Journal International Wine Marketing Supplement,* 16(6): 97-108.

Beverland, M. B. and Lockshin, L. S. (2001). "Organizational Life Cycles in Small New Zealand Wineries." *Journal of Small Business Management,* 39(4): 354-362.

Brown, S. L. and Eisenhardt, K. M. (1998). *Competing on the Edge: Strategy As Structured Chaos.* Boston, MA: Harvard Business School Press.

Carson, D. (2001). "Marketing for Small to Medium Enterprises." In Baker, M. J. (Ed.), *The Marketing Books,* Fourth Edition (pp. 621-639). London: Butterworth Heinemann.

Collins, J. C. and Porras, J. I. (2000). *Built to Last: Successful Habits of Visionary Companies.* London: Random House.

Fullerton, R. A. (1988). "How Modern Is Marketing? Marketing's Evolution and the Myth of the 'Production Era.'" *Journal of Marketing,* 52(1): 109-125.

Geene, A., Heijbroek, A., Lagerwerf, A. and Wazir, R. (1999). *The World Wine Business.* The Netherlands: Rabobank International.

Grönroos, C. (1996). "Relationship Marketing Logic." *Asia-Australia Marketing Journal,* 4(1): 19-24.

Keith, R. (1960). "The Marketing Revolution." *Journal of Marketing,* 24(January): 35-38.

Kotler, P. (2000). *Marketing Management: The Millennium Edition.* Sydney: Prentice Hall International.

Loubere, L. A. (1990). *The Wine Revolution in France: The Twentieth Century.* Princeton, NJ: Princeton University Press.

Mintzberg, H., Ahlstrand, B., and Lampel, J. (1998). *Strategy Safari.* London: Financial Times Prentice Hall.

Pettigrew, A. M., Woodman, R. W., and Cameron, K. S. (2001). "Studying Organizational Change and Development: Challenges for Future Research." *Academy of Management Journal,* 44(4): 697-713.

Porter, M. E. (1980). *Competitive Strategy.* Ontario: Free Press.

Rachman, G. (1999). "Christmas Survey: A Rum Business." *The Economist,* 353(8150): 101-103.

Swaminathan, A. (2001). "Resource Partitioning and the Evolution of Specialist Organizations: The Role of Location and Identity in the U.S. Wine Industry." *Academy of Management Journal,* 44(6): 1169-1185.

Swaminathan, A. and Delacroix, J. (1991). "Differentiation Within an Organizational Population: Additional Evidence from the Wine Industry." *Academy of Management Journal,* 34(3): 679-692.

Varadarajan, P. R. and Jayachandran, S. (1999). "Marketing Strategy: An Assessment of the State of the Field and Outlook." *Journal of the Academy of Marketing Science,* 27(2): 120-143.

Webster, F. E. (2000). "Understanding the Relationships Among Brands, Consumers and Resellers." *Journal of the Academy of Marketing Science,* 28(1): 17-23.

Chapter 8

Niche Marketing for Hotel Managers

Ron Morritt
Walden University

ABSTRACT

This chapter examines the strategy of niche marketing for competitive advantage in the consolidation phase of the 1990s hotel market. It tracks the evolution of segmentation strategy in the U.S. hotel market from price segmentation to integrated niche marketing. Different types of segmentation used in both the U.S. and Caribbean hotel markets are cited as examples of successful segmentation and niche marketing in the hotel industry. Benefits and liabilities associated with niche marketing are summarized. The need for empirical support for the selection of a target niche is emphasized using different types of market research. The chapter concludes with a review of four niche selection methods for hotel managers and owners. These methods include the following:

1. Adapt and modify a successful segmentation formula.
2. Use your hotel guest history/database to profile your best customers.
3. Identify segmentation gaps in your local market.
4. Contract with a reputable consulting firm to do a segmentation study.

The use of at least two of these methods is recommended.

INTRODUCTION

The focus of this chaper is niche marketing as a strategy for smaller[1] resort hotels, but the strategic implications of niche marketing are generalizable over the entire hotel industry. The tourist hotel market in Jamaica, not unlike the global market, is involved in a consolidation phase associated with the later stages of a mature market. There is fierce competition, commoditization of products, price cutting, declining revenues, and declining profitability. Morritt (1995) has argued that the key to smaller hotels competing successfully in this market is related to three programs: market segmentation, strategic alliances, and automation. This chapter will focus on niche marketing as a segmentation strategy for smaller hotels.

A Brief Overview of Niche Marketing Strategy

Market segmentation is the process of classifying customers and prospects into groups with similar needs and purchasing behavior (Kotler, 1991; Weinstein, 1995). Effective segmentation allows the firm to select those groups that can be served most profitably and positions the firm to effectively service the needs of those groups. Niche marketing is perhaps best defined by Dalgic and Leeuw (1994):

> We may conclude that niche marketing could be defined as positioning into small, profitable homogeneous market segments which have been ignored or neglected by others. This positioning is based on the integrated marketing concept and the distinctive competencies the company possesses.

How does niche marketing (NM) lead to competitive advantage?

- If you have selected carefully, little competition exists for your target niche. (The niche may not be large enough to be feasible for larger hotels or it may not be synergetic with its other products.)
- Your hotel should have a competitive advantage in servicing this niche since it was selected because it fits the resources and key competencies of your hotel.
- You can serve this niche better than other hotels by specializing in understanding and serving its needs.
- Niche marketing is associated with higher margins since servicing niches better meets the needs of niche customers (greater price elasticity).

- Niche marketing is a strategy that hotels such as Marriott and Club Med have already proven to be effective in competing in the hotel industry.
- There is greater opportunity for cross-marketing because of the intimate knowledge of niche customers contained in your customer database (e.g., tours, rental cars).
- Here, as elsewhere, greater market returns are associated with greater risks. Risks and limitations associated with NM are as follows:

  —There is more investment risk for smaller hotels targeting a single niche since you are not diversified.
  —NM is more expensive; it requires more information about your customers and greater customization of products and services.
  —NM requires the use of customer databases to continuously track, monitor, evaluate, and control operations to profitably maximize service, quality, and value, as defined by the customer.
  —NM will not make up for fundamental hotel problems (poor service, low quality, poor facilities, and lack of operational controls).
  —NM is more dependent on customer retention (since it is a small market); therefore, perceived service and value must be excellent.
  —NM requires the full support and commitment of both upper management and employees who must buy into the marketing concept that NM implies. What is this marketing concept? It is that the mission of your hotel (and every employee) is to provide the facilities and service that best serves the needs and expectations of your target customers.

Segment selection needs to be supported by periodic market research and analysis of guest histories and surveys. A priori selection of segments without empirical support exposes the hotel to the risk of selecting a segment that is of insufficient size, that will not be attracted to the hotel product being offered, or is not sufficiently profitable. If you are targeting more than one segment, you will need to be concerned about possible interactions (conflicts/synergies) between segments.

SEGMENTATION PRACTICES
IN THE HOTEL INDUSTRY

Writers often distinguish between "a priori" (predetermined) and "post hoc" segmentation. The latter identifies market segments based on market research including market surveys. A priori segmentation, on the other hand, usually involves selecting groups from the market and then finding out if they are true segments, often without new research (Struhl, 1992). Until recently all segmentation in the U.S. hotel industry was a priori segmentation, which was an attempt to appeal to different customer segments by a differentiation strategy. The U.S. hotel industry has evolved from price segmentation to product segmentation and is now experimenting with market segmentation and niche marketing. Niche marketing strategy is often accompanied by a "relationship marketing" strategy, whereby hotels utilize integrated customer databases to build long-term interactive and mutually profitable relationships with their best customers.

Stage 1: Price Segmentation

Call it marketing genius or marketing madness, but Marriott International is turning its 782-room Miami Airport Marriott into three hotels. When an $8.5 million renovation project is completed there in October, guests will find a 365-room full-service Marriott, a 125-room Courtyard by Marriott, and a 285-room Fairfield Inn. The original hotel, built in 1972 as a Marriott Motor Inn, had a main tower and two low-rise buildings in the back. The hotel became outdated in the 1980s as guests began to prefer the main tower with its indoor corridor to the hotel's two smaller buildings with their outside corridors. Eventually the two smaller buildings housed mostly airline crews. Each of the remodeled hotels will have a lobby, front desk, hotel staff, and complementary airport shuttle. The three hotels will share a pool and a fitness center. The Courtyard and the Marriott will each have a restaurant that will serve guests of all three hotels. Rates will differ:

Marriot is $99 a night; Courtyard, $79; Fairfield Inn, $49 to $59. Travelers call the regular Marriott number to make reservations for any of the three.

Until the 1980s the U.S. hotel industry had developed with four basic price segments: luxury, convention, first class, and economy. Usually a hotel company specialized in one of these categories (Schultz, 1994).

Stage 2: Product Segmentation

Product segmentation revolutionized the U.S. hotel industry in the 1980s. Major U.S. hotel chains used this strategy to counter the competitive effects of a mature market and to more effectively serve diverse economic segments. This was the first attempt by the hotel industry to create hotels to mirror consumers' lifestyles rather than to be all things to all people (Schultz, 1994). The most successful of these new products were the all-suite hotels and the "limited service" hotels ("super segments" in Kotler's terminology). Hotel chains developed segmentation portfolios to reach critical mass. Five hotel segments reported by one hotel marketing analyst (Dev and Hubbard, 1989) for eleven major hotel chains are the following:

1. Traditional (full service, comfort, food service, moderate price: Holiday Inn, Marriott)
2. Economy (limited to no-service, no-frills facilities, low price: Fairfield Inn, Sheraton Inns)
3. All suites (apartments, the most successful of the segments, moderate price, offering homelike accommodations: Embassy Suites, Residence Inns)
4. Casino (moderate prices, subsidized by casino operations: Harrah's, Tropicana)
5. Upscale (high service level, comfort, food service, expensive: Crowne Plaza, Towers)

Stage 3: Special Interest Segmentation

In recent years hotels have experimented with special interest segmentation, a niche marketing strategy that targets special interest groups. However, too often this is an a priori strategy and does not take advantage of the benefits of market research and the new technology afforded by computerized guest databases. Special interest groups targeted by hotels include

- Hotels that cater to the 50+ traveler (Choice hotels). Customized features include lever handles on door, brighter lights, larger buttons on remote controls, ground-floor locations (*Lodging Hospitality,* 1993).
- Hotels targeting nature lovers (ecotourism) (Campamento Camani, 13 units). David Anderson (president of the Anderson Group) said that ecotourism is the world's fastest growing tourist market (Deneen, 1993).
- Hotels that accommodate guests needing to stay for a month or more (the 84-room Sutton in New York City). This hotel offers maid service, free health club, fully equipped kitchens, and apartment-sized closets and storage areas (Selwitz, 1992b).
- Hotels that cater to culture buffs (e.g., Boston's Four Seasons hotel which markets arts packages tied to the city's cultural institutions and theater (Selwitz, 1992a).
- Hotels that exploit historical attractions of places (Club Med has "villages" in Mexico and Asia that promote tours of famous archeological sites) (Club Med, 1995).
- Hotels that cater to gourmets and aficionados (e.g., Omni Hotels just launched its cigar dinner program, the first in a series of "smoking soirees" that will take place at 17 Omni properties in the United States (*Hotel & Motel Management,* 1995).
- Hotels that cater to the auto/truck traveler (Forte Hotel's Thrift Lodge brand) (Escalera, 1994).
- Hotels that have created a new business: residential life-care communities targeting the growing mature (65+) population (Marriott made use of psychographic segmentation found useful in segmenting the elderly market for the development of these communities) (Camacho, 1988).
- Hotels that have entered the time-share and condominium markets. Time-sharing and condominium conversions stabilize revenues and bring in capital. (You sell your units but still get to rent and manage the property.) Jamaica's upscale Half Moon re-

sort has a time-share plan on rooms and villas where the units revert to the owners in 25 years. (GMS, 1993)

Niche marketing allows a hotel to successfully compete against larger hotels by its superior ability to service its chosen niche. This is no accident but is based on a niche marketing strategy that includes market research and transformation of the hotel culture to deliver what this niche considers value in an unexcelled and profitable manner.

If you owned a small resort hotel in Jamaica, you would not want to compete with an international chain such as Wyndham for business clients. They have superior resources and are better positioned for this market, having conference facilities, marketing departments, relationships with many large corporations, and large marketing budgets. You do not have the resources to compete effectively in this segment so you need to target a different, perhaps smaller, niche that is more consistent with your abilities and resources. An example of one small hotel in Jamaica that successfully targeted a niche market is Negril Gardens in Jamaica,[2] which achieved excellent occupancy rates as well as insulated themselves from the last U.S. recession by targeting the European market (16 percent of present market).

Negril Gardens effectively served middle-class European tourists who were comfortable with a small, moderately priced beachfront hotel which adopted European standards of higher service quality, continental cuisine, nightly entertainment, clothing-optional beaches, relaxed atmosphere (no scheduled activities), multilingual staff, and no phones in the rooms. An added and unique benefit of this hotel was that Europeans associated with other European guests who had similar values and lifestyles. Thus they avoided the "ugly American" problem. Negril Gardens has achieved a competitive advantage in the Jamaican tourism market. If you wished to vacation in Negril (world-famous seven-mile-long beach) and desired a European-type ambiance in a moderately priced hotel, Negril Gardens was one of the few places to achieve these goals. While most small hotels were struggling with marginal occupancy rates during this period, Negril Gardens had occupancy rates exceeding 90 percent and, due to its target niche, was relatively immune to the U.S. recession at the time (GMS, 1993).

Stage 4: Integrated Niche Marketing

We define integrated niche marketing as niche marketing that is integrated with customer databases, quality control systems,[3] and relationship marketing[4] to achieve a sustained competitive advantage by offering unexcelled products and services to target customers. This entails knowing how your target customers define value and consistently delivering this value in an efficient, friendly, and cost-effective manner.

Integrated niche marketing enables you to better achieve and maintain a competitive advantage in servicing your target niche. Customer databases, relationship marketing, and quality control systems are tools to customize, optimize, and control all hotel operations in servicing your target niche.

A recent example of successful integrated niche marketing is Baldridge award winner Ritz-Carlton hotel (Mene, 1994; Partlow, 1993), which services the super-luxury market niche. Hotel manager Mene used Baldridge award criteria, guest databases, and guest surveys to improve hotel processes and personally build teamwork and transform the culture of the hotel to deliver what guest surveys indicated constituted value[5] to their guests and significantly minimized service defects (reported by committed employees as well as guests).

Employees were trained, empowered, evaluated, and rewarded according to satisfaction of corporate goals of service quality and teamwork, and the conversion process was "top down," led by the general manager. Use of a computerized guest database that provides detailed information on 240,000 frequent guests was used to help employees become familiar with individual guests' likes and dislikes, resulting in personalized quality service and long-term relationships with customers.

SEGMENTING YOUR LOCAL MARKET

Market Structure

It is important to first understand the major forces, trends, and critical success factors that drive the present market. The market for Jamaican resort hotels, for example, has a particular structure at any given time, which is uncovered by researching the answers to the following questions:

- Who are the major and minor buyer groups?
- Where do they come from?
- What are the competing products?
- How successful are these products?
- What are the major reasons why buyers purchase this product?
- How is this product used?
- What are the standard variations of this product?
- What is the industry life cycle stage in this market?

The major geographical sources of tourism for Jamaica have been the United States, Canada, and Europe. Thus in the first two months of 1995 the United States constituted 66 percent of the market; Canada, 13 percent; Europe, 16 percent; and others, 6 percent (CTO, 1995).

The Jamaican market has long been divided into the "all-inclusive" hotel group (which, following the Club Med model, offers a package that includes meals, entertainment, sports, and often an air package) and the noninclusive hotel group, which charges separately for meals and often do not have entertainment or a great variety of sports. In recent years the most profitable hotels have tended to be of the "all-inclusive" variety of which Sandals is representative (GMS, 1993).

The major tourist centers in Jamaica are Montego Bay, Negril, and Ocho Rios. The average occupancy rate over the past five years has been below the break-even point of 65 percent for most noninclusive independent hotels. This situation, associated with the mature life cycle stage of the tourism market, was exacerbated by recessions in the United States and Europe, the Gulf War, overbuilding in major tourist areas such as Montego Bay, competition from other Caribbean tourist destinations, and government cutbacks on tourism marketing. Adding to this problem is an image problem associated with an inaccurate perception of inadequate security propagated by the media and travel agents.

The major hotel products in the Jamaican market consist of all-inclusive hotels (Sandals, Ciboney) which target the younger active couples segment, hotels that target businesspeople and convention business (Wyndham, Holiday Inn), hotels that cater to the affluent market (Half Moon, Lido), a few hotels that target the European market (Negril Gardens), condo hotels that offer suites (Montego Bay Club, Turtle Towers, Seawind), and many small hotels on or near the beach that do not target anyone.

The larger and international hotel chains have decided competitive advantages in this market not only by economies of scale and deeper pockets, but by expert management teams, computerized hotel systems, staff training programs, and international brand equity. Many of these larger hotels are operating sophisticated database marketing systems and frequent guest programs. Smaller hotels have an increasingly difficult time competing in the latest shakeout phase of the Jamaican tourist market and most have occupancy levels below the break-even level of 65 percent (Morritt, 1995).

Tourists come to Jamaica for many different reasons that can be exploited by a niche marketing strategy for smaller hotels (benefit segmentation). Some of these reasons are the tropical climate, lush vegetation, magnificent beaches, water sports, snorkeling and scuba diving on the coral reef, sports fishing, world-class golf and tennis facilities, the Jamaican culture (including reggae music and the historical celebrity of Port Royal), and the friendly people. Often, affluent tourists come to be pampered in elegant spalike surroundings and never get to see Jamaica or its people at all outside the sterile surroundings of an "international hotel." There are presently no casino hotels. Jamaica, famous for bauxite and tourism, is the home of some of the best coffee (Jamaican Blue Mountain) and cigars (Royal Jamaican) in the world.

MARKET TRENDS

The Dominance of the "All-Inclusive Vacation" Package

Many tourists prefer an all-inclusive package, which includes airfare, meals, accommodations, drinks, airport transportation, and tips. This successful pricing strategy, originated by Club Med, is now used successfully by Sandals and other all-inclusive hotels worldwide. Statistical data continue to show that all-inclusive hotels, as a group, have higher occupancy rates than noninclusive hotels in Jamaica (Caribbean Tourism Organization, 1995).

Ecotourism: The Fastest-Growing Sector of Tourism

Ecotourism describes the recent trend toward concern for environmental protection, cleanliness, safety, and health as well as the enjoyment of natural beauty including parks, forests, lakes, rivers, oceans (whale watching), coral reefs (diving and snorkeling), and wildlife. A growing number of tours are springing up in countries such as Jamaica for tourists to see the unspoiled back country as well as to enjoy activities such as glass-bottom boat rides, scuba diving, and snorkeling at the coral reefs.

According to the Travel Industry Association of America, 43 million U.S. individuals are self-proclaimed "ecotourists," who are willing to pay 8.5 percent more for environmentally friendly travel suppliers. The potential is cited by one travel writer for the creation of the "Eco-hotel" or Ecotel, which would tap this huge market (Rushmore, 1993).

Health Tourism

Health tourism is defined by Goodrich (1994) as the attempt on the part of a hotel or destination to attract tourists by promoting its health care services and facilities in addition to its regular amenities. Goodrich cites such services as medical treatments and special diets. I shall use the term "health tourism" in a wider sense to include spa and fitness facilities as well as special meal plans to target health-conscious tourists.

Caribbean tourists and locals often enjoy ocean-bathing as a healthy activity, and islands such as the Bahamas, Cuba, and Jamaica have mineral springs and health resort facilities such as the Silver Reef Health Club in Grand Bahama Island and Doctors Cave Beach in Jamaica (Goodrich, 1994).

Furthermore certain all-inclusive hotels in Jamaica (Ciboney and Swept Away) have successfully differentiated themselves by offering spa and/or fitness facilities including "spa food" (fresh-ingredient, low-calorie gourmet meals) to tourists who are health conscious.

The targeting of health-conscious tourists is an especially interesting niche for smaller hotels in the Caribbean since the relatively inexpensive modification of facilities also has the potential to bring in local business for restaurants and fitness facilities. Several hotels in Jamaica have special diet facilities, such as Lady Diane (macrobiotic food) and Ciboney (spa food).

Cultural Tourism

The rise of "cultural tourism" promotes the local culture, history, and archeology of the tourist destination.

Kotler, Haider, and Rein (1993) speak of a major trend in place revival called heritage development: "the task of preserving the history of places, their buildings, their people and customs, the machinery, and other artifacts that portray history" (p. 209). I mentioned previously that Club Med has special archeological villages in Mexico and Asia and also that Boston's Four Seasons hotel offers cultural packages tied to local cultural institutions such as theater, concerts, and opera. One example of the attraction of historical landmarks is New York's famous South Street Seaport (including the museum, restored giant clipper ships, and concerts of old sea chanteys).

IMPLICATIONS OF U.S. POPULATION TRENDS FOR THE HOTEL INDUSTRY

Demographic trends indicate a significant increase in the 65+ population (baby boomers maturing), the distribution of wealth skewing toward the older population, the increase in the percentage of dual-income families, increased business travel for women, and an increased proportion of nontraditional households (Yesawitch, 1991). Other trends include

- The trend toward shorter, more frequent vacations. U.S. vacations average four to five days versus European vacations, which average 10 to 14 days (CTO, 1995).
- Greater numbers of visitors from Germany and the Pacific Rim, as higher disposable incomes of people from these countries, and currency devaluation, make countries such as the United States, Mexico, and Jamaica a better value.
- Greater competition from cruise ships (growing twice as fast as the hotel industry in the Caribbean) and strong competition from other Caribbean Islands such as Puerto Rico, Dominican Republic, Cuba, and the Bahamas (CTO, 1995).

SEGMENT SELECTION

As Figure 8.1 illustrates, a rigorous segment selection procedure involves using primary and secondary market research using selected segmentation criteria (e.g., benefits, lifestyles, usage, and "special interests") and market structure analysis to target potentially profitable segments in your local market. The subsequent "short list" of potentially most profitable segments is further screened by the criteria of "fit" with the resources, culture, and special competencies of your hotel, actionability (how reachable are your customers?), and structural attractiveness (growth of, profitability of, and competition for this segment).

Risks of Segment Selection

Because most hotel segmentation at the time of this writing consists of a post hoc differentiation strategy called "product segmentation," any discussion of hotel industry segmentation must address the risks of a "product segmentation" that is not supported by market research, as opposed to pursuing a market-based segmentation strategy such as niche marketing.

Attracting true segments by both methods is possible (segment is defined as a group with similar needs and purchasing behavior). However, a priori segmentation, unless supported by market research, involves special risks.

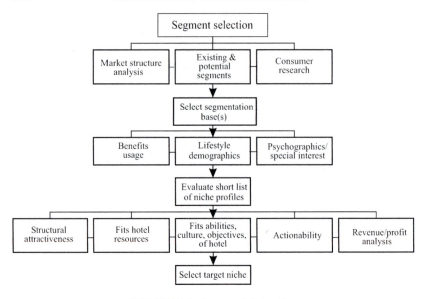

FIGURE 8.1. Segment Selection

The selection of a product segment that is not a true segment is possible. Because the group does not exhibit similar needs and purchasing behavior (e.g., the decision to specialize in mature tourists [55+], Europeans, or affluent tourists) does not address a true market segment since these groups are not homogenous,[6] the size, growth, needs, preferences, and/or purchasing behavior of your target segment may change. Without ongoing market research, you will be "flying blind" with your marketing and strategic planning.

In addition, you may miss significant new market trends, competitive threats, unidentified or neglected market niches, and major differences between competitive products in a product class (Struhl, 1992).

Segmentation Bases (Segmentation Variables)

We cited earlier the following segmentation variables used by the hotel industry to target segments and niche markets:

- Price segmentation (traditional, economy, upscale, ultra)
- Benefit segmentation (limited service hotels, business hotels)

- Psychographic/lifestyle segmentation (VALS, younger, active, health-conscious couples)
- Demographic segmentation (country, age, income, family size)
- Usage segmentation (frequent guest programs, RFM analysis used in relationship marketing)
- Special interest segmentation (ecotourists, culture tourists, health tourism)

Once we have examined our market structure and determined the available segment options, we must then undertake the task of segment selection. What criteria should be used for selecting your target segment?

Selection Methods for Smaller Resort Hotels

Smaller resort hotels are typically limited in their financial, technical, physical, and marketing resources. Therefore, there is an acute need for practical segmentation methods that are market based, relatively inexpensive, cost-effective, require a minimum of technical sophistication, and can be fitted to the resources and culture of the smaller resort hotel.

1. *Modify a successful target segmentation.* Choose a successful target segmentation that fits the selection criteria cited previously (including empirical support) and modify it to your particular market and hotel. Then position your hotel, services, promotions, and communications to this segment. The success of the Sandals chain in targeting young, active couples who prefer all-inclusive pricing is an example of selecting a niche that was built on an already proven model. This was the model responsible for the success of the French international resort hotel company known in the United States as Club Med, which originated the all-inclusive vacation concept. This "bundling" strategy has the added advantage (in addition to cost savings) that guests do not need to worry about money or extra costs during their vacations. This concept was modified to include couples only, and Sandals is now the most successful hotel company in Jamaica (Club Med, 1995).

2. *Use your guest register/customer database to profile your best customers.* Major service companies use database marketing to target

their best companies by RFM[7] and "lifetime value" analysis and build a relationship with these customers by tracking relevant guest data such as demographics, usage, family members, guest preferences (room type, child care facilities, business facilities, etc.) when they travel, their needs or requests, as well as their credit and purchase history. Larger hotels such as Marriott and Holiday Inn offer "frequent guest" programs that provide special benefits to guests for frequent stays. Furthermore, the achievement of successful niches allows for additional revenues from cross-marketing and the sale of additional products to your target niche.

3. *Find a gap in the present industry segmentation of the market.* Find a gap in the present industry segmentation of the market that meets the segment selection requirements outlined previously. By creating a perceptual map of your local market, using such attributes as product segmentation, price, target profile, customer preferences, and purchase intentions (Struhl, 1992), you may find unsatisfied gaps in your local market. Some of these gaps may be empirically verified to represent significant demand for your current or projected resort hotel offering. For example, (at the time of this writing) few resorts in Jamaica seem to be targeting singles, culture-oriented tourists, health and ecotourists, and tourists who would like clean, comfortable economy hotels (e.g., Motel 6)[8] while touring the country.

4. *Hire a market research consulting firm to do a segmentation study.* Hire a reputable consulting firm to research the attractive segments available in your particular market that conform to the selection criteria cited previously, confirm attractive a priori segments, and analyze your current customer base. Although a segmentation study can be relatively expensive, the investment often pays off over the long term in future revenues. You can inexpensively purchase secondary (previous) research from trade associations such as the Caribbean Tourism Association and the Jamaican tourist board. You can also reduce costs by forming strategic marketing alliances with other smaller hotels (Dev and Ellis, 1991). You may also want to talk to your consultants about setting up a guest database that is integrated with the reservation system.[9] This will enable you to automatically obtain guest information critical to selection of target niches, monitoring their profiles, needs, preferences, attitudes, and perceptions of your hotel. This information is used to continuously improve and

customize your promotions, services, and facilities to the needs and desires of your target niche.

NOTES

1. Hotels with fewer than 125 rooms.

2. I am indebted to Pat Morgan, the (European) manager of this hotel, for her assistance.

3. Monitoring, continuous improvement of customer satisfaction, employee performance, morale, and hotel processes.

4. Building long-term, mutually profitable interactive relationships with customers usually with the help of a customer database and personalized marketing.

5. Speedy, friendly, personalized service; long-term relationships with customers; responsiveness to complaints; a "good feeling" associated with the hotel.

6. For a contrary view that treats the affluent as a homogenous segment of the hotel market despite an opening remark dividing the affluent into three segments, see Mann (1993), "Marketing to the affluent: A look at their expectations and service standards," *Cornell Hotel and Restaurant Administration Quarterly,* 24(4) (February), 55-59.

7. Recency, Frequency, and Monetary value. This is a procedure adapted from direct marketing firms who, with considerable success, identify their best customers (using a weighted algorithim) related to the recency of their visits, the frequency of their visits, and their total amount of purchases. *Lifetime value analysis* computes the lifetime value of each customer (estimated revenues less costs over a five-to-ten-year time frame). Then all marketing projects are evaluated on their incremental effects on the lifetime value of the targeted customers (Hughes, 1994, pp. 87-104, 46-47).

8. For an interesting account of the Motel 6 success story based on solid market research using focus groups and guest surveys, see Cunningham and Dev (1992), "Strategic marketing: A lodging end run," *Cornell Hotel and Restaurant Administration Quarterly,* (August), 36-43.

9. For information on database marketing strategies for hotels, see Durr, 1989; Francese and Renaghan, 1990; Durocher and Niman, 1991; Nowakowski, 1991; Mondy and Hollingsworth, 1984; and Sparks, 1993.

BIBLIOGRAPHY

Bieber, T. (1989). Guest history systems: Maximizing the benefits. *Cornell Hotel and Restaurant Administration Quarterly,* 30(3) (November), pp. 20-22.

Camacho, F. (1988). Meeting the needs of senior citizens through lifecare communities: Marriot's approach to the development of a new service business. *Journal of Services Marketing,* 2(1) (Winter), pp. 49-53.

Caribbean Tourism Organization (CTO) (1995). Available online at www. transafrica forum.org/reports/tourism_issuebrief0700.pdf+Caribbean+Tourist+Organization +1995.

Club Med (1995). Annual Report.

Copulsky, J. and Wolf, M. (1991). Relationship marketing: Positioning for the future. *Journal of Business Strategy,* (July 8), pp. 16-26.

Cunningham, M. and Dev, S. (1992). Strategic marketing: A lodging "end run." *Cornell Hotel and Restaurant Administration Quarterly,* (August), pp. 36-43.

Dalgic, T. and Leeuw, M. (1994). Niche marketing revisited: Concept applications and some European cases. *European Journal of Marketing,* 6, pp. 69-82.

Deneen, S. (1993). Marketing Mother Nature. *Hotel and Motel Management,* 208(5) (March), p. 25.

Dev, C. and Ellis, B. (1991). Guest histories: An untapped service resource. *Cornell Hotel and Restaurant Administration Quarterly,* 52(2) (August), pp. 28-37.

Dev, C. and Hubbard, J. (1989). A strategic analysis of the lodging industry. *Cornell Hotel and Restaurant Administration Quarterly,* 30(1) (May), pp. 19-23.

Durocher, J. and Niman, N. (1991). Automated guest relations that generate hotel reservations. *Information Strategy: The Executives Journal,* 17(3) (Spring), pp. 27-30.

Durr, J. (1989) The value of the guest register. *Direct Marketing,* 52(5), pp. 48-55.

Escalera, K. (1994). Special-interest marketing builds business for hotels. *Hotel and Motel Management,* 209(19) (November), p. 50.

Francese, P. and Renaghan, L. (1990). Database marketing: Building consumer profiles. *Cornell Hotel and Restaurant Administration Quarterly,* 31(1) (May), pp. 60-63.

GMS (1993). Raw survey of Jamaican smaller resort hotels.

Goodrich, J. (1994). Health tourism: A new positioning strategy for tourist destinations. *Journal of International Consumer Marketing,* 6(3), pp. 227-238.

Hepworth, M. and Mateus, P. (1994). Connecting customer loyalty to the bottom line. *Canadian Business Review,* 21(4) (Winter), pp. 40-43.

Hotel and Motel Management (1995). Omni Hotels plays up to aficionados. 210(6) (April 24), p. 53.

Hughes, A. (1994). *Strategic Database Marketing.* Chicago: Probus Publishing Co.

Hunter, V. (1995). Database marketing revisited. *Target Marketing,* 18(5), pp. 59-74.

Kotler, P. (1991). *Marketing Management.* Englewood Cliffs, NJ: Prentice Hall.

Kotler, P., Haider, D., and Rein, I. (1993). *Marketing Places.* New York: Free Press.

Lewis, R. (1985). Predicting hotel choice: The factors underlying perception. *Cornell Hotel and Restaurant Administration Quarterly,* 25(4) (February), pp. 82-96.

Lewyn, M. (1994). Database: A new potent tool for selling. *BusinessWeek,* (September 5), pp. 56-62.

Liljander, V. and Strandvik, T. (1995). The nature of customer relationships in services. In Swartz, T., Bowen, D., and Brown, S. (Eds.), *Advances in Services Marketing and Management,* Volume 4. London: JAI Press.

Lodging Hospitality (1993). Rodeway seniors get choice room. 49(12), p. 11.

Mann, I. (1993). Marketing to the affluent: A look at their expectations and service standards. *Cornell Hotel and Restaurant Administration Quarterly,* 34(5) (October), pp. 55-59.

Mene, P. (1994). The winning practices of Baldridge award winner Ritz-Carlton Hotel Co. *Tapping the Network Journal,* 5(1) (Spring), pp. 10-14.

Mondy, R. and Hollingsworth, W. (1984). Getting the most from your club survey. *Cornell Hotel and Restaurant Administration Quarterly,* 24(4) (February), pp. 77-80.

Montague, D. (1991). Current guests are your best prospects. *Hotel and Motel Management,* 206(10) (June), p. 20.

Morritt, R. (1995). *Jamaica's Resort Hotels: Competing in the '90s in Caribbean and Latin American Economic Development: Progress and Challenges.* Ed. Lawson and Little, New York: St. Johns University Press, pp. 261-270.

Nascenzi (1988). Segmentation: The ideal way to find and target customers. *Bank Marketing* (February), pp. 36-39.

Nowakowski, J. (1991). The jewels of technology. *Lodging Hospitality,* 47(2) (Feburary), pp. 66-68.

Partlow, C. (1993). How Ritz-Carlton applies "TQM." *Cornell Hotel and Restaurant Quarterly,* 34(4) (August), pp. 16-24.

Raphel, M. (1994). The notebook in the host's pocket. *Direct Marketing,* 57(1) (May), pp. 18-20.

Rushmore, S. (1993). Beyond recycling: The ecotel. *Lodging Hospitality,* 49(9) (August), p. 20.

Schultz, R. (1994). A decade of segmentation. *Lodging Hospitality,* 50(10) (October), p. 20.

Selwitz, R. (1992a). Boston Four Seasons cultural connections help boost business. *Hotel and Motel Management,* 207(3) (February 24), pp. 2, 16.

Selwitz, R. (1992b). New York boutique hotel fills extended-stay market niche. *Hotel and Motel Management,* 207(21) (December 14), pp. 3, 39.

Sparks, B. (1993). Guest history: Is it being utilized? *International Journal of Contemporary Hospitality Management,* 5(1), pp. 22-27.

Struhl, S. (1992). *Market segmentation: An introduction and review.* Chicago: American Marketing Association.

Weinstein, A. (1995). *Market segmentation: Using demographics, psychographics, and other niche marketing techniques to predict and model customer behavior.* Chicago: Probus Publishing Co.

Yesawitch, P. (1987). Hospitality marketing for the '90s: Effective market research. *Cornell Hotel and Restaurant Administration Quarterly,* 28(1), pp. 48-57.

Yesawitch, P. (1991). Who are the guests of the '90s? *Lodging Hospitality,* 47(10) (October), p. 50.

Young, L. and Feigin, B. (1978). Some practical considerations in market segmentation. *Journal of Marketing Research,* 15(3) (August), pp. 405-412.

Chapter 9

Out in the Market: The History of the Gay Market Segment in the United States

Blaine J. Branchik

ABSTRACT

In recent years, the American gay market segment has been recognized by publications and businesses as large and lucrative. This widespread corporate interest and associated targeting activities are less than 30 years old. However, whether purposefully, or inadvertently, U.S. businesses have been marketing to gay consumers for well over 100 years. This market segment has developed as a result of a series of historical and societal events, paralleling the development of the gay community, and involving activities on the part of both buyers and sellers. This paper traces the evolution of the gay market segment from the late-nineteenth century to the beginning of the twenty-first century through three historical phases: (1) the Underground Phase, pre-1941; (2) the Community-Building Phase, 1941-1970; and (3) the Mainstream Phase, 1970-2000. A conceptual framework linking buyer and seller activities to historic events in these three phases is presented along with examples of products and services marketed to gay Americans within each phase.

This chapter was originally published in B. Branchik, *Journal of Macromarketing,* (June 2002), pp. 86-97, copyright 2002 by Sage Publications, Inc. Reprinted by permission of Sage Publications, Inc.

The author thanks Dr. Eric H. Shaw for his course in the development of marketing thought, which provided the genesis for this paper, and for his invaluable editorial advice and support.

211

INTRODUCTION

Numerous books and articles have been written recently about the gay market in the United States (e.g., Chasin 2000; Fejes 2000; Gluckman and Reed 1997; Kates 1998; Lukenbill 1999; Wardlow 1996). These works address the demographics of the gay market segment (Kates 1998; Lukenbill 1999), discuss the lengths to which firms are going to target their products at them (Fejes 2000; Peñaloza 1996), and provide advice on how to succeed with this "affluent dream market" segment (Kates 1998; Lukenbill 1999). Advertisements for a variety of broad-based products from furniture to automobiles target the gay market segment. Television shows such as *Will and Grace* and *Queer As Folk* bring gay viewers to network programs and their associated commercial sponsors.

This well-acknowledged market, so written about and addressed of late, appears to be a recent phenomenon. Although various works in the literature argue whether a gay market segment exists (Peñaloza 1996; Fejes 2000) or does not exist (Fugate 1993), the reality is that, whether inadvertently or purposefully, American businesses have been marketing products and services to gays for over 100 years.

The development and growth of this market segment parallels the development of the gay community and gay rights movement in the United States, and is punctuated with key historical and societal events that acted as catalysts to propel the segment forward in terms of recognition, size, and identifiability.

Definitions

To avoid confusion, it is important to define terms used in this paper. The term *gay* refers to male homosexuals. A four-dimensional definition of the term includes desire for and attraction to other men, behaviors associated with that desire, identification as gay or homosexual (Laumann et al. 1994), and a perception of belonging to a larger gay community (Herdt 1992; Laumann et al. 1994; Thompson 1988).

The term "gay" has been in use since the early twentieth century to denote homosexual men. There are instances of the word "gay" being used to describe gay men throughout the 1930s and 1940s. A 1933 dictionary of slang defines a gay cat as a homosexual boy (Ersine 1935). In 1941, gay is defined as an "adjective used almost exclusively by homosexuals to denote homosexuality" (Lighter 1994). A diary entry recalls that two gay men meeting on a train, for example, might ask each other if there are "any gay spots" in the destination city (Painter 1941, p. 170). Another diary entry from October 22, 1946, discusses how one young man threw ". . . a few words like 'gay'. . . to follow the lead on" (Finch 1946). By the early 1950s, it had become the popular term used by gay men to describe themselves (Chauncey 1994).

Two other terms that must be specified for purposes of this paper include *marketing* and *market segment*. This paper is based on the premise that marketing is a process involving both buyers and sellers (Alderson 1957; Kotler and Levy 1973). Alderson notes "buyers no less than marketing executives come into the market to solve problems" (Alderson 1957, p. 163), and that "exchange takes place because each party to the transaction has a surplus of one product and a deficit of another" (Alderson 1957, p. 195). The purchasing aspect of marketing has become so neglected in defining the term "marketing" due to the advent of marketing management, that Kotler and Levy (1973) had to remind marketing academicians and practitioners that "Buying Is Marketing, Too!" Within this context, a market segment results from the process of sellers differentiating products and services to appeal to the specific needs of groups of buyers as well as buyers searching out sellers who offer the product/service variations that best meet their needs (Alderson 1957). The notion of proactive consumers is important because for the first 50 to 75 years of the history of the U.S. gay market segment, sellers mostly serviced the gay market inadvertently. Consequently, it was gay consumers who drove the segment and therefore conducted the bulk of effort in the marketing relationship.

Phased Historical Framework

The purpose of this paper is to chronicle the development of the American gay market segment from the late-nineteenth century to the present day. It is divided into three sections, each comprising an historic phase in the development of the U.S. gay market segment:

(1) The Underground Phase, pre-1941; (2) the Community-Building Phase, 1941-1970; and (3) the Mainstream Phase, 1970-2000. A framework containing key information presented in this paper can be found on Table 9.1. This table includes the phases, associated historical drivers, and summaries of activities undertaken by buyers and sellers during the respective historical phase.

This paper is intended to contribute to the marketing history literature by its development of the above conceptual framework, applicable to the study of any market segment, that incorporates both buyer and seller activities within a multiphased historical context. As discussed above, key to this framework is the notion that both buyers and sellers interact to create a market segment. In addition, it is intended to demonstrate how the development of a market segment is not necessarily a gradual evolutionary process. Rather, its growth is erratic, punctuated by historic events and eras.

This paper also highlights the multidimensional nature of a segment's development in terms of multiple product and service categories and multiple facets of society. These facets include demographic, social, sexual, economic, geographic, political, technological, public health, material culture, communication, and commercial considerations. Finally, this study reveals the interdependence of the relevant product and service categories and facets of society.

Each section of this paper overviews the cultural or historical milestones that characterize that phase, summarizes activities undertaken by both sellers and buyers as a result of those historical drivers, and provides examples of product or service categories and offerings that businesses marketed to the gay niche during that phase.

PRE-1941: THE UNDERGROUND PHASE

Urbanization resulting from the industrial revolution and mass immigration was undoubtedly key to the creation of an identifiable gay community in the United States (D'Emilio 1983) and, in turn, the gay market segment. Beginning in the mid-nineteenth century, men were no longer tied to the farm in order to live. Further, they no longer had the accompanying need to produce offspring to work the farms. As a result, good jobs and the promise of a better life lured men from the

TABLE 9.1. Gay Market Segment Framework of Historical Drivers and Buyer/ Seller Activities

Phase	Historical Drivers	Buyers	Sellers
I. Underground Pre-1941	Urbanization; Industrial revolution; *Gay migration to cities, seeking out others, forming relationships**	Gathering; Seeking out others; Establishing shopping patterns in new cities; Driving segmentation as function of gathering & self-revealing; Vendor selection based on convenience & location	No targeting; Unaware—inadvertent servicing of the segment; Accommodating/tolerating; Exceptions: bars and sex-oriented venues; Service businesses growing to service new arrivals
II. Community Building 1941-1970	WWII relocations; ONE vs. Oleson Supreme Court ruling; Stonewall gay riots; *Establishment of gay-friendly neighborhoods and gay-owned businesses**	Establishment of self-sustaining neighborhoods; Using mail-order for access to gay literature, gay-targeted products	Gay-owned businesses forming— bars, magazine, mail-order; No mainstream targeting; Continued accommodation by some businesses; Gay press develops with associated need for advertisers
III. Mainstream 1970-2000	Gay rights movement; Sexual revolution; Consumer movement; Formation of religious right; AIDS; *Gay acceptance by and integration into mainstream consumer economy**	Integration into larger society; Becoming visible to marketers; Patronizing sellers who target gays	Increasing social acceptance; Studies completed on size and wealth of market; Fear of boycotts; Proactive mainstream targeting; Advertising in mainstream media; AIDS industry formation

*Italicized entries in the historical drivers column denotes results of the drivers directly related to the development of the gay community and gay market segment.

household economy into the workplace. At the same time, people began buying goods—such as foodstuffs—that had formerly been produced at home. Cities grew and populations shifted from field to factory.

As urbanization took place, a class of men freed from the constraints of small-town life recognized their attraction to other men and acknowledged that interest as a characteristic that distinguished them from others. Once arrived in cities with their dense populations, these strangers followed basic human drives to seek out others like themselves, to make themselves known to each other, and to form relationships (Maslow 1954; Alderfer 1972) with those whom they shared characteristics including, but not limited to, their sexuality. Similar patterns were taking place with gay men in cities and towns across the United States. Although by the beginning of the twentieth century, homosexuality was seen as a phenomenon of mostly larger cities (Parke 1906; Ellis 1942), as early as 1889, an American physician wrote that there was "in every community of any size a colony of male sexual perverts; they are usually known to each other, and are likely to congregate together" (Lydston 1889, p. 254). Magnus Hirschfield, the German physician who established the first Institute of Sexual Science in Berlin in 1920, found homosexuality widespread in Philadelphia and Boston, two cities where he focused his studies of homosexuality (Hirschfield 1920).

As this gathering took place, these men were contending with the practicalities of food, clothing, shelter, and employment. Marketers, unaware for the most part of this nascent community and market segment, only serviced the segment inadvertently or unknowingly. Three notable exceptions were bathhouses, brothels, and bars. With their majority-gay clientele, proprietors of these businesses were the first to actually target the gay market segment. Notwithstanding these exceptions, however, the effort expended in the marketing process was overwhelmingly left to the buyer. In addition to bathhouses, brothels, and bars, this section also examines clothiers, lodgings, restaurants, and a gay-friendly resort town.

Bathhouses and Brothels

Gay brothels and bathhouses have existed since the late-1800s. As early as 1879, a Saint Louis newspaper reported that a house of prostitution had been raided and that four of eight prostitutes arrested were men (Burnham 1973).

In the 1890s in New York, an in-depth investigation of brothels, gambling houses, and saloons by Reverend Charles Parkhurst uncovered a multitude of brothels featuring male prostitutes servicing male clientele, including the Golden Rule Pleasure Club (Gardner 1931), Manila Hall, The Black Rabbit, The Palm, and Paresis Hall (Gardner 1931; Mazet 1897). In 1902, a bathhouse in New York, the Ariston Baths, was documented by police reports (Jerome 1905).

In San Francisco in the 1930s, Jack's Turkish Baths and Third Street Baths opened, servicing an exclusively gay clientele (Higgs 1999).

Bars

Along with bathhouses and brothels, gay bars were among the first businesses that serviced gay clientele, at a time when homosexual gatherings themselves were illegal. In 1908, Vito Lorenzo's Saloon was charged with being a "fairy place" (Canal 1908).

On the West Coast, Dash, a dance hall and saloon that featured female impersonators, became San Francisco's first identifiable gay bar in 1908 (and closed in the same year). About 1910, following the rebuilding of San Francisco after the 1906 earthquake, San Francisco society and many gay bars relocated to the Fillmore District. One of the gay bars to relocate was the Lion's Pub, which exists to this day (Higgs 1999).

By the 1920s, there were so many gay bars and clubs in cities like New York that they began differentiating their offerings to various market segments much like businesses in any maturing industry. In the case of New York bars, differentiation was based on their target clients' social class or "type" (D'Emilio 1983). In the early 1940s, the oval-shaped bar of the upscale Astor Hotel in New York was known to have a gay side and a heterosexual side (Kaiser 1997).

In the early 1930s, a speakeasy located on East 28th Street in New York that wanted to attract gay patrons noted suggestively that it was located "in the Gay 20's" (Chauncey 1994, p. 19).

Following raids, the New York State Liquor Authority reports and court testimony from the 1930s describe such gay bars as Gloria's (Gloria 1940) and Consolidated Bar and Grill (Horowitz 1939). Gloria's and another bar called Benny's were accepted in a 1939 diary entry (Finch 1946).

Clothing

During this period, as throughout gay history, gay men used clothing as a way of signaling their "gayness" to other gay men. One prime example from the 1890s into the 1940s was a red tie (Chicago 1911; Werther 1922; Kiernan 1916; Kaiser 1997). In his landmark, two-volume *Studies in the Psychology of Sex,* first published in the United States in 1905, psychologist Havelock Ellis, described as the foremost living authority on the psychology of sex in the foreword to the 1936 edition of the work, noted that ". . . there has been a fashion for a red tie to be adopted by inverts (gay men) as their badge." He went on to state "this is particularly marked among the 'fairies' (as a fellator is there termed) in New York" (Ellis 1942, p. 300). He then goes on to state that a few of his presumably heterosexual medical school colleagues ". . . had the courage to wear a red tie . . ." as an experiment. Those who did "never repeated the experiment again," due to the propositions or harassment they received (Ellis 1942, p. 300). In the 1930s green suits, tight-cuffed trousers, flowered bathing trunks, and one-half length flaring topcoats were considered distinctively gay attire (Painter 1941). Gay men managed to find clothing merchants to sell them these relatively specialized items of clothing that had little demand in the broader male market.

Rooming Houses and Apartments

All of the single young men arriving in large cities at this period required housing. Rooming houses and other housing options were created to meet that pressing market need. Inadvertently, the YMCA became one of the key housing providers for gay men newly arrived in large cities, such as New York. The YMCA began building men's dormitories in 1896, and by the 1920s there were seven YMCA residential hotels in New York alone. The "Y" provided low-cost, private accommodation. At the Y, young single men living alone were not considered strange at all. In fact, that was the market segment to which the dormitories were targeted. Many diaries, accounts, and interviews throughout this period indicate that the Y dormitories were well-known housing options for gay men in large cities through World War II (Chauncey 1994; Bérubé 1990).

As gay men entered the workforce and became more affluent, a variety of resident-hotels in New York were built early in the twentieth century differentiating themselves from offerings such as the Y, with more luxurious accommodations for wealthier, more established single men. Apartments followed the resident hotels in the 1920s and 1930s. Gay men tended to choose accommodations in specific buildings located in neighborhoods desirable to them. As a result of friendly referrals and word of mouth, certain apartment buildings soon had large numbers of gay tenants.

Restaurants

Gay men living in apartments or rooming houses were seldom knowledgeable about cooking and generally took meals out. Whether expressly or accidentally, restaurateurs in areas where gay men tended to live, work, and socialize found themselves catering to the gay market.

Early in the twentieth century, low-cost restaurants in New York such as Life Cafeteria and Child's (first opened in 1899, with over 44 New York City locations by 1939) appealed to the gay clientele living in rooming houses and apartments. They differentiated themselves from other eating options with low prices and fast service. Although not expressly targeting gay consumers, several Child's locations became meeting spots for gay men based on their locations (Chauncey 1994). *Vanity Fair's* 1931 guide to New York informed readers that the Child's Restaurant located in New York's Paramount Theater building was particularly interesting because it "features a dash of lavender" (Shaw 1931, p. 40), a color long associated with homosexuality. One gay man stated in an interview that after midnight the location was "taken over" by gay men (Chauncey 1994, p. 166). Other Child's locations on 5th Avenue at 59th Street and another at 49th Street were said to be gay meeting places according to interviews and the newspaper *Broadway Brevities* (Kahan 1926). Enrico's, an Italian restaurant in New York City, had a reputation for being a hangout for "perverts" and was put under surveillance in one of a myriad of crackdowns on prostitution and perversion (New York City Investigator's Report 1919).

In the 1920s and 1930s, restaurants began differentiating themselves to reach different consumer segments. Examples in New York included Louis' Restaurant on West 49th St. and Jewel Restaurant on West 48th St. These restaurants became meeting spots for successful, more established gay men. An important development in the gay market in the 1920s was that restaurants described above and others were not only tolerating gay clientele, they were becoming predominantly gay. Many were noted as such both in vice squad reports and in a Broadway gossip sheet, which referred to them as a rendezvous for the "queer smart trade" (Chauncey 1994, p. 175).

A 1936 article in the publication *Current Psychology and Psychoanalysis* described how "boy(s) assuming the usual feminine characteristics . . ." ". . . usually known as 'pansies'" congregated at a large, brightly lit cafeteria in Greenwich Village (Duberman 1991, p. 161).

Describing Stewart's and the Life Cafeteria, two eating establishments on Christopher Street in Greenwich Village, the 1939 WPA Guide to New York City described it as one of the "few obviously Bohemian spots in the Village," and went on to explain that in the "evenings the more conventional occupy tables in one section of the room and watch the 'show' of the eccentrics on the other side" (WPA Guide to New York City 1939). Other accounts in tour books indicate that restaurants were not only catering to gay men as patrons, but were in essence using them to draw gawkers and tourists to view "real" bohemian life.

Resorts

Businesses such as restaurants, guesthouses, bars, and shops in resort towns have targeted or at least welcomed gay customers as early as the turn of the twentieth century. Provincetown, Massachusetts, was a haven for artists and writers, attracting many gays as both seasonal and year-round residents (Weathers et al. 1979).

1941-1970: THE COMMUNITY-BUILDING PHASE

The period in the development of the gay market that spans the years 1941 to 1970 can be referred to as the Community-Building Phase. This phase includes World War II, the post-World War II backdrop of McCarthyism, the rapid expansion of the gay press, the sexual revolution, and consumer movement, and culminates in the 1969 Stonewall riots that symbolically launched the gay liberation movement in the United States. During this period, gay neighborhoods and communities grew in large U.S. cities.

World War II had a significant impact on the development of the gay community and associated market segment. Within six months of the Japanese attack on Pearl Harbor, 14,000 men were entering 250 different training centers every day (Bérubé 1990), one of the greatest relocations and concentrations of men in gender-segregated living situations in history. With this gathering of men from all parts of the country, gay men were able to find others like themselves. In addition, they were able to see various parts of the country, including large port cities that led to the establishment or growth of gay neighborhoods after the war in cities like San Francisco and New York. With the growth of gay neighborhoods came the expansion of gay-owned businesses catering to gay clients within gay neighborhoods and a movement within the gay community and its businesses to take care of their own.

In its 1958 decision *Publication* ONE *vs. Oleson,* the U.S. Supreme Court ruled that gay-related materials were not obscene per se, opening the way for an explosion in local gay press and the distribution of gay-oriented materials via mail (Streitmatter 1995). This decision led to the rapid development of gay newspapers in communities around the country. With the growing scope of the gay press, marketers and their advertisements could target gay consumers as never before. This landmark was key in the development of the gay market segment. To this day, advertising in the gay press remains the most common way for firms to reach the gay market niche.

Finally, on June 27, 1969, a routine police raid of the Stonewall Inn gay bar in Greenwich Village in New York erupted into a days-long gay riot. By June 28, 1969, amidst graffiti throughout Greenwich Village calling for "gay power" and with the formation of the Gay Liberation Front, the American gay rights movement had its symbolic beginning (D'Emilio 1983).

These landmark events, aided by the sexual revolution of the 1960s, led to the development of the gay community. As a result, American gays entered the Community-Building phase as an underground, albeit growing, market segment and ended the phase as a large, identifiable target market.

Bars and Restaurants

Spurred by the concentration of men in large and port cities resulting from the Second World War, gay bars were flourishing in the 1940s, with supply in these cities struggling to keep pace with growing demand. By the 1940s, San Francisco's Finocchio's, which featured female impersonators, became the city's most popular site for gay men and women (Higgs 1999, p. 171). Money to fund these bars often came from shady sources. In the East, gay bars were stated to be owned and controlled by organized crime (Doty 1963). However, in San Francisco, 25 to 30 percent of gay bars were actually owned by gay men and lesbians (Escoffier 1997).

By the 1940s, gay bars were opening in small cities across the United States, including Kansas City, Missouri; Worcester, Massachusetts; San Jose, California (D'Emilio 1983); and Richmond, Virginia (Swisher 1988).

As in previous decades, subtle signals and codes continued to be used by businesses targeting gay patrons. The Cyrano Restaurant in Manhattan let gay men know that they were welcome at the restaurant by billing itself "Where the Gay Set Meet for Dinner" (Cherry Grove Arts Council 1951).

In a 1963 article describing the raids of two gay bars in New York, the Fawn and the Heights Supper Club were described as "notorious congregating points for homosexuals" by the chairman of the New York State Liquor Authority (Doty 1963).

The Gay Press, Literature, and Magazines

The late 1940s and 1950s saw the emergence of the gay-oriented press, a milestone in the history of the gay market segment and, according to a well-known gay historian, the "only significant victory (for the gay rights movement) during the 1950s" (D'Emilio 1983, p. 115). These publications played a seminal role in enabling businesses to target the gay market via advertising. Finally, there was a means to reach this invisible market.

In 1954, what is thought to be the first advertisement in a gay publication was run in *ONE,* a Los Angeles-based gay publication with peak mail-based circulation of 5,000, begun in 1952 with mostly political and social commentary. The advertisement was for men's pajamas and underwear (Streitmatter 1995).

This advertisement was noteworthy not only for its historical context, but also for its ultimate impact on the gay press and associated advertising. It was this particular issue of *ONE* that inadvertently created an explosion in gay publications nationally. After a letter from U.S. Senator Alexander Wiley of Wisconsin to Postmaster General Arthur Summerfield resulted in the issue's confiscation by postal officials who described the publication as "obscene, lewd, lascivious and filthy" (Streitmatter 1995, p. 33), charges were filed against the publication under the Comstock Law, an 1873 law dealing with obscene materials in the U.S. mails. The *ONE* trial ultimately made its way to the U.S. Supreme Court. In 1958, the court sided with *ONE,* in essence opening the way for local gay publications all over the United States. According to *Our Own Voices: A Directory of Lesbian and Gay Periodicals,* by 1972, there were 150 gay publications being produced nationally (Streitmatter 1995). Accompanying this publishing explosion was the growing need—and outlet—for advertisers. And by the late-1960s, local gay publications were turning a profit based on advertisements from mostly local gay businesses (Chasin, 2000).

Although physical culture magazines had been finding their niche in the gay market since the turn of the twentieth century, two gay magazine publishers, Bruce of Los Angeles and The Athletic Model Guild, began publishing physical culture magazines, the most popular of which, *Physique Pictorial,* began in 1951. These were pocket-sized magazines created for a gay audience containing photos of scantily clad men. By 1958, there were several dozens of physique magazines with titles such as *Guild Pictorial, Adonis,* and *American Apollo* serving as many as 70,000 readers (Streitmatter 1995).

Gay Neighborhoods

By the 1940s, in New York City, which along with San Francisco formed the centers of urban gay America, gays were already creating identifiable gay-friendly neighborhoods. Gay male residential and commercial enclaves in New York included the Bowery, Greenwich Village, Times Square, and Harlem. In these neighborhoods, a variety of businesses sprang up to service gay residents. Although many moral crusaders were shocked, small entrepreneurs ignored the "disreputable" nature of their gay patrons—primarily because they were a significant source of revenue. And a growing number of small businesses actively encouraged the patronage of openly gay men because once they became known as gay-welcoming businesses, they attracted other gay customers (Chauncey 1994).

In the 1950s and 1960s, the growth of gay neighborhoods accelerated as gay World War II veterans settled in cities they had seen during the war. These expanding neighborhoods spawned various gay businesses to service their residents. In San Francisco, the Italian neighborhood of North Beach became the gay neighborhood, attracting bohemian gay artists and poets. The group of gay and bisexual poets and writers known as the Beat Generation, including Allen Ginsberg, William Burroughs, Jack Kerouac, and Neal Cassidy, gathered at the Northern Lights Bookstore to read their works. Ginsberg, who discussed his homosexuality and that of his beat colleagues in several interviews, read his groundbreaking poem "Howl" there for the first time in 1955 (Young 1974; Wallace and Stiller 1986). The Black Cat Café in the same neighborhoods served as a bar and gathering place for drag queens and transvestites (Higgs 1999).

By the late 1950s and the early 1960s, as gay neighborhoods began to form true communities, gays began setting down roots and seeing themselves as a minority who needed to "take care of their own" in an economic sense as well as a social sense. This was another important development in the history of the American gay market. Bars, baths, adult bookstores, and mail order services explicitly or subtly targeted the gay market segment in cities throughout the United States. Gay entrepreneurs owned many of these businesses (Gluckman and Reed 1997).

A 1963 *New York Times* article discussing the "problem of homosexuality" estimated that one-half of the estimated 100,000 to 600,000 gay men in New York City were drawn to the East Greenwich Village, parts of the East Side, the "West 70s," and the area around Eighth Avenue and 42nd Street. In the first three areas, the *Times* article states that " . . . the homosexuals have their own restaurants and bars . . ." and clothing stores (Doty 1963).

In response to ongoing raids on their businesses and scandals involving payoffs to police officers, gay bar owners formed the Tavern Guild in San Francisco in 1961. Their goal was to ensure the safety and continued operations of their businesses targeting the gay market in the city which *Life* magazine named the "Gay Capital" of the United States in 1964 (Higgs 1999, p. 176).

In 1969, the Stonewall riots changed the course of gay history, sparking the gay rights movement and changing how gays saw themselves and ultimately how the public, including marketers, saw them.

1970-2000: THE MAINSTREAM PHASE

Following on the heels of the 1969 Stonewall riots, the Mainstream Phase saw an exponential growth in the visibility and acknowledged desirability of the gay market that paralleled the exploding gay liberation movement. For the first time, mainstream national news media were speaking about the size and affluence of the gay market—a market increasingly targeted by mainstream sellers. Multinational corporations launched marketing campaigns aimed at the gay market. Concurrently, the rise of the religious right in the United States had a dampening effect on the euphoria the gay community felt about its power, and the enthusiasm that corporations felt about its financial potential.

With the onset of the AIDS epidemic in the early to mid-1980s and the growing clout of socially conservative groups, businesses moved more cautiously, uncertain of the impact AIDS would have on the gay niche market and continually concerned about possible product boycotts by the religious right. This phase also saw the formation of a product/service category built around AIDS and the provision of products and services to appeal to gay men with AIDS.

In the 1990s, as a result of promising AIDS treatments, the end of the conservative Reagan/Bush era, and society's growing acceptance of homosexuality, businesses began to realize that the gay market would not disappear. Recognized now by businesses as an affluent minority market with relatively high disposable income, the gay market has been targeted by an ever-growing variety of industries, portrayed in growing numbers of films and television shows, and profiled in a multitude of articles and books targeted at businesses wanting to reach this market. Several examples of these gay-targeted marketing activities are provided below.

A Desirable Market Segment

By the mid-1970s, mainstream business publications were acknowledging the size and the desirability of the gay market, noting "gays have gained the attention of marketers in such mainstream corporations as Adolph Coors Company, Chartered Bank of London, and Hertz Corp" (Weathers et al. 1979).

A 1977 market survey found that the average income for readers of *The Advocate,* a gay magazine, was about 50 percent above the national average. In addition, 79 percent of readers used commercial airlines for an average of nearly four trips a year, 80 percent ordered drinks by brand name, and 70 percent were college graduates. Another study indicated that gays controlled an amazing 19 percent of spendable income in the United States (Weathers et al. 1979).

In 1988, a market survey by Simmons Market Research mailed to readers of eight gay and lesbian newspapers that belonged to the National Gay Newspaper Guild generated significant publicity about the gay market. Simmons reported the average per capita gay income of $36,800, versus $12,287 for the population as a whole; 60 percent versus 18 percent with college degrees; 49 percent versus 16 percent in managerial or professional positions. Showing similar results was a 1990 survey by Overlooked Opinions, a Chicago-based marketing company focused on the gay market (Baker 1997).

In the early 1980s the national gay population based on Kinsey Institute's 1960s estimates was about 8 to 10 million. The combined gay populations of New York, San Francisco, Los Angeles, and Washington totaled only 1.35 million. That meant that 7 to 8 million gays and lesbians lived outside these major areas, and could be an untapped niche-within-the-niche.

Mainstream Businesses Target the Market Segment

A myriad of mainstream corporations began marketing to the gay segment in the 1970s. Budget Rent a Car advertised in *The Advocate* in the 1970s. Fidelity Savings & Loan Association, one of the top 15 savings and loans in California at the time, sponsored a printing of a gay business owners' guide in San Francisco.

In 1979, the first Absolut vodka advertisement ran in *The Advocate*. This represented the first launch of a mainstream national brand to the gay market segment. As in the case of most if not all mainstream campaigns to target the gay market, the move was based on pragmatic business judgment. Carillon Importers of New Jersey, who imported Absolut, were willing to take this risk because they were responsible for launching a new, unknown brand into a crowded market. Their mission was to find a desirable niche market and gain a foothold there. The gay market was their chosen niche.

The 1990s was the decade that saw an explosion in gay market targeting by mainstream organizations in a variety of industries such as technology, financial services, telecommunications, travel, and even furniture.

In 1990, Ikea, an international furniture company, aired what is thought to be the first national television advertisement featuring an openly gay couple. Part of Ikea's "life-stages campaign," the ad featured a gay couple shopping for a dining room table (Gallagher 1994).

Apple Computer began advertising its Powerbook in national gay magazines in 1993, the first Silicon Valley firm to invest significant amounts in marketing to the gay community. In 1993, MCI targeted a very large direct mail effort at the gay market for their residential long distance services, followed by AT&T in 1994. It is interesting to note that the AT&T mailer, though a follower to MCI's, was the more successful of the two. The AT&T piece was far more open about the gay and lesbian focus of the campaign and used more obvious language and images and included information on its own gay and lesbian employee organization (Gallagher 1994).

In 1994, People's Bank of Bridgeport issued the first of two "affinity" credit cards, Uncommon Clout Mastercard and Visa. The PointOne credit card, also targeting the gay market, was launched soon after that. American Airlines created a unit in its marketing department dedicated to marketing to gays and lesbians. Although American's gay and lesbian marketing group's budget was a mere $300,000, the incremental revenues that the airline attributed directly to this marketing expenditure totaled $193.5 million by 1999 (Hussein 2000).

Between 1991 and 1993 alone, *American Demographics, The Wall Street Journal, New York Times, Advertising Age,* and other mainstream publications featured articles about the gay market niche (Chasin 2000). Among the scores of articles that appeared in publications nationwide addressing the gay market, titles included "The Gay Market: Nothing to Fear But Fear Itself"; "Untapped Niche Offers Marketers Brand Loyalty"; and "Mainstream's Domino Effect: Liquor, Fragrance, Clothing Advertisers Ease into Gay Magazines" (Gluckman and Reed 1997). And in 1998 and 1999, two different books targeted at mainstream corporations on how to capture the gay market were published: *Untold Millions: Secret Truths About Marketing to Gay and Lesbian Consumers* (c.f. Lukenbill 1999) and *Twenty Million New Customers! Understanding Gay Men's Consumer Behavior* (c.f. Kates 1998).

In 1998, Fannie Mae, AT&T, Sony, IBM, Wells Fargo, and America Online, all big, well-known corporations, sponsored the Media Awards hosted by the Gay and Lesbian Alliance Against Defamation (GLAAD) in New York (Lukenbill 1999).

With all the marketing campaigns targeting potential gay patrons, it must be said that there is still a long way to go to have blanket targeting of the gay market by most mainstream companies on all levels. Gay publications were still attracting only a few well-paying national advertisers, like Absolut vodka and Remy Martin cognac (Gay Press Looks, 1990).

Gay Literature, Newspapers, and Magazines

The gay media, which had its tentative beginnings in the 1940s and healthy growth in the 1960s, exploded in the 1970s on a national basis. Examples of gay-owned media companies that began in the early 1970s are Liberations Publications—publishers of *The Advocate* national gay news magazine; Washington's Lambda Rising bookstore chain and mail order service; other bookstores, such as A Different Light in San Francisco and Oscar Wilde Memorial Bookstore in New York; community newspapers like *The New York Native* and the *Washington Blade* (originally the *Gay Blade*); and Bob Damron's guide to gay bars, baths, and sites of interest. Even venerable travel writers Fodor's began offering *Fodor's Gay Guide* series to Amsterdam, Los Angeles, New York, San Francisco, South Florida, and U.S. regions in the mid-1990s. These firms and publications represented not only businesses targeting the gay market, but also served as vehicles to permit advertisers to reach the gay market segment as well.

In response to the availability of mainstream ad dollars, the years 1992 to 1995 saw the launch of a series of glossy, national publications targeting the gay and lesbian reader. These included *Out, Genre, Ten Percent, POZ, Urban Fitness, Mens' Style, Wilde,* and *50/50.*

Theater, Television, and Cinema

A 1971 attempt by the film industry to deal with the subject of homosexuality and to target a gay audience failed. A critically acclaimed film by Academy Award-winning director John Schlesinger, *Sunday Bloody Sunday,* about a heterosexual couple attracted to the same man, failed financially. Gay characters experienced more success on television. From 1977 to 1981, actor/comedian Billy Crystal played a groundbreaking role as a gay man in the very successful television show *Soap* (Poniewozik 2000).

By the early pre-AIDS 1980s, the film company executives forgot their tentative and unsuccessful early steps and began targeting the gay market with many feature films. Included were Paramount Pictures' *Partners* about two New York City policemen, one gay, one straight; 20th Century Fox's *Making Love,* about a doctor who leaves his wife for a man; Warner Bros.' *Personal Best,* about two female Olympic athletes who fall in love; *Deathtrap,* about two lovers who murder one of their wives; and MGM/UA's *Victor/Victoria,* which featured Julie Andrews as a male female impersonator (Chasin 2000).

The succession of gay-themed films produced in the pre-AIDS early 1980s was cut short by the epidemic. From 1984 through the end of the decade, the number of gay-themed films declined, with the exception of those dealing with AIDS. This was in reaction both to the conservatism of the Reagan era and the AIDS epidemic, which brought gays center stage but not in the way that fostered marketers' interest (Chasin 2000).

By the end of the 1990s, gays had made great strides on television series. At that time, there were more than 30 gay or lesbian characters on prime-time television shows such as *Will and Grace, Mission Hill, Oh Grow Up, Wasteland,* and *Action* (Poniewozik 1999).

Travel and Tourism

The 1970s saw the rapid growth of tourism marketing targeted at gay travelers. In 1970 Linblad Travel, Inc., started offering tour packages for gay men. A former vice president, Hanns Ebensten, stated that "people were appalled" and straight publications rejected his firm's ads targeting gay travelers. However, by the late 1970s, ads for his firm were running in straight as well as gay publications (Bianco 1999, pp. 214-215).

By the 1970s, several resort towns began competing for the gay vacationer's dollars. In Provincetown, Massachusetts, 50 percent of income-producing property was owned by and catered to gays. The properties housed guesthouses, bars, restaurants, boutiques, and gift shops. However, according to one *Newsweek* report, people were very worried that the town would be taken over by gays (Weathers et al. 1979). At The Pines on Fire Island, New York, discos catering to gay clientele had become so successful, they were attracting a growing straight clientele. Guerneville, California, 85 miles north of San Francisco, had several gay-targeted resorts. Fort Lauderdale, Florida, had 15 gay hotels and motels, 17 gay nightclubs, nine gay restaurants, and even a gay church. In Key West, Florida, the gay influx was blamed for skyrocketing property values (Weathers et al. 1979).

These examples illustrate that travel and leisure industry vendors and municipalities, eager for tourist dollars, recognized the size and affluence of the gay market segment and were able to match their amenities and sites to the segment's needs.

Growth of the Religious Right and Mainstream Marketing

Starting with Anita Bryant's campaign to remove sexual orientation from the Dade County Florida Human Rights Ordinance in the late 1970s, the religious right realized its power relative to gays and lesbians early in the 1980s. Certain religious groups decried a moral decay in the United States and saw gay men as one of the groups most responsible. With the power of the religious right came fears by mainstream marketers of an antigay backlash. This fear manifested itself in the unwillingness of mainstream marketers to use gay celebrities in endorsements. When it was discovered in 1981 that tennis great Billie Jean King had had a lesbian affair, for example, lucrative endorsement deals dried up.

To avoid these concerns, firms created ad campaigns targeting gays but resorted to tactics they had used 50 years earlier by using subtle gay-oriented signals. Calvin Klein jean advertisements were a classic example of this "gay window" advertising. The ads featured young shirtless men in a variety of poses for different Klein fashion lines. At the time, Calvin Klein spokespeople claimed that they were trying to appeal to a much broader target.

Paco Rabanne, a maker of men's cologne, had a series of suggestive ads featuring a man on a bed talking on the phone. At the time, Ogilvy & Mather, the firm that designed the ad campaign, said the ads were not specifically targeting gay men. However, they admitted that gays were an important market for them.

Fear of a religious right boycott was not the only reason that corporations did not target the gay market directly. Personal prejudices and discomfort played a role as well. Joe DiSabato, an advertising executive (Stabiner, 1982), was frustrated by his attempts to get his male client executives to target gay markets directly. A man will approach this with one of three different attitudes, assuming that the product is appropriate for the market: (1) he's had thoughts of homosexuality and is scared to death of confronting them, so he doesn't want to deal with it; (2) he's gay and he's closeted, so he doesn't want to deal with it; (3) he's straight and has no problem with it, in which case he can deal with it. However, there were not many of the straight executives who fit into the "no problem" category (Stabiner 1982).

Unique Niche Products

One interesting case pinpoints how some clever marketing managers found ways to target their products to the gay market segment. In 1981, a Pfizer, Inc., pharmaceutical product manager was responsible for marketing an anti-crab-lice product. He obtained research showing that gay men in urban areas were more sexually active than the general population. He then surveyed public health clinics in zip codes thought to have high gay male concentrations and found that there was a high incidence of crab lice in those clinics. He then targeted his sales efforts at pharmacies in those zip codes and ran ads in gay newspapers (Chasin 2000). The campaign was successful.

AIDS

All developments related to the gay community in the 1980s, including target marketing, were overshadowed by the AIDS crisis, which by 1984 was grabbing headlines and changing the way the gay community saw itself and how others saw gay men. AIDS increased the visibility of the gay community and individual gay men more than anything else in U.S. history. This ironically made it easier for marketers to find gays and market to them.

One unintended consequence of the AIDS epidemic was the creation of an AIDS product and service category targeting infected gay men and marketed mostly through gay publications and gay community events. Calistoga and Perrier advertised the purity of their water for those with weakened immune systems. Viatical settlement company advertisements appeared in practically every gay publication, offering HIV-infected readers immediate cash in exchange for naming those firms as their life insurance policy beneficiaries. Advera promoted its nutritional supplements specifically developed for people with AIDS (Streitmatter 1995).

Gay Businesses Cater to the Gay Community

As had been the case since the 1940s, gay-owned businesses—including many of those mentioned in this section—continued to service the gay market. What had changed from the 1940s/1950s to the

1980s/1990s was that the scope of gay-owned businesses went far beyond restaurants, bars, and bathhouses.

In October 1991, *Shocking Gray: The Catalog for the Other 25 Million People* was established. This catalog company broke new ground by offering a variety of products, most of which would appeal to many different types of audiences—clothing, home accessories, jewelry, designer furniture, artwork, luggage, track lighting, and gourmet food—but marketed exclusively to gays and lesbians. The catalog layouts featured same-sex couples walking dogs, making meals, and spending time with friends. Even though not all suppliers of goods to the catalog were gay-owned, all vendors were required to donate a portion of their proceeds to gay and lesbian organizations (Plummer 1992).

During the 1990s, the breadth of product and service offerings targeting the lesbian and gay had grown to such an extent that gay and lesbian market expos began. The year 1994 saw the first Gay Expo in New York. These trade shows were intended to highlight gay and lesbian-owned and mainstream businesses that target the gay/lesbian market niche (Plummer 1992).

Beverage Companies Continue to Lead

Heublein and Seagram, noting Absolut's success with the gay market in the late 1970s, began advertising in gay publications. Seagram's Boodles Gin advertisements featured a "famous men in history" campaign. This campaign included historical figures that were purported to be gay, such as Oscar Wilde and Walt Whitman (Baker 1997).

Carrying on the industry's interest born in the 1970s and continued into the 1980s, other beverage firms including Coors, Philip Morris, Anheuser-Busch, Hiram Walker, Schieffelin and Somerset Co., and William Grant followed suit in the 1990s (Plummer 1992). Reversing the 1980s marketer concern about directly targeting the gay segment because of fears of religious right boycotts, beverage company marketers realized not only that gay men were a lucrative market, but also that evangelical Christians were typically not big drinkers and therefore their boycotts would have little impact on the bottom line.

Boycotts

The strength of a market segment can be demonstrated by its ability to affect policy related to products and services offered it. The gay community had used boycotts since the 1970s to flex its consumer muscle to punish marketers who were hurting the cause of gay rights. In 1992, gay consumers targeted the state of Colorado. Colorado voters had passed Amendment 2, which outlawed any sort of civil rights protections for gays and lesbians throughout the state (Colorado's Aspen ski resort was the site of a large and lucrative annual gay and lesbian ski week event). The boycott received a large amount of publicity and cost the state millions of dollars in tourism revenues. The Colorado Supreme Court eventually invalidated the law. Meanwhile, the gay market had put other tourist jurisdictions on notice (Bianco 1999).

SUMMARY AND CONCLUSIONS

Beginning in the late-nineteenth century and continuing into the twentieth century, a series of historical events including urbanization, Prohibition and its repeal, two World Wars, the advent of the gay press, the growth of gay ghettos, AIDS, and society's growing acceptance of homosexuality impacted the gay market segment, which can be chronicled in three distinct phases, each of which includes a variety of activities undertaken by both sellers and buyers. These phases include (1) the Underground Phase, pre-1941; (2) the Community-Building Phase, 1941-1970; and (3) the Mainstream Phase, 1970 to 2000. These three identifiable phases cover roughly 100 years, incorporating historical drivers and marked by activities of both buyers and sellers as summarized in the conceptual framework, led to the recent maturing of the gay market segment unimaginable even 40 years ago.

Today, American Express has built an entire program around the gay consumer, including the development of gay-specific advertisements for its promotional campaigns (Hussein 2000). Web sites dedicated to marketing to gays and lesbians are very popular. The two leading online gay portals, gay.com and PlanetOut, are each accessed by several hundred thousand unique visitors each month. According to figures from Internet media research group Media Metrix, PlanetOut's unique monthly visitors topped the 1 million mark in April 2000.

Even Office Max, the Cleveland-based office supplies retailer, started advertising on gay Web sites. According to Steve Baisden, a spokesman for Office Max, "We're here to serve our customers. We don't care whether they're white, black, yellow, gay, or lesbian" (www.jobcircle.com/career/articles/x/njtc/2915.xml).

These examples of mainstream corporations embracing and targeting the gay market and myriad other examples presented in this paper do not represent a recent phenomenon. They are the result of more than 100 years of the growth and recognition of the U.S. gay market segment. As illustrated in this paper, however, this growth has not taken place in a gradual and consistent evolutionary nature. Rather, it has resembled Gould's notion of punctuated equilibria (Eldredge and Gould 1972). This biological theory describes evolution as including long periods of stasis punctuated by episodes of very rapid change (Futuyma 1986). In the case of the American gay market segment, these episodes of rapid change were driven by historical and societal events and eras described in this study. This same punctuated equilibria view may well describe the development of many, if not all, market segments. Its application presents a rich opportunity for broader study of market segment history and development of related macromarketing theory.

In addition, this study has undertaken a macro, multidimensional view of the gay market segment. Micromarketing analyses typically conceive of a market segment in terms of a given product or service category. In contrast to this narrow view, this study's macromarketing perspective has focused on multiple categories, including bathhouses, brothels, bars, clothing, housing, neighborhoods, restaurants, resorts, print and electronic media, telecommunications, and tourism. Moreover, given their concurrent nature and dynamic impact upon one another, this analysis suggests that the development of these categories is interdependent. This approach can be seen as reflecting an Aldersonion view of how consumers construct their lives in terms of assortments. Utilizing this paper's conceptual framework to organize historical events and activities and to place them in proper chronological order, this approach presents additional opportunities for continuing study.

As we enter the twenty-first century, the American gay market segment is confronted with two opposing forces that could impact its future. One is the growing acceptance of homosexuality in the United States, witnessed by gay rights legislation, corporate domestic partner benefits, and gay character depictions in popular entertainment. The other force is the ongoing "culture wars" being waged by some conservative groups against gays and other groups and phenomena seen as responsible for the moral decline of American society. Which of these two forces prevails will have a significant impact on the future of the gay market.

At the same time, as with many niche markets, the diversity within the gay market segment is as significant as its shared characteristics. Already "subniches"—groups within the larger gay market segment that share their own demographic and psychographics—are forming. These include men and women, urban and rural, young and senior citizens. This progression may result in the formation of not one, but several gay market subsegments. Conversely, the integration of gays into American society might ultimately result in the disappearance of the gay market niche altogether. Time alone will tell if the gay market segment's growth and development in the next 100 years will continue to be driven by periodic historical and societal events, whether increasing societal acceptance of gays will result in an integration of the gay market segment into larger demographic or psychographic segments, or whether some movement will suppress the desire or ability of businesses to reach out to what today is a thriving market segment.

BIBLIOGRAPHY

Alderfer, Clayton (1972). *Existence, Relatedness, and Growth: Human Needs in Organizational Settings.* New York: Free Press.

Alderson, Wroe (1957). *Marketing Behavior and Executive Action, A Functionalist Approach to Marketing Theory.* Homewood, IL: R.D. Irwin.

Baker, Dan (1997). "A History in Ads: The Growth of the Gay and Lesbian Market." In Gluckman, A. and Reed, B. (Eds.), *Homo Economics: Capitalism, Community, and Lesbian and Gay Life* (pp. 11-21). London: Routledge.

Bérubé, Allan (1990). *Coming Out Under Fire: The History of the Gay Men and Women in World War II.* New York: Free Press.

Bianco, David (1999). *Gay Essentials: Facts for Your Queer Brain.* Los Angeles: Alyson Books.

Bullough, Vern L. (1976). *Sexual Variance in Society and History.* New York: John Wiley & Sons.

Burnham, John (1973). "The Physicians' Discovery of a Deviate Community in America, Medical Aspects of Human Sexuality." (Cited in Bullough, 1976.)

Canal St. Report (207) (1908). Court of Special Sessions, Box 65. Committee of Fourteen papers. New York Public Library. (Cited in Chauncey, 1994.)

Chasin, Alexandra (2000). *Selling Out: The Gay and Lesbian Movement Goes to Market.* New York: Palgrave.

Chauncey, George (1994). *Gay New York: Gender, Urban Culture, and the Making of the Gay Male World, 1890-1940.* New York: Basic Books.

Cherry Grove Arts Council theater program advertisement. 1951.

Chicago Vice Commission (1911). "The Social Evil in Chicago." Chicago: Gunthorp-Warren Printing Co. (Cited in Bullough, 1976.)

D'Emilio, John (1983). *Sexual Politics, Sexual Communities: The Making of a Homosexual Minority in the United States, 1940-1970.* Chicago: The University of Chicago Press.

Doty, Robert C. (1963). "Growth of Overt Homosexuality in City Provokes Wide Concern." *New York Times* (December 17) 113:38, 678, p. 1.

Duberman, Martin (1991). *About Time: Exploring the Gay Past.* New York: Meridian.

Eldredge, N. and S. J. Gould (1972). "Punctuated Equilibria: An Alternative to Phyletic Gradualism." In T. J. M. Schopf (Ed.), *Models in Paleobiology* (pp. 82-115). San Francisco: Freeman, Cooper.

Ellis, Havelock (1942). *Studies in the Psychology of Sex,* Volume 1, Part 4. New York: Random House.

Ersine, Noel (1935). *Underworld and Prison Slang.* Upland, IN: A. D. Freese & Son.

Escoffier, Jeffrey (1997). "The Political Economy of the Closet." In Gluckman, A. and Reed, B. (Eds.), *Homo Economics: Capitalism, Community, and Lesbian and Gay Life* (pp. 123-135). New York: Routledge.

Fejes, Fred (2000). "Market Niche at Last, Market Niche at Last, Thank God Almighty, We're a Market Niche at Last: The Political Economy of Lesbian/Gay Identity." Unpublished paper.

Finch, Will (1946). Diary. Kinsey Institute for Research in Sex, Gender, and Reproduction Library, Indiana University, Bloomington. (Quoted in Chauncey, 1994.)

Fugate, D. L. (1993). "Evaluating the U.S. Male Homosexual and Lesbian Population as a Viable Target Market Segment: A Review with Implications." *Journal of Consumer Marketing,* 10(4), 46-57.

Futuyma, Douglas J. (1986). *Evolutionary Biology,* Second Edition. Sunderland, MA: Sinauer Associates, Inc.

Gallagher, John (1994). "Ikea's Gay Gamble: Why Did a National Home-Furnishings Chain Build a Television Ad Around a Gay Couple?" *Advocate,* May 3.

Gardner, Charles W. (1931). "The Doctor and the Devil or the Midnight Adventures of Dr. Parkhurst." New York: Vanguard Press. (Cited in Bullough, 1976, and Katz, 1992.)

"Gay Press Looks to Madison Ave." (1990). *New York Times* (December 17), D11:4.

Gloria Record on Review (1940). New York State Liquor Authority transcript 259 A.D. 813. (Cited in Chauncey, 1994.)

Gluckman, A. and Reed, B. (Eds.) (1997). *Homo Economics: Capitalism, Community, and Lesbian and Gay Life.* New York: Routledge.

Herdt, Gilbert (Ed.) (1992). *Gay Culture in America: Essays from the Field.* Boston, MA: Beacon.

Higgs, David (Ed.) (1999). *Queer Sites: Gay Urban Histories Since 1600.* New York: Routledge.

Hirschfield, Magnus (1920). "Die Homosexualität." Berlin: Louis Marcus. (Cited in Bullough, 1976.)

Horowitz, Morris (1939). Testimony in Times Square Garden and Grill, Inc., v. Bruckman, et al., 256 A.D. 1062 (1st Dep't.). (Cited in Chauncey, 1994.)

Hussein, Imtiyaz (2000). "Marketing to the Gay Community." *The Harbus* (April 17).

Jerome, District Attorney Wm. T. to the Governor (1905). File with *People v. Galbert* (CGS 1903). JJC. (Cited in Chauncey, 1994.)

Kahan, H. (1926). Committee of Fourteen papers, NY Public Library; September 26; Jeffrey Gottfried, interview; *Broadway Brevities,* October 1926, 48-49; *Broadway Brevities,* November 16, 1931. (Cited in Chauncey, 1994.)

Kaiser, Charles (1997). *The Gay Metropolis: 1940-1996.* Boston: Houghton Mifflin Company.

Kates, Steven M. (1998). *Twenty Million New Customers! Understanding Gay Men's Consumer Behavior.* Binghamton, NY: The Haworth Press.

Kiernan, James (1916). "Classifications of Homosexuality." *Urologic and Cutaneous Review,* 20, 350.

Kotler, Philip and Levy, Sidney J. (1973). "Buying Is Marketing, Too!" *Journal of Marketing,* 37 (January), 54-59.

Laumann, Edward O., Gagnon, John H., Michael, Robert T., and Michaels, Stuart (1994). *The Social Organization of Sexuality: Sexual Practices in the United States.* Chicago: University of Chicago Press.

Lighter, J.E. (Ed.) (1994). *Random House Historical Dictionary of American Slang,* Volume 1. New York: Random House.

Lukenbill, Grant (1999). *Untold Millions: Secret Truths About Marketing to Gay and Lesbian Consumers.* Binghamton, NY: The Haworth Press.

Lydston, G. Frank (1889). "Sexual Perversion, Satyriasis and Nymphomania." *Medical and Surgical Reporter,* 61.

Maslow, A. (1954). *Motivation and Personality.* New York: Harper & Row.

Mazet Committee Report, New York State (1897). Frank Moss. The American Metropolis. New York: Collier. 3:163, 222. (Cited in Chauncey, 1994; verbatim committee testimony re: Paresis Hall in Katz, 1992.)

New York City Investigator's Report (1919). June 30.

Painter, Thomas (1941). "The Prostitute" (typescript). 168-169. Kinsey Institute for Research in Sex, Gender, and Reproduction Library. Indiana University, Bloomington.

Parke, J. Richardson (1906). "Human Sexuality: Medico-Literary Treatise." Professional Publishing Co. 251. (Cited in Bullough, 1976.)

Peñaloza, Lisa (1996). "We're Here, We're Queer, and We're Going Shopping: A Critical Perspective on the Accommodation of Gays and Lesbians in the U.S. Marketplace." In Wardlow, D. (Ed.) *Gays, Lesbians and Consumer Behavior* (pp. 9-41). Binghamton, NY: Harrington Park Press.

Plummer, Douglas M. (1992). "Marketing to the Gay Community." *The Harbus,* January 21.

————. (1999). "TV's Coming-Out." *Time* (October 25), 116-118.

————. (2000). "It's Here, It's Queer. Get Used to It." *Time* (November 27), 78-79.

Shaw, Charles G. (1931). *Nightlife:* Vanity Fair's *Intimate Guide to New York.* New York: John Day.

Stabiner, Karen (1982). "Tapping the Homosexual Market." *New York Times Magazine* (May 2).

Streitmatter, Rodger (1995). *Unspeakable: The Rise of the Gay and Lesbian Press in America.* London: Faber and Faber.

Swisher, Bob (1988). "One Big Community: Gay Life in Richmond After 1944." *Southern Exposure,* 14 (Fall), 29.

Thompson, Mark (1988). *Gay Spirit: Myth and Meaning.* New York: St. Martin's Press.

Wallace, Sam and Nikki Stiller (1986). "Interview with Allen Ginsberg." *The Newark Review,* 1 (April 22), 3.

Wardlow, Daniel L. (Ed.) (1996). *Gays, Lesbians and Consumer Behavior.* Binghamton, NY: Harrington Park Press.

Weathers, Diane, Reese, Michael, et. al. (1979). "Where the Boys Are." *Newsweek,* July 30.

Werther, Ralph (1922, reprint 1975). *The Female-Impersonators.* New York: Arno Press.

WPA Guide to New York City (1939).

Young, Allen (1974). *Gay Sunshine Interview: Allen Ginsberg with Allen Young.* Bolinas, CA: Grey Fox Press.

Index

Page numbers followed by the letter "f" indicate figures; those followed by the letter "t" indicate tables.

Order a copy of this book **with this form or online at:**
http://www.haworthpress.com/store/product.asp?sku=5475

HANDBOOK OF NICHE MARKETING
Principles and Practice

_____in hardbound at $49.95 (ISBN-13: 978-0-7890-2329-2; ISBN-10: 0-7890-2329-6)

_____in softbound at $29.95 (ISBN-13: 978-0-7890-2330-8; ISBN-10: 0-7890-2330-X)

Or order online and use special offer code HEC25 in the shopping cart.

COST OF BOOKS_____

☐ **BILL ME LATER:** (Bill-me option is good on US/Canada/Mexico orders only; not good to jobbers, wholesalers, or subscription agencies.)

☐ Check here if billing address is different from shipping address and attach purchase order and billing address information.

POSTAGE & HANDLING_____
(US: $4.00 for first book & $1.50 for each additional book)
(Outside US: $5.00 for first book & $2.00 for each additional book)

Signature_____

SUBTOTAL_____

☐ **PAYMENT ENCLOSED: $**_____

IN CANADA: ADD 7% GST_____

☐ **PLEASE CHARGE TO MY CREDIT CARD.**

STATE TAX_____
(NJ, NY, OH, MN, CA, IL, IN, PA, & SD residents, add appropriate local sales tax)

☐ Visa ☐ MasterCard ☐ AmEx ☐ Discover
☐ Diner's Club ☐ Eurocard ☐ JCB

Account # _____

FINAL TOTAL_____
(If paying in Canadian funds, convert using the current exchange rate, UNESCO coupons welcome)

Exp. Date_____

Signature_____

Prices in US dollars and subject to change without notice.

NAME_____

INSTITUTION_____

ADDRESS_____

CITY_____

STATE/ZIP_____

COUNTRY_____ COUNTY (NY residents only)_____

TEL_____ FAX_____

E-MAIL_____

May we use your e-mail address for confirmations and other types of information? ☐ Yes ☐ No
We appreciate receiving your e-mail address and fax number. Haworth would like to e-mail or fax special discount offers to you, as a preferred customer. **We will never share, rent, or exchange your e-mail address or fax number.** We regard such actions as an invasion of your privacy.

Order From Your Local Bookstore or Directly From
The Haworth Press, Inc.
10 Alice Street, Binghamton, New York 13904-1580 • USA
TELEPHONE: 1-800-HAWORTH (1-800-429-6784) / Outside US/Canada: (607) 722-5857
FAX: 1-800-895-0582 / Outside US/Canada: (607) 771-0012
E-mail to: orders@haworthpress.com

For orders outside US and Canada, you may wish to order through your local
sales representative, distributor, or bookseller.
For information, see http://haworthpress.com/distributors

(Discounts are available for individual orders in US and Canada only, not booksellers/distributors.)

PLEASE PHOTOCOPY THIS FORM FOR YOUR PERSONAL USE.
http://www.HaworthPress.com   BOF04